Isaac Amada Cornelison

The relation of religion to civil government in the United States of America

a state without a church, but not without a religion

Isaac Amada Cornelison

The relation of religion to civil government in the United States of America
a state without a church, but not without a religion

ISBN/EAN: 9783744736916

Printed in Europe, USA, Canada, Australia, Japan

Cover: Foto ©Lupo / pixelio.de

More available books at **www.hansebooks.com**

THE

RELATION OF RELIGION

TO

CIVIL GOVERNMENT

IN

THE UNITED STATES OF AMERICA

A STATE WITHOUT A CHURCH, BUT NOT WITHOUT A RELIGION

BY

ISAAC A. CORNELISON

G. P. PUTNAM'S SONS

NEW YORK   LONDON
27 WEST TWENTY-THIRD ST.   24 BEDFORD ST., STRAND

The Knickerbocker Press

1895

The Knickerbocker Press, New York

PREFACE.

It has seemed to the author, that it would be proper for him to give to his readers, beforehand, what the astromomers would call, his "personal equation," upon the subject he is now undertaking to discuss.

He would, therefore, say that, in the study of the early history of our government, his sympathies have been wholly with the distinctive political views of Washington and Hamilton ; and not with those of Jefferson and Madison. His highest admiration is given to those who secured the formation and adoption of the Constitution of the United States,—a Federalist measure—which transformed a weak and unstable confederacy of independent States, into a vigorous and indissoluble Union ; leaving the several States in their integrity, while constituting the people of all the States, a Nation. But, that being secured, and unalterably established, the author has found himself drifting away from Federalism. By reason of a mental bent, produced by accidental circumstances, or of a mental type, received by inheritance, he will have to be classed with that school in politics which is negative and restrictive in its policy, rather than with one that is positive and aggressive. On all questions relating to the functions of civil government and the extent of its

iii

power, he finds himself affected with an antecedent, perhaps a predeterminate inclination to the negative ; that is, to the reduction of the functions of civil government to their lowest terms ; and the restriction of its powers to their narrowest limits. He finds himself opposed to centralization and paternalism in our own government. While he is ready to concede that paternalism was the primitive form of government, he maintains that the laws of social development have tended, and do necessarily tend, to a progressive reduction of its powers.

The individual independence of democracy, as a theory, opposed to the fostering paternalism of monarchy, seems to him to be now on trial ; that trial forming the political problem of the present epoch. Were it his lot to be living at the conclusion of the trial, he trusts that he would be able to accept the result with good grace, if it should happen to be adverse ; but he thinks that in the meantime the theory, on trial, should be consistently carried out, and not be complicated with its opposite. In a democracy, the many may not claim to be better judges of the personal interests of the one than the individual himself. They may not, therefore, compel him to act in a matter relating only to his own interest, against his own judgment, and in accordance with theirs. It may be that, in the use of his liberty, he will do himself harm ; but the discipline of responsibility will tend to strengthen and elevate the man, which would be far better than that he should escape a particular harm by the surrender of his liberty and the transfer of his responsibility to others. This being the principle upon which the divine government of the world is conducted, it must be regarded as founded in the highest wisdom and benevolence, and therefore as best fitted (at least in the case of adults) to promote the welfare of mankind. The Creator has made special provision in nature for the paternal government of the young ; but he has made it plain that it is the proper aim of that government to secure its own early extinction by developing in the young the power of self-government. This divine intention is manifested, with especial clearness, in the lower animal creation, for there the dam does not recognize her offspring, or even know them as her own, after they have come to maturity.

The authority of civil government, when it interferes with the liberty of the individual, for the purpose of securing his own good, and not merely for the purpose of preventing his interference with the liberty of his fellowman, is pedagogic, fulfilling an office like that of the freedman or slave who, in ancient times, was given authority to conduct the child from the home to the school. The authority of the pedagogue over the child was legitimate and proper for a time, but when he had delivered the child to the teacher his authority ceased. The fulfilment of the function of his office was the very thing which brought his authority to an end. Even the Mosaic law, the apostle Paul argues, was of this character. "Therefore the law was our pedagogue (παιδαγωγος, child-conductor, not διδάσκαλος, school-master or teacher, as it is given in the A. V.) to bring us to Christ." Gal. iii., 24. He affirms therefore that "The law of the Spirit of life in Christ Jesus hath made me free from the law of sin and death." Rom. viii., 1., and exhorts the Galatians to "stand fast, therefore, in the liberty wherewith Christ hath made us free." Gal. v., 1.

Paternalism is neither an evil nor a wrong, in itself ;

but it is both when it proposes to make itself perpetual. Monarchies are not all to be denounced as sinful usurpations, not all even of the most absolute. Impulses, however, are operating in them all towards the individual freedom of democracy, and these impulses, notwithstanding the efforts of the rulers to repress them, are daily gaining strength. No one who observes carefully the course of modern history will fail to see that the Ruler of the nations is guiding the course of events, among civilized peoples, towards that high consummation. Among the monarchies of Europe may be seen to-day examples of the various stages of progress to that end. Monarchy, if it fulfil its mission, will accomplish its own extinction. If its aim and effort be to make itself perpetual it will be found fighting against God, and, as the times ripen, its thrones will be dashed to pieces. Paternalism, under whatever form of government, if subject to the Spirit that rules the world, will aim, not at the perpetuation, but at the extinction of its authority.

In the author's view it cannot be a permanent function of civil government to make the citizen prosperous, intelligent, moral, or religious. In his view, true wisdom will be ever looking for, and ever ready to embrace, opportunity for the relinquishment of this function. Therefore, while desiring not to be an impracticable theorist, the author would be inclined to restrict the fostering power of the government, in all directions, rather than to enlarge it, in any direction. It may be very readily inferred that he is not in favor of a union of Church and State. He rejoices in the fact that we have, in this country, a grand system of political institutions, entirely separate from all ecclesiastical institutions. He rejoices also in the fact that, upon this question, there is no diversity of sentiment among American citizens.

The question still remains, however, whether a State, without a Church, is also without a Religion. The question of the union of Church and State, not being of any practical interest in this country, he does not propose to discuss. The discussion will be confined exclusively to the former question. That question is beginning to work like a ferment in the public mind ; and, as in all other fermentations, so in this : there will be at first commotion, turbidness, and heat. In due time, the crudities will settle away and the mass will become quiet and clear. It ought to be the desire of every patriot and philanthropist to contribute to the hastening of this result. It is with such desire the author enters upon this discussion of the relation of Religion to Civil Government, in the United States of America.

The best thought upon the subject is to be found in the decisions of the various courts, Federal and State, owing, no doubt, to the fact that it has been wrought out by vigorous minds, specially disciplined, and acting under a strong sense of duty. But the enunciations of principle, in these decisions, having been made, in connection with a great variety of particular cases, and being scattered through a great many series of Reports, do not form a complete and harmonious system. The author has found it necessary, in the investigation of his subject, to traverse these enunciations, and to attempt an informal digest of their contents. For readers of the legal profession, mere references to the decisions of the courts would have been sufficient, but he has thought best to make large extracts from the leading decisions on the subject, and to include them in the body of the work, rather than to consign them to an appendix. He entertains the hope that what, at first sight, might seem to be an encumbrance of the work, will prove to be one of the most interesting parts of it. Indeed, he is led to believe, that it would be no small help, in forming a satisfactory opinion on the subject, if all the decisions of the courts that bear in any way upon it were collected and published together in full.

It may be inferred from this latter observation, that the author does not flatter himself with the assurance, that he has succeeded in unravelling all the intricacies, and solving all the difficulties, of the subject he has undertaken to treat. He feels that he needs, especially, to maintain a modest demeanor in the presence of the judiciary and other learned members of the legal profession. If what he has done shall, in the least degree, help others to the formation of a satisfactory opinion for themselves ; or shall provoke them to contribute something towards the ascertainment of the absolute truth and the establishment of perfect justice, he will feel that he is amply compensated for his labor.

The author has had recourse, for information, as far as he could find it possible, to original sources ; when that was not possible, he has drawn from other sources regarded as trustworthy. The various authorities from whom he has made quotations are indicated in connection with the quotations. The extracts made from Charters and Constitutions are taken from *The Federal and State Constitutions, Colonial Charters and other Organic Laws of the United States, compiled under the order of the United States Senate, by Ben Perley Poore.* Published at the Government Printing-Office at Washington, D. C., 1877.

Washington, Ill., March, 1895.

CONTENTS.

PART I.

PART II.

PART III.

Contents.   xi

PART I.

A question of history. What has been the relation of religion to civil government, in the world at large; and especially in the colonies which, after the Declaration of Independence in 1776, became States of the United States of America?

CHAPTER I.

AMONG all the nations of antiquity, and among all the heathen nations of the present day, we find the religious institutions of the people incorporated with their civil and political institutions.

As soon as it appeared that Christianity was destined to supplant paganism among the Roman people, as it did in the time of Constantine I., Christianity was made the religion of the Empire. Offences against the Church were regarded as crimes against the State, and were punished with fines, imprisonment, banishment, and death.

This relation of Christianity to the State has been maintained, with various modifications, in all the countries of Europe, down to the present day. It existed in England, the fountain head of our own national life; and it might have been expected that in the course of historic continuity it would prevail in the colonies of England in America; unless special causes should operate to prevent it. The expeditions fitted out in England for the founding of settlements in the new world, had a religious, as well as a commercial, purpose; that purpose being distinctly expressed in the charters and grants given.

3

Sir Humphrey Gilbert, half brother of Sir Walter Raleigh, was sent out on an expedition of exploration and occupation, in 1578 ; and one object of the expedition, stated in his commission, was " compassion of poore infidels, captived by the devil, and the establishment of a system of government not against the true Christian faith professed in the Church of England."

In the Letters Patent granted to Sir Walter Raleigh by Queen Elizabeth in 1584, he was authorized to " discover, search, find out, and view such remote heathen and barbarous lands, countries, and territories, not actually possessed of any Christian prince, nor inherited by any Christian people ; . . . to have, hold, occupy and enjoy, to him, his heirs and assigns forever, with all prerogatives, commodities, jurisdictions, royalties, privileges, franchises and pre-eminences . . . as we, or any of our royal progenitors have, heretofore, granted to any person or persons, bodies politic or corporate." In giving him authority to establish government and make laws, it was provided, "So always as the said statutes, laws, and ordinances . . . be not against the true Christian faith, now professed in the Church of England."

The three Charters of Virginia, given by James I. in 1606, 1609, and 1611–12, respectively, disposed of all the territory lying between the mouth of the St. John's River in Florida and the middle of Nova Scotia, and extending westward to the " South Sea." The grantees were to be divided into two companies ; the one to have its location in London, its colony to be known as The First Colony of Virginia ; and to possess, under the third charter, the territory lying between 30° and 41° N. latitude, the parallels of the mouth of the St. John's River, Florida, and New York City. The other was to have its location in Plymouth ; its colony to be known as The Second Colony of Virginia ; and to possess the territory lying between 38° and 45° N. latitude—the parallels of Washington City and St. Andrews, Nova Scotia. In the charter of these two companies the King says : " We, greatly commending, and graciously accepting of their desires for the furtherance of so noble a work, which may, by the Providence of Almighty God, hereafter tend to the glory of His Divine Majesty, in propagating Christian religion to such people as yet live in miserable ignorance of the true knowledge and worship of God ; and may, in time, bring the infidels and savages living in those parts to civility, and to a settled and quiet government ; do, by these our Letters Patent, graciously accept of, and agree to their humble and well-intended desires."

" Articles, Instructions, and Orders, made, set down, and established by us, twentieth day of November, in the year of our reign of England, France, and Ireland, the fourth (1606), and of Scotland, the fortieth, for the good order and government of the two several colonies and plantations to be made by our loving subjects in the country commonly called Virginia, and America, between thirty-four and forty-five degrees from the equinoctial line. . . . And we do especially ordain, charge, and require the said presidents and Council and the ministers of the said several colonies, respectively, within their several limits and precincts, that they, with all diligence, care, and respect, do provide that the true word and service of God and Christian faith be preached, planted, and used, not only within every of the said several colonies, but also, as much as they may, amongst the savage people which do, or shall, adjoin unto them or border upon them, according to the doctrine, rites, and religion now professed and established within our realm of England ; and that they shall not suffer any person or persons to withdraw any of the subjects or people inhabiting, or which shall inhabit within any of the said several colonies and plantations, from the same or from their due allegiance unto us, our heirs and successors."

The Plymouth Company received, at their request, a new charter from James I. in 1620, " for the planting, ruling, ordering and governing, of New England, in America " ; and granting them the territory between 40° and 48° N. latitude, the parallels of Philadelphia, Pa., and New Carlisle, in northern New Brunswick. In this charter the king says : " We, according to our princely inclination, favoring much their worthy disposition, in hope, thereby, to advance the enlargement of Christian religion, to the glory of God ; as, also, by that means, to stretch out the bounds of our dominions ; and to replenish those deserts with people, governed by laws and magistrates, for the peaceable commerce of all. . . ."

CHAPTER II.

THE COLONIES.

1. Virginia. The first settlement was made by the London Company, on James River, in 1607, and among the first laws made by the Assembly of Virginia, which met in 1619—the first laws enacted within the territory now occupied by the United States—it was enacted :

" 1. That there shall be, in every plantation, where the people use to meet for the worship of God, a house or room, sequestered for that purpose, and not to be for any temporal use whatever ; and a place em-paled in, sequestered only to the burial of the dead.

" 2. That whosoever shall absent himself from divine service any Sunday, without an allowable excuse, shall forfeit a pound of tobacco ; and he that absenteth himself a month shall forfeit fifty pounds of tobacco.

" 3. That there be an uniformity in our church, as near as may be, to the canons in England, both in sub-stance and circumstance ; and that all persons yield ready obedience unto them under pain of censure.

" 5. That no minister be absent from his church above two months in all the year, upon penalty of forfeiting half his means ; and whosoever shall be absent above four months in the year shall forfeit his whole means and cure.

" 6. That whosoever shall disparage a minister, with-out bringing sufficient proof to justify his reports, whereby the minds of his parishioners may be alienated from him, and his ministry prove the less effectual, by their prejudication, shall not only pay five hundred pounds of tobacco, but also ask the minister so wronged, forgiveness publicly in the congregation. . . .

" 19. The proclamations for swearing and drunken-ness, set out by the Governor and Council, are con-firmed by the Assembly; and it is further ordered, that the church-wardens shall be sworn to present them to the commanders of every plantation ; and that the for-feitures shall be collected by them, to be for public uses." [1]

---

[1] *The Statutes at Large, being a collection of all the Laws of Virginia, from the first session of the Legislature in the year 1619. Published pursuant to an Act of the General Assembly of Virginia, passed on the fifth day of February one thousand eighteen hundred and eight.* By William Waller Hening, vol. i., pp. 67, 68, 122, 123.

By Act VIII. of the General Assembly, held the 16th day of October, 1629,

"It is ordered that there be an especial care taken by all commanders and others, that the people do repair to their churches on the Sabbath day, and to see that the penalty of one pound of tobacco, for every time of absence, and fifty pounds for every month's absence, set down in the Act of the General Assembly 1623, be levied, and the delinquents to pay the same ; as also to see that the Sabbath day be not ordinarily profaned by working in any employments or by journeying from place to place."[1]

By Act II. of the Grand Assembly of 1631–32, the commanders, captains, and church-wardens, were, in God's name, earnestly required and charged, "that they shall endeavor themselves, to the uttermost of their knowledge, that the due and true execution hereof may be done and had through this colony, as they will answer before God for such evils and plagues wherewith Almighty God may justly punish his people for neglecting this good and wholesome law" (the law requiring attendance upon church on Sunday).[2]

The same Assembly adopted the following, viz.:

Act IV. "And it is further ordered and thought expedient, according to a former order, made by the Governor and Council, that all church-wardens shall take this oath, and that it be administered before those that are of the commission for monthly courts, viz. :

"You shall swear that you shall make presentments of all such persons as shall lead a profane or ungodly life ; of such as shall be common swearers, drunkards, or blasphemers ; that shall ordinarily profane the Sabbath days, or contemn God's holy word or sacraments.

[1] *Ibid.*, p. 124.   [2] *Ibid.*, p. 155.

You shall also present all adulterers or fornicators, or such as shall abuse their neighbors, by slandering, tale carrying, or backbiting, or that shall not behave themselves soberly and orderly in the church during divine service. Likewise, they shall present such masters and mistresses as shall be delinquent in the catechising the youth and ignorant persons. So help me God."

Act VIII. " It is also thought fit, that upon every Sunday the minister shall, half an hour or more before evening prayer, examine, catechise, and instruct the youth and ignorant persons of his parish, in the commandments, the articles of the belief, and in the Lord's Prayer; and shall diligently hear, instruct, and teach them the catechism, set forth in the Book of Common Prayer. And all fathers, mothers, masters, and mistresses shall cause their children, servants, or apprentices, which have not learned the catechism, to come to the church, at the time appointed, obediently to hear, and to be ordered by the minister, until they have learned the same. And if any of the said fathers, mothers, masters, and mistresses, children, servants, or apprentices shall neglect their duties, as the one sort, in not causing them to come ; and the other, in refusing to learn, as aforesaid, they shall be censured by the courts in those places holden. And the Act to take beginning on Easter next." [1]

Article XI. " Ministers shall not give themselves to excess in drinking or riot, spending their time idly, by day or night, playing at dice, cards, or any other unlawful game ; but, at all times convenient, they shall hear or read somewhat of the Holy Scriptures ; or shall occupy themselves with some other honest study or exercise ; always doing the things which shall apper-

[1] *Ibid.*, pp. 156, 157.

tain to honesty, and endeavor to profit the church of God ; always having in mind that they ought to excel all others, in purity of life, and should be examples to the people to live well and Christianly." [1]

Article XIV. "The Governor and Council, together with the burgesses, in the present Grand Assembly, upon the petition of the ministers within this colony, have taken into their consideration by what way there might be a sufficient means allowed unto the said ministers for their better subsistence and encouragement in their ministry ; and thereupon, have ordained and enacted that there shall be paid, unto the said ministers, the former allowance of ten pounds of tobacco, and a bushel of corn, in such manner as formerly hath been done ; and, because of the low rates of tobacco, at this present, it is further granted and ordered, that there shall be likewise due to the ministers, from the first day of March next ensuing, the 20th calf, the 20th kid of goats, and the 20th pig, throughout all plantations within this colony . . . and this Act, to continue in force until the next meeting of the General Assembly, at which time there may fall out just cause of alteration, either by the advancement of tobacco, or some other means, for that formerly the ancient allowance of ten pounds of tobacco and a bushel of corn hath been a sufficient proportion for their maintenance in their calling. . . .

"And no planter or parishioner may neglect the bringing of the tobacco or corn, upon the penalty, that if any make default, they shall forfeit double the quantity of the tobacco and corn, levied by distress, by authority from the commander ; and likewise, by distress, all arrearages of tobacco and corn due to the

[1] *Ibid.*, p. 158.

minister as duties, shall, or may be recovered by virtue
of this order of this Assembly. And if the church-
wardens shall fail in the execution of their office hereby
enjoined, then the commander shall take order that it
be levied by distress out of the church-wardens' goods
and chattels."

Article XV. " It is ordained and enacted, that in all
such places where any churches are wanting or de-
cayed, the inhabitants shall be tied to contribute
towards the building of a church or repairing any de-
cayed church ; the commissioners, together with the
ministers, church-wardens, and chief of the parish, to
appoint, both the most convenient place for all parts to
assemble together, and also, to hire and procure any
workmen, and order such necessaries as are required to
be done in such works. This they are to effect before
the feast of the nativity of our Savior Christ, or else
the said commissioners, if they be deficient in their
duties, to forfeit fifty pounds in money, to be employed
as the whole body of the Assembly shall dispose.
. . . "

Article XVIII. " It is ordered that all the council
and burgesses of the Assembly shall, in the morning,
be present at divine service, in the room where they
sit, at the third beating of the drum, an hour after sun-
rise, upon the penalty of one shilling to the benefit of
the marshall of James City. . . ." [1]

The Grand Assembly of 1642–43 adopted the following, viz. :

Act XXXV. " Be it also enacted and confirmed, for
the better observance of the Sabbath, that no person or
persons shall take a voyage upon the same, except it
be to church or for other causes of extreme necessity,

[1] *Ibid.*, p. 162.

upon the penalty of the forfeiture, for such offence, of twenty pounds of tobacco, being justly convicted for the same.

"Be it further enacted and confirmed, for the better observance of the Sabbath, and for the restraint of divers abuses, committed in the colony, by unlawful shooting on the Sabbath day, as aforesaid, unless it shall be for the safety of his or their plantation or corn-fields, or for defence against the Indians, he or they, so offending, shall forfeit for his or their first offence, being thereof lawfully convicted, if he be a freeman, the quantity of twenty pounds of tobacco ; and, if a servant, to be punished at the discretion of his master. And if masters of any such servants be remiss and negligent in the punishment of his servant for the offence aforesaid, he shall be liable to the forfeiture of twenty pounds of tobacco, being justly convicted for the same." [1]

Act LI. "Whereas, It was enacted, at an Assembly in January, 1641 . . . that it should not be law-ful, under the penalty aforesaid [forfeiture of one thousand pounds of tobacco] for any popish priest, that shall hereafter arrive, to remain above five days, after warning given for his departure, by the Governor or commander of the place where he or they shall be, if wind and weather hinder not his departure ; and that the said Act should be in force ten days after the pub-lication thereof at James City, this present Grand Assembly, to all intents and purposes, doth hereby confirm the same." [2]

Act LXIV. "For the preservation of the purity of doctrine and unity of the church, it is hereby enacted that all ministers, whatsoever, which shall reside in

[1] *Ibid.*, p. 261.   [2] *Ibid.*, p. 268.

the colony, are to be conformable to the orders and constitutions of the Church of England, and the laws therein established ; and not, otherwise, to be admitted to teach or preach, publicly or privately. And that the Governor and Council do take care that all non-conformists, upon notice of them, shall be compelled to depart the colony with all convenience." [1]

The Assembly of 1659–60 adopted the following Act entitled *An Act for the Suppressing the Quakers*, viz. :

" *Whereas,* There is an unreasonable and turbulent sort of people, commonly called Quakers, who, contrary to the laws, do daily gather unto them unlawful assemblies and congregations of people, teaching and publishing lies, miracles, false visions, prophecies, and doctrines, which have influence upon the community of men, both ecclesiastical and civil, endeavoring and attempting thereby to destroy religion, laws, communities, and all bonds of civil society, leaving it arbitrary to every vain and vicious person whether men shall be safe, laws established, offenders punished, and governors rule ; hereby disturbing the public peace and just interest : to prevent and restrain which mischief,

" It is enacted that no master or commander of any ship or other vessel, do bring into this colony any person or persons called Quakers, under the penalty of one hundred pounds sterling, to be levied upon him and his estate, by order of our Governor and Council, as the commissioners in the several counties where such ships shall arrive. That all such Quakers as have been questioned, or shall hereafter arrive, shall be apprehended wheresoever they shall be found, and they be imprisoned, without bail or mainprise, till

[1] *Ibid.*, p. 277.

they do abjure this country or put in security with all speed to depart the colony and not return again. And if they should dare to presume to return hither, after such departure, to be proceeded against, as contemners of the law and magistracy, and punished accordingly, and caused again to depart the country. And if they should the third time be so audacious and imprudent as to return hither, to be proceeded against as felons. That no person shall entertain any of the Quakers that have heretofore been questioned by the Governor and Council, or which shall hereafter be questioned, or permit, in or near his house, any assemblies of Quakers, in the like penalty of one hundred pounds sterling. That commissioners and officers are hereby required and authorized, as they will answer the contrary at their peril, to take notice of this Act, to see it fully effected and executed. And that no persons do presume, on their peril, to dispose or publish their books, pamphlets, or libels, bearing the titles of their tenets and opinions." [1]

The Assembly of 1661-62 enacted, "That, for the preservation of the purity and unity of doctrine and discipline in the church, and the right administration of the sacraments, no minister be admitted to officiate in this country, but such as shall produce to the Governor a testimonial that he hath received his ordination from some bishop in England, and shall then subscribe to be conformable to the orders and constitutions of the Church of England and the laws there established, upon which the Governor is hereby requested to induct the said minister into any parish that shall make presentations of him ; and, if any other person, pretending himself a minister, shall, contrary to this Act,

[1] *Ibid.*, p. 532.

presume to teach or preach publicly or privately, the
Governor and Council are hereby desired and empowered to suspend and silence the person so offending ;
and, upon his obstinate persistence, to compel him to
depart the country with the first conveniency, as it hath
been formerly provided by the 77th Act, made at James
City, the second of March, 1642.[1]

Act III. " Whereas many schismatical persons, out
of their averseness to the orthodox established religion,
or out of the new-fangled conceits of their own heretical inventions, refuse to have their children baptized,
Be it therefore enacted, by the authority aforesaid, that
all persons that, in contempt of the divine sacrament
of baptism, shall refuse, when they may carry their
child to a lawful minister in that country to have them
baptized, shall be amerced two thousand pounds of
tobacco ; half to the informer, half to the public." [2]

The Assembly, September 12, 1663, adopted the
following resolution, viz. :

" *Whereas*, Mr. John Hill, high sheriff of Lower
Norfolk, hath represented to the House that Mr. John
Porter, one of the burgesses of that county, was loving
to the Quakers, and stood well affected towards them,
and had been at their meetings, and was so far an Anabaptist as to be against the baptizing of children, upon
which representation the said Porter confessed himself
to have and be well affected to the Quakers, but conceived his being at their meetings could not be proved,
upon which the oaths of allegiance and supremacy were
tendered to him, which he refused to take ; whereupon
it is ordered that the said Porter be dismissed this
House." [3]

This Assembly made the law against Quakers,

[1] *Ibid.*, vol. ii., p. 46.   [2] *Ibid.*, p. 163.   [3] *Ibid.*, p. 198.

against persons entertaining them, and masters of ships bringing them into the country, more specific and stringent, and included " other separatists " in its prohibitions and penalties.[1]

The Assembly of 1667–68, taking it into serious consideration that " the many sins of this country may justly provoke the anger of Almighty God against us, and draw down his judgments upon us unless diverted by a timely and hearty repentance," appointed the 27th day of August to be set apart as a day of humiliation, " strictly requiring all persons on that day to repair to their respective churches, with fasting and prayers, to implore God's mercy, and deprecate the evils justly impending upon us " ; and enacted, " that if any person or persons, in contempt thereof, shall be found on that day working, gaming, or drinking (works of necessity only excepted) he or they, so offending, upon presentment of the church-warden, and proof thereof made to the vestry, shall be fined by them one hundred pounds of tobacco."[2]

The Lord's Commissioners for Foreign Plantations submitted certain " Enquiries to the Governor of Virginia," the twenty-third of which was, " What course is taken about instructing the people, within your government, in the Christian religion ; and what provision is there made for the paying of your ministry ? "

The answer returned by Sir William Berkeley, then Governor (1671), was as follows, viz. :

" The same course that is taken in England out of towns ; every man, according to his ability, instructing his children. We have forty-eight parishes, and our ministers are well paid, and by my consent should be

[1] *Ibid.*, p. 180. [2] *Ibid.*, p. 260.

better, if they would pray oftener and preach less. But, of all other commodities, so of this, the worst are sent us, and we had few that we could boast of since the persecution of Cromwell's tyranny drove divers worthy men hither. But I thank God, there are no free schools nor printing, and I hope we shall not have these hundred years, for learning has brought disobedience, and heresy, and sects into the world, and printing has divulged them and libels against the best government. God keep us from both." [1]

The General Assembly of 1691 enacted: "That no person or persons whatsoever shall, from henceforth, swear, curse, or profane God's holy name; and if any person or persons shall offend therein, and shall thereof be convicted, by the oath of two witnesses, or by confession of the party, then every such offender shall, for every time so offending, forfeit and pay the sum of one shilling; and forasmuch as, nothing is more acceptable unto God than the true and sincere service and worship of him, according to his holy will, and that the holy keeping of the Lord's day is a principal part of the true service of God, which, in very many places of the dominion, hath been and is now profaned and neglected by a disorderly sort of people;

"Be it enacted . . . That there shall be no meetings, assemblies, or concourse of people out of their own parishes on the Lord's day; and no person or persons whatsoever shall travel upon the said day; and that no other thing or matter whatsoever be done on that day which tends to the profanation of the same; but that the same be kept holy in all respects, upon pain, that every person and persons so offending, and being convicted as aforesaid, shall lose and forfeit twenty shil-

[1] *Ibid.*, p. 517.

2

lings. . . . If offender or offenders be unable to pay
the fine, to be committed to the stocks for every offence,
there to remain for the space of three full hours." [1]

The following Act, entitled, *An Act for the more
effectual suppressing of Blasphemy, Swearing, Cursing,
Drunkenness, and Sabbath-breaking,"* was adopted by
the General Assembly of 1699, viz. :

" Whereas, Notwithstanding many good and wholesome laws already made for the punishment and re-
straining of vice, many wicked, blasphemous, disso-
lute, and vicious persons still continue their impious
and abominable practices, and avow their horrid and
atheistical principles, greatly tending to the dishonor
of Almighty God, and may prove destructive to the
peace and welfare of his Majesty's colony and dominion, for the more effectual suppression of the said
detestable crimes ;

" Be it enacted,—That if any person or persons,
brought up in the Christian religion, shall, by writing,
printing, teaching, or advisably speaking, deny the
being of a God, or the Holy Trinity, or shall assert or
maintain that there are more Gods than one, or shall
deny the Christian religion to be true, or the Holy
Scriptures of Old and New Testament to be of divine
authority, and be thereof lawfully convicted, upon indictment or information in the general court of this his
Majesty's colony and dominion, by the oaths of two or
more creditable witnesses, such person or persons, for
the first offence, shall be adjudged incapable or disabled in law, to all intents and purposes whatsoever,
to hold or enjoy any office or employment, ecclesiastical, civil, or military, or any part of them, or any
profit or advantage to them appertaining, or any of

[1] *Ibid.*, vol. iii., p. 72.

them. And if any person or persons, so convicted as aforesaid, shall, at the time of his or their conviction, enjoy or possess any office, place, or employment, such office, place, or employment shall be void, and is hereby declared void. And if such person or persons shall be a second time lawfully convicted as aforesaid, that then he or they shall, from henceforth, be disabled to sue, prosecute, plead, or use any action or information in any court of law or equity, or to be guardian to any child, or to be executor of any person, or to bear any office ecclesiastical, civil, or military, forever within this his Majesty's colony and dominion, and shall also suffer, from the time of such conviction, three years imprisonment without bail or mainprise. . . .

" Be it further enacted,—That if any person or persons shall profanely swear or curse, or shall be drunk, he or they so offending, for every such offence, being thereof convicted by the oath of one or more witnesses (which oath any justice of the peace is hereby empowered and required to administer), or by confession before one or more justice or justices of the peace, in the county where such offence shall be committed, shall forfeit and pay the sum of five shillings or fifty pounds of tobacco, for every such offence ; or if the said offence or offences be committed in the presence or hearing of one or more justice or justices of the peace, or in any court of record, in this his Majesty's colony and dominion, the same shall be sufficient conviction without any other evidence. And the said offender, upon such conviction, shall forfeit and pay the sum of five shillings or fifty pounds of tobacco, for every such offence, which said sum or sums shall be paid to the church wardens of that parish where the offence shall be committed, who shall be accountable for the same to the vestry of such parish, to

the use of the poor of the parish. And if any person
or persons shall refuse to make present payment, or
give sufficient caution for the payment of the same, at
the levying of the next parish levy, after the said
offence committed, then the said fines and penalties
shall be levied upon the goods of such person or persons by warrant or precept from any justice of peace
before whom the same conviction shall be, which warrant may be directed to the sheriff of the county or to
the constable, in his respective precincts, to be appraised
and valued as another distress. And if the offender or
offenders be not able to pay the said sum or sums, then
he, or they, shall have or receive ten lashes on his, her,
or their bare back, well laid on, for every such offence.

"And for the prevention of Sabbath breaking; Be it
enacted—That if any person or persons, of the age of
twenty-one years or more, do neglect or refuse to resort
to their parish church or chapel once in two months, to
hear divine service upon the Sabbath day, every person
or persons so neglecting or refusing, and being thereof
lawfully convicted, by confession or otherwise, before
one or more justice or justices of the peace where such
offences shall be committed, shall forfeit and pay for
every such offence the sum of five shillings or fifty
pounds of tobacco, to be paid to the church-wardens
of that parish wherein the said offence shall be committed, who shall be accountable for the same to the
vestry for the use of the said parish.

"Provided always, that if any person or persons can
show or make known to their justice or justices such
cause or causes of his, her, or their absence from
church, at any time or times, as the said justice or justices shall adjudge true and reasonable, then the said
pains and penalties shall be remitted to such person or

persons for such time and times and no longer, anything in this Act to the contrary notwithstanding.

"Provided always, that if any person or persons dissenting from the Church of England, being every way qualified, according to one Act of Parliament, made in the first year of the reign of our sovereign lord the King that now is, and the late Queen Mary, of blessed memory, entitled, *An Act for Exempting their Majesties' Protestant Subjects, Dissenting from the Church of England, from the Penalties of Certain Laws*, shall resort and meet at any congregation or place of religious worship, permitted and allowed by the said Act of Parliament, once in two months, that then the said penalties and forfeitures inforced by the Act for neglecting or refusing to resort to their parish church or chapel, as aforesaid, shall not be taken to extend to such person or persons, anything in this Act to the contrary notwithstanding."[1]

In the fifth revisal of the laws of the colony, which was made by the General Assembly in 1705, the foregoing law was re-enacted as Chapter XXX., with the following additions, viz. :

"The person brought up in the Christian religion who should by writing, printing, teaching, or advisedly speaking, deny the being of God, etc., should be liable to the additional disability of being incapable of acting as administrator of any person, and of making any deed of gift or legacy.

"Provided always, that every prosecution, by virtue of this Act for swearing, cursing, or for being drunk, shall be made within two months after the offence committed, and not afterward."

The limit allowed for absence from church was made

[1] *Ibid.*, p. 168.

to be one month instead of two months, and all persons being of the age of twenty-one years or upwards, who "shall not when there (at church) in a decent and orderly manner, continue until the said service is ended ; and if any person shall, on that day, be present at any disorderly meeting, gaming, or tippling, or shall, on the said day, make any journey or travel upon the road, except to and from church (cases of necessity and charity excepted) or shall, on the said day, be found working in their corn or tobacco, or any other labor of their ordinary calling other than is necessary for the sustenance of man and beast,—every person failing or making default in any of these premises (so that prosecution be made within two months after such default) shall forfeit and pay for every such offence the sum of five shillings or fifty pounds of tobacco."

"And be it further enacted,—That this Act shall be publicly read two several times in the year in all parish churches and chapels within this colony by the minister, clerk, or reader, of each parish, immediately after divine service ; that is to say, on the first or second Sunday in April ; and on the first or second Sunday in September, under the penalty of twenty shillings for every such omission and neglect ; and the church-wardens of every parish are hereby required to provide a copy of this Act at the charge of the parish." [1]

An Act of the Assembly of 1661, Chapter III., required "that there be a glebe laid out in every parish, and a convenient house built for the abode of the minister, and that a maintenance be provided for him which shall be worth eighty pounds per annum, besides his perquisites and glebe."

An Act of the Assembly of 1748, Chapter XXXIV.,

[1] *Ibid.*, pp. 358, 362.

Sec. 5, directs that the glebe shall contain two hundred acres of good land, at least; and that there shall be built on it a convenient mansion house, kitchen, barn, stable, dairy, meat house, corn house, and garden; the expense of which is to be levied on the tithable persons of the parish.[1]

In the case of *Godwin et al v. Lunan*, Godwin et al, vestrymen of the upper parish of Nansemond, filed a libel in the General Court, as a court of ecclesiastical jurisdiction, against Lunan, setting forth that he was of evil fame, profligate in manners, much addicted to drunkenness, often drunk at church, unable to go through the service, to baptize or marry, officiated in ridiculous apparel; was a disturber of the peace, quarrelling and fighting, a common profane swearer; that he exposed his private parts, solicited negro and other women to commit fornication and adultery with him; declared that he did not believe in the revealed religion of Christ, that he cared not of what religion he was, so he got the tobacco; nor what became of the flock, so he got the fleece."

Objection was made by the defendant to the jurisdiction of the Court, but the Court decided that it was possessed of jurisdiction; and that as an ecclesiastical court, it might proceed to censure or deprive the defendant.[2]

The Church of England continued to be the established church of Virginia; and the laws regulating the religious life of the people continued without essential modification to be in force throughout the colonial period.

2. **Plymouth.**—The next settlement after that on the James River was made by the Pilgrims, who landed

[1] Jefferson's *Reports*, pp. 104, 105. [2] *Ibid.*, p. 96.

on Plymouth Rock, December 11, 1620. Before leaving Europe they obtained a grant of land from the London Company, but afterwards decided to settle in the territory of the Plymouth Company. They obtained several patents from that company, but failed to obtain confirmation of them by the King. On the 11th day of November, 1620, on board the *Mayflower*, they made the following agreement : " In the name of God, amen. We whose names are underwritten, the loyal subjects of our dread sovereign lord King James, by the grace of God of Great Brittain, France, and Ireland, King, Defender of the faith, etc., having undertaken for the glory of God, and the advancement of the Christian faith, and the honor of our King and country, a voyage to plant the first colony in the northern parts of Virginia ; do, by these presents, solemnly and mutually, in the presence of God and one another, covenant and combine ourselves into a civil body politic, for our better ordering and preservation, and furtherance of the ends aforesaid, and by virtue hereof to enact, constitute, and frame such just and equal laws, ordinances, acts, constitutions, and offices, from time to time, as shall be thought most meet and convenient for the general good of the colony, unto which we promise all due subjection and obedience. In witness whereof we have hereunder subscribed our names, at Cape Cod, the eleventh of November (O. S.) in the year of the reign of our sovereign lord King James of England, France, and Ireland, the eighteenth, and of Scotland the fifty-fourth. Anno Dom. 1620." This colony, partly from a feeling that it was under some obligation to recognize the jurisdiction of the London Company, which was known to favor the Church of England, and partly from conviction forced

upon them by bitter experience, at first kept their civil
and ecclesiastical organizations apart ; but within a
little over thirty years from the time of their landing,
the Church is found united to the State and supported
by taxes upon the people.

The belief, then almost universal, that civil government had not only a religious character, but a religious
function, made its appearance very early in the history
of the colony. It was enacted by the General Court,
June 10, 1650, "that whosoever shall profane the
Lord's day, by doing servile work, or any like abuses,
shall forfeit, for every such default, ten shillings, or be
whipped."

It was enacted on June 6, 1651, "that whatsoever
person or persons shall neglect the frequenting the
public worship of God, that is according to God, in
the places where they live ; or do assemble themselves,
upon any pretence whatsoever, contrary to God and
the allowance of the government, tending to the subversion of religion and churches ; or palpable profanation of God's holy ordinances ; being duly convicted,
viz. : every one that is a master or dame of a family, or
any other person at their own disposing, to pay ten
shillings for every such default."[1]

In 1665 the following law was enacted, viz. :

"Whereas, complaint is made to the Court of great
abuse, in sundry towns of this jurisdiction, by persons
there behaving themselves profanely, by being without doors at the meeting house, on the Lord's day, in
time of exercise, and there misdemeaning themselves
by jesting, sleeping, or the like ; It is enacted by the
court, and hereby ordered that the constables of each
township of this jurisdiction, shall, in their respective

[1] *Plymouth Colonial Records*, vol. xi., p. 57.

towns, take special notice of such persons, and to admonish them; and, if notwithstanding, they shall persist in such practices, that he shall set them in the stocks, and in case this will not reclaim them, that they return their names to the Court." [1]

In July, 1669, it was enacted, that "unnecessary violent riding on the Lord's day" should be reported to the next court after the offence. Also, "that any person or persons that shall be found smoking of tobacco, on the Lord's day, going to, or coming from the meetings, within two miles of the meeting house, shall pay twelve pence, for every such default, to the colony's use." [2]

In June, 1670, the following was enacted, viz. :

"For the further prevention of the profanation of the Lord's day, it is enacted, by the Court and the authority thereof, that the selectmen of the several towns of this jurisdiction, or any one of them, may or shall, as there be occasion, take with him the constable or his deputy, and repair to any house or place where they may suspect that any slothfully do lurk at home, or get together in companies, to neglect the public worship of God, or profane the Lord's day; and, finding any such disorder, shall return the names of the persons to the next court; and give notice also of any particular miscarriage that they have taken notice of, that it may be inquired into." [3]

In 1682 the following was enacted, viz. :

"To prevent profanation of the Lord's day by foreigners or any others, unnecessarily travelling through our towns on that day; It is enacted by the Court that a fit man, in each town, be chosen unto whom whosoever hath necessity of travel on the Lord's day, in case

[1] *Ibid.*, p. 214.   [2] *Ibid.*, pp. 224, 225.   [3] *Ibid.*, p. 228.

of danger of death or such necessitous occasions, shall
repair, and making out such occasions satisfyingly to
him, shall receive a ticket from him to pass on about
such like occasions, which, if the traveller attend not
unto, it shall be lawful for the constable or any man
that meets him, to take him up, and stop him until he
is brought before authority, or pay his fine for such
transgression, as by law in that case is provided. And
if it after shall appear that his plea was false, then may
he be apprehended at another time, and made to pay
his fine as aforesaid. . . .

" It is enacted that none shall presume to attend servile work or labor, or attend any sports, on such days
as are, or shall be, appointed by the Court for humiliation by fasting and prayer, or for public thanksgiving,
on penalty of five shillings." [1]

In 1691 Plymouth colony was united with the colony
of Massachusetts Bay.

3. **Massachusetts Bay.**—A charter was granted
by Charles I., March 4, 1629, to Sir Henry Rosewell
and others, making them a body politic, by the name
of " The Governor and Company of the Massachusetts
Bay, in New England," giving them the territory between the Charles and the Merrimac Rivers, with a
margin of three miles beyond both of these limits. In
the charter it is said that authority is granted to
" establish all manner of wholesome and reasonable
orders, laws, statutes, and ordinances . . . for the
directing, ruling, and disposing of all other matters and
things whereby our said people, inhabitants there, may
be so religiously, peaceably, and civilly governed, as
their good life and orderly conversation may win and
incite the natives of the country to the knowledge and

[1] *Ibid.*, p. 258.

obedience of the only true God, and Savior of mankind, and the Christian faith, which, in our royal intention, and the adventurer's free profession, is the
principal end of this plantation."

This colony, in 1631, three years after the arrival of
the first settlers, enacted that "to the end the body of
the commons may be preserved honest and good men, it
was likewise ordered and agreed that, for time to come,
no man shall be admitted to the freedom of this body
politic but such as are members of some of the churches
within the limits of the same." [1]

The General Court, April 17, 1629, adopted the following action, viz. : " And to the end the Sabbath may
be celebrated in a religious manner, we appoint that
all that inhabit the plantation, both for the general
and particular employments, may surcease their labor
every Saturday throughout the year, at three of the
clock in the afternoon, and that they spend the rest of
that day in catechising and preparation for the Sabbath, as the minister shall direct." [2]

On September 6, 1638, the General Court adopted
the following, viz.: " This Court, taking into consideration the necessity of an equal contribution to all common charges in towns, and observing that the chief
occasion of the defect herein ariseth from hence, that
many of those who are not freemen nor members of
any church do take advantage thereby to withdraw
their help in such voluntary contributions as are in use.

" It is, therefore, hereby declared that every inhabitant in any town is liable to contribute to all charges,
both in church and commonwealth, whereof he doth
or may receive benefit.   And withal, it is ordered that

[1] *Records of the Colony of Massachusetts*, vol. i., p. 87.
[2] *Ibid.*, p. 395.

every such inhabitant who shall not voluntarily contribute proportionably to his ability, with other persons of the same town, to all common charges, as well for upholding the ordinances of the churches as otherwise, shall be compelled thereto by assessment and distress, to be levied by the constable or other officer of the town, as in other cases." [1]

Roman Catholics were denied toleration in the colony by the charter. In 1644, Baptists, who should openly condemn or oppose the baptizing of infants, or go about secretly to seduce from the approbation or use thereof, were, if wilfully and obstinately persistent therein, to be sentenced to banishment. [2]

In 1646, the following law was enacted, viz. : Chapter XXXIX. Section 14. "Forasmuch as, the open contempt of God's word, and messengers thereof, is the desolating sin of civil states and churches ; It is ordered that if any Christian (so-called) within this jurisdiction, shall contemptuously behave himself towards the Word preached or the messengers thereof, called to dispense the same in any congregation, when he doth faithfully exercise his service and office therein, according to the will and word of God, either by interrupting him in his preaching or by charging him, falsely, with any error ; or, like a son of Korah, cast upon his true doctrine or himself any reproach to the dishonor of the Lord Jesus who hath sent him, and to the disparagement of his holy ordinance, and making God's ways contemptible and ridiculous, that every such person or persons (whatsoever censure the church may pass), shall for the first scandal be convented and rebuked openly by the magistrate at some lecture, and bound to their good behavior. And if a second time they break forth into

[1] *Ibid.*, pp. 240, 241.   [2] *Ibid.*, vol. ii., p. 85.

the like contemptuous carriages, they shall either pay five pounds to the public treasury, or stand two hours openly upon a block or stool, four feet high, on a lecture day, with a paper pinned to his breast, written in capital letters, *An open and obstinate contemner of God's holy ordinances*, that others may hear and be ashamed of breaking out into the like wickedness."

Section 15. "Wheresoever the ministry of the Word is established, according to the order of the gospel, throughout this jurisdiction, every person shall duly resort and attend thereunto, respectively, upon the Lord's days, and upon such public fast days, and days of thanksgiving, as are to be generally held by the appointment of authority. And if any person, within this jurisdiction, shall, without just and necessary cause, withdraw himself from hearing the public ministry of the Word, after due means of conviction used, he shall forfeit, for his absence from every such public meeting, five shillings."

Section 14 required that a convenient habitation for the minister be provided by tax.

On November 4, 1646, the following was enacted, viz. :

" Though no human power be lord over the faith and conscience, yet, because such as bring in damnable heresies, tending to the subversion of the Christian faith and destruction of the souls of men, ought to be duly restrained from such notorious impiety ;

" It is therefore ordered and decreed by this Court, that if any Christian, within this jurisdiction, shall go about to subvert or destroy the Christian faith and religion, by broaching or maintaining any damnable heresy, as denying the immortality of the soul ; or the resurrection of the body ; or any sin, to be repented of in the regenerate; or any evil, done by the outward man, to be accounted sin ; or denying that Christ gave himself a ransom for our sins ; or that we are justified by his death and righteousness, but by the perfection of our own works ; or denying the morality of the fourth Commandment ; or any other heresy of such nature and degree ; shall pay to the common treasury, for the first six months, twenty shillings a month ; and if any person shall endeavor to seduce others to the like heresy and apostacy from the faith and religion of our Lord Jesus Christ, he shall forfeit to the treasury for every several offence five pounds." [1]

In 1650 a book, published by William Pyncheon, was, by order of the Court, burned by the common hangman in Boston Common. The book was entitled, *Meritorious Price of Christ's Redemption*, and controverted the orthodox view of the atonement. Mr. Pyncheon was a man of eminence in the colony ; he had come over with John Winthrop ; was the first treasurer of the colony and chief magistrate of Springfield ; but he was deposed from his magistracy and was required to attend the General Court at Boston and report progress from time to time in his conversion to correct views of the atonement. [2]

In 1653 the following was enacted, viz.:

"Upon information of sundry abuses and misdemeanors, committed by several persons, on the Lord's day, not only by children playing in the streets and other places, but by youths, maids, and other persons, both strangers and others, uncivilly walking the streets and fields, travelling from town to town, going on ship-

[1] *The Charters and General Laws of the Colony and Province of Massachusetts Bay*, pp. 102, 103, 177.
[2] Palfrey's *History of New England*, vol. ii., p. 395.

board, frequenting common houses, and other places, to drink, sport, and otherwise to misspend that precious time ; which things tend much to the dishonor of God, the reproach of religion, and the profanation of his holy Sabbath, the sanctification whereof is sometimes put for all duties immediately respecting the service of God, contained in the first table ; It is therefore ordered, by this Court and authority, that no children, youths, maids, or other persons, shall transgress in the like kind, on the penalty of being reputed great provokers of the high displeasure of Almighty God, and further incurring the penalties hereafter expressed ; namely, that the parents and governors of all children above seven years old, (not that we approve of younger children in evil,) for the first offence in that kind, upon due proof before any magistrate, own commissioner, or selectmen of the town, where such offence shall be committed, shall be admonished ; for a second offence, upon due proof as aforesaid, shall pay a fine of five shillings ; for a third offence, upon due proof as aforesaid, ten shillings ; and if they shall again offend in this kind, they shall be presented to the County Court, who shall augment punishment, according to the merit of the fact.''

Upon all youths and maids, above fourteen years of age, and all elder persons, who shall be convicted ''either for playing, uncivilly walking, drinking, travelling from town to town, going on ship-board, sporting, or any way misspending that precious time,'' similar penalties were to be inflicted, and it was provided that, ''if any be unable or unwilling to pay the aforesaid fines, they shall be whipped by the constable, not exceeding five stripes for ten shillings fine.'' [1]

[1] *Records Massachusetts Bay*, vol. iii., pp. 316, 317.

In 1658 a law was enacted requiring that Quakers should be banished from the colony, and that they should be put to death if they returned after banishment.[1] The latter part of the enactment, happily, remained in force only two years, which, unhappily, was long enough to compass the death of four persons. It was thought that none would return under such a penalty and that there never would be occasion for its infliction, but William Robinson, Marmaduke Stevenson, William Leddra, and Mary Dyer, having been banished, returned, under a supposed revelation of the Spirit requiring them to testify to the truth by the sacrifice of their lives. All were hanged on Boston Common. Mary Dyer was offered suspension of the sentence and release while under the gallows and accepted the offer, but afterwards, repenting of her unfaithfulness, returned to seek death.[2]

In 1667 it was enacted by the General Court, "that all laws for sanctification of the Sabbath, and preventing the profaning thereof, be twice in the year, viz., in March and in September, publicly read by the minister or ministers on the Lord's day, in the several respective assemblies within this jurisdiction ; and all people, by him, cautioned to take heed to the observance thereof. And the selectmen are hereby ordered to see to it that there be one man appointed to inspect the ten families of his neighbors, which tithing man, or men, shall, and hereby have power in the absence of the constable to apprehend all Sabbath-breakers and disorderly tipplers, or such as keep licensed houses, or others that shall suffer any disorders in their houses on the Sabbath day, or evening after, or at any other time. . .   And

[1] *Ibid.*, iv., pp. 349, 367.
[2] Palfrey's *History of New England*, vol. ii., pp. 478-480.

3

for the better putting a restraint and securing offenders
that shall any way transgress against the laws, *title*,
Sabbath, either in the meeting house, by abusive carriage or misbehavior, by making any noise or otherwise, or during the daytime, being laid hold on by any
of the inhabitants, shall by the said person appointed
to inspect this law be forthwith carried forth and put
into a cage in Boston, which is appointed, forthwith, by
the selectmen to be set up in the market place, and in
such other towns as the County Court shall appoint ;
there to remain till authority shall examine the person
offending, and give order for his punishment, as the
matter may require, according to the laws relating to
the Sabbath.'' [1]

On November 3, 1675, the following law was enacted,
viz. :

"Whereas, There is so much profaneness amongst
us, in persons turning their backs upon the public
worship before it be finished and the blessing pronounced ; It is ordered by this Court that the officers
of the church or selectmen shall take care to prevent
such disorders by appointing persons to shut the meeting house doors, or some other meet way to attain that
end. . . .

" And, touching the law of importation of Quakers,
that it may be more strictly executed and none transgressing to escape punishment ; It is hereby ordered
that the penalty of that law averred be in no case less
than twenty pounds.'' [2]

On October 15, 1679, the following enactment was
made, viz. :

[1] *Records of the Colony of the Massachusetts Bay in New
England*, vol. v., p. 133.
[2] *Ibid.*, p. 60.

" For the prevention of the profanation of the Sabbath and disorders, on Saturday night, by horses and carts, passing late out of the town of Boston, It is ordered and enacted that there be a ward, from sunset on Saturday night until nine of the clock or after, consisting of one of the selectmen or constables of Boston, with two or more meet persons, who shall walk between the fortification and the town's end, and upon no pretence whatsoever suffer any cart to pass out of the town after sunset ; nor any footman nor horseman, without such good account of the necessity of his business as may be to their satisfaction ; and all persons attempting to ride or drive out of town after sunset, without such reasonable satisfaction given, shall be apprehended and brought before authority, to be proceeded against as Sabbath-breakers, and all other towns are empowered to do the like as need shall be."

" It is ordered by this Court and the authority thereof, that the order with respect to ministers reading the laws respecting the Sabbath once in the year publicly on the Lord's day, be henceforth repealed ; and it is further ordered that the constable or town clerk of the town perform the same upon some public meeeting of the inhabitants." [1]

Sections 18 and 20 of the statute of 1679 are as follows, viz. :

" It being the great duty of this Court to provide that all places and people within our gates be supplied of an able and faithful minister of God's holy word ; Be it therefore enacted by this Court, and the authority thereof, that the county courts within their respective precincts do diligently and carefully attend on the execution of such orders of this Court as concerns the

[1] *Ibid.*, pp. 239, 240, 243.

maintenance of the ministry, and the purging of their towns and peculiars from such ministry and public preachers as shall be found vicious in their lives or perniciously heterodox in their doctrine ; that they use their best endeavor for the procuring and settling of such faithful laborers in God's vineyard ; and that the charges of their procuring and settling be levied on the inhabitants as the law for the maintenance of ministers directs ; and that for the future, there may be no neglect hereof, the presidents of each county court shall duly from time to time give it in charge to the grand juries of their respective courts to present all abuses and neglects of this kind ; and that with all care and diligence the same be redressed, that so the name of the Lord our God being known in our dwellings and exalted in our gates, He may still delight in us."

" It is ordered by the Court and the authority thereof, that no persons whatever, without the consent of the freemen of the town where they live, first orderly had and obtained, at a public meeting assembled for that end, and license of the County Court, or defect of such consent and license, by the special order of the General Court, shall erect or make use of any house as above said (for a meeting house) ; And in case any person or persons shall be convicted of transgressing this law, every such house or houses wherein such persons shall so meet more than three times, with land whereon such house or houses stand, and all private ways leading thereunto, shall be forfeited to the use of the county, and disposed of by the county treasurer by sale, or demolishing as the court that gave judgment in the case shall order." [1]

[1] *Charters and General Laws of the Colony and Province of Massachusetts Bay*, pp. 104, 105.

It was enacted that if a town should neglect to provide for the support of the ministry, " upon complaint made to the Quarter Sessions of the peace the said court of Quarter Sessions shall and hereby are empowered to order a competent allowance unto such minister according to the statute and ability of the town, the same to be imposed upon the inhabitants by the warrant from the Court." [1]

A fine, not exceeding forty shillings, was imposed on each person in the town which neglected to provide for the maintenance of the ministry. Upon a second conviction, a fine of four pounds was imposed on each person, and a like sum for every other conviction. [2]

It was enacted in 1679, "that all masters of families do once a week (at the least) catechise their children and servants in the grounds and principles of religion ; and if any be unable to do so much, that then at least they procure such children and apprentices to learn some short orthodox catechism without book, that they may be able to answer unto the questions that shall be propounded to them out of such catechism by their parents or masters or any of the selectmen, when they shall call them to trial of what they have learned in that kind." [3]

" It is required of the selectmen that all children and youth under family government . . . be taught some orthodox catechism." [4]

By Act of 1700, Jesuits and Romish priests were required to depart the colony, under penalty of imprisonment for life if they returned.

In 1742, upon complaint of the members of the Church of England, a law was enacted without limitation, which had been twice before (1727 and 1735)

[1] *Ibid.*, p. 244.   [2] *Ibid.*, p. 256.

[3] *Ibid.*, p. 74.   [4] *Ibid.*, p. 197.

enacted, with a limitation of five years, allowing the town treasurer to pay to ministers of the Protestant Episcopal Church the taxes received from the members of that church. In order to obtain such payment it was required that the member should present a certificate from the minister and church wardens that he usually and frequently attended that church. [1]

Similar laws were enacted, with limits of various periods, at different times in behalf of the Baptists and Quakers. In 1770 a similar law was enacted in favor of all dissenters, but the treasurer was not allowed to pay over any taxes for the support of a dissenting minister "unless such person shall have been educated at some university, college or public academy for the instruction of youth in the learned languages and in the arts and sciences; or shall have received a degree from some university, college or public academy; or shall have obtained testimonials from the major part of the settled ministers of the gospel in the county that they approved him to be of sufficient learning to qualify him for the work of such ministry." [2]

It appears that such vexatious regulations were prescribed for the administration of the law, that it was difficult for the dissenter to get out of the public treasury the portion due him for the support of his minister. The Baptists objected, on principle, to the requirement of a certificate of membership in their own church in order to get from the town treasury their portion of the taxes; holding that to give certificates implies an acknowledgment that civil rulers have a right to set up one religious sect above another; holding, also, that civil rulers are not representatives in religious matters, and therefore have no right to im-

[1] *Ibid.*, p. 537.　　　　　[2] *Ibid.*, p. 622.

pose religious taxes. They presented their grievances to the Continental Congress in 1774, but failed to obtain any action for their relief.[1]

In 1760, all former laws relating to Sunday were repealed, and a new code adopted, which continued in force throughout and after the colonial period. The preamble to the new code was as follows, viz. :

" And, whereas, It is the duty of all persons upon the Lord's day carefully to apply themselves, publicly and privately, to religion and piety ; the profanation of the Lord's day is highly offensive to Almighty God ; of evil example and tends to the grief and disturbance of all pious and religiously disposed persons ; Therefore. . . ."

The following are some of the provisions of the new law, viz. :

Work or play on land or water ; travelling by any one, except in extreme necessity, and then only far enough for immediate relief; are forbidden, under a penalty of not less than ten, nor more than twenty shillings.

Licensed public-house keepers are forbidden to entertain any except travellers, strangers, and lodgers, in or about their premises, for the purpose of drinking, playing, lounging, or doing any secular business whatever, on penalty of ten shillings ; and the person drinking, playing, lounging, or doing secular business was to be fined five shillings.

Loitering, walking, or gathering in companies, in streets, fields, orchards, lanes, wharves, etc., was forbidden, under penalty of five shillings.

Absence from public worship, for one month, was to be punished with a fine of ten shillings.

[1] *Church and State in New England*, Lauer, pp. 80-83.

The observance of Sunday was to commence at sunset on Saturday.

Twelve wardens were to be appointed in each town to execute these laws. They were to look after all infringements, enter all suspected places, examine or inquire after all suspected persons. In Boston, they were to patrol the streets every Sunday (very stormy or cold days excepted), and diligently watch and search for offenders. These laws were to be read at the March meeting of the towns each year.[1]

4. **Maine.**—The Plymouth Company, on the 10th of August, 1622, gave a patent to Sir Ferdinando Gorges and Captain John Mason for certain territory in New England. Charles I., by a charter issued to Sir Ferdinando Gorges, April 3, 1639, confirmed the previous patent, granting him the territory from Pascataway Harbor to the Kennebec River, and one hundred and twenty miles inland, which was to be called "The Province or County of Mayne." To him were granted in this charter "All Patronages and Advowsons, Free Dispositions and Donacons, of all and every such churches and chapels as shall be made and erected within the said Province and Premises, or any of them, with full power, lycense, and authority to builde, erect, or cause to be builte and erected, so many churches and chappels there as to the said Sir Ferdinando Gorges, his heirs and assigns, shall seeme meete and convenient ; and to dedicate and consecrate the same, or cause the same to bee dedicated and consecrated, according to the Established Lawes of this our Realme of England ; together, alsoe, with all and singular, and as large and ample Rights, jurisdictions . . . as

[1] *Acts and Laws of the Province of Massachusetts Bay,* pp. 392, 397.

the Bishopp of Durham, within the Bishopricke or Countie Palatine of Duresme, in our kingdome of England, now hath, useth, or enjoyeth, or, of right, he ought to have, use, or enjoye.   .   .   ."

While the Church of England was by this charter made the established church of the colony, it appears that Massachusetts, by its enterprise and its aggressions, effected the establishment of the Congregational Church in many of the towns of Maine. Its ecclesiastical policy was made regularly predominant by the purchase of the Gorges Charter in 1677 ; and finally also by the new charter, granted by William and Mary in 1691, which merged all the provinces of Plymouth, Massachusetts, Maine, Sagadohoc, and Acadia into one, under the title of The Province of Massachusetts Bay.

5. New Hampshire.—The first settlements in New Hampshire, Dover, Portsmouth, and Exeter, were independent governments ; but being unable to defend themselves against the Indians, they united with the colony of Massachusetts, in 1641. This union continued till 1679, when New Hampshire was constituted and declared to be a separate province. Charles II., in the Commission constituting the President and Council of the Province of New Hampshire, September 18, 1679, said, " And, above all things we do by these presents, will, require, and command our said Council, to take all possible care for the discountenancing of vice, and encouraging of virtue and good living ; and that by such examples, the infidel may be incited and desire to partake of the Christian religion ; and for the greater ease and satisfaction of the said loving subjects in matters of religion, we do hereby require and command that liberty of conscience shall be allowed unto all Protestants ; that such especially as shall be conformed to the rights of the Church of England shall be particularly countenanced and encouraged." [1]

Among the laws enacted in 1680 are the following, viz. :

" If any person within the province professing the true religion, shall wittingly and wilfully presume to blaspheme the holy name of God the Father, Son and Holy Ghost, with direct, express, presumptuous or high-handed blasphemy, either by wilful or obstinate denying the true God, or his creation, or government of the world ; or shall curse God the Father, Son or Holy Ghost, such person shall be put to death. Leviticus, xxiv., 15, 16." [2]

" Upon information of sundry abuses and misdemeanors, committed by divers persons on the Lord's day, it is therefore ordered and enacted by this General Assembly, that what person soever within this government shall profane the Lord's day by doing unnecessary servile work or travel ; or by sports or recreations ; or by being at ordinaries in time of public worship ; such person or persons shall forfeit ten shillings, or be whipped, for every such offence ; and if it appear that the sin was proudly or presumptuously or with a high hand committed against the known command and authority of the blessed God, such person, therein despising and reproaching the Lord, shall be severely punished at the judgment of the Court. . . . Forasmuch as the open contempt of God's word and the messengers thereof is the desolating sin of several States and churches ; it is therefore enacted that if any Christian, so called, in this province, shall speak contemptuously of the holy Scriptures, or of the holy pen-

[1] *Provincial Papers*, vol. i., p. 378.   [2] *Ibid.*, p. 363.

men thereof, such person or persons shall be punished by fine or corporal punishment, as the Court shall see reason, so as it extend not to the life or limb ; or shall behave himself contemptuously toward the Word of God preached, or any minister thereof, called and faithfully discharging the same in any congregation, either by manifest interrupting him in his ministerial dispensations, or falsely or presumptuously charging him with teaching error, to the disparagement and hindrance of the work of Christ in his hands ; or manifestly or contemptuously reproach the ways, churches, or ordinances of Christ ; being duly convicted thereof, he or they, for the first transgressions, be amerced twenty shillings to the province, or to sit in the stocks not exceeding four hours ; but if he or they go on to transgress in the same kind, then to be amerced forty shillings, or to be whipped for every such traugression." [1]

By the law of 1682, it was " ordered that the constable with some other meet person, whom he shall choose, shall in the time of public worship go forth to any suspected place " and apprehend those who idly straggle abroad.[2]

" Be it enacted,—That it shall and may be lawful for the freeholders of every respective town, convened in public town meeting, as often as they shall see occasion, to make choice of, and by themselves, or any other person or persons by them appointed, to agree with a minister or ministers for the supply of the town, and what annual salary shall be allowed him ; and the minister so made choice of shall be accounted the settled minister of that town ; and the selectmen, then for the time being, shall make rates and assessments upon the inhabitants of the town for the payment of

[1] *Ibid.*, pp. 387, 388.　　　　[2] *Ibid.*, p. 446.

the minister's salary, as aforesaid, in such manner and form as they do for defraying of other town charges, which rates, by warrants from a justice of the peace, with the selectmen, to the constable or constables of the town, shall be by him or them collected and paid, according to the direction of the selectmen, for the end aforesaid.   Provided always that this Act do not interfere with their Majesties' grace and favor in allowing their subjects liberty of conscience, nor shall any person under pretence of being of a different persuasion be excused from paying toward the support of the settled minister or ministers of the town ; but only such as are conscientiously so, and constantly attend the public worship of God on the Lord's day according to their own persuasion, and they only shall be excused from paying towards the support of the minister of the town." [1]

It was voted by the House of Representatives, January 6, 1725, " That the petititioners (of Sandy Beach) are obliged to maintain an able orthodox minister of the gospel, at their own charges." [2]

6. **Connecticut.**—The first permanent settlements in Connecticut were made at Windsor, Hartford, Weathersfield, and Springfield, by emigrants from Massachusetts.   A provisional government was instituted, under a commission from the General Court of Massachusetts, March 3, 1636, issued to eight of the persons who " had resolved to transplant themselves and their estates unto the river Connecticut ; . . . that commission taking rise from the desire of the people that removed, who judged it inconvenient to go away without any frame of government ; not from any claim of the Massachusetts of jurisdiction over them by virtue of Patent." Springfield withdrew from the association in 1637, and

[1] *Ibid.*, vol. iii., pp. 189, 190.   [2] *Ibid.*, vol. iv., p. 414.

the remaining towns formed a written compact or constitution in 1639, entitled, *The Fundamental Orders of
Connecticut*, which was the first constitution "written
out as a complete form of civil order in the new world."
In this constitution they say : "We . . . do for ourselves, and our successors, and such as shall be ad-
joined to us at any time hereafter, enter into combination and confederation together, to maintain and
preserve the liberty and purity of the gospel of our
Lord Jesus, which we now profess ; as also the discipline of the churches, which, according to the truth
of the said gospel, is now practised amongst us." It
is provided in Article I., that the magistrates "shall
have power to administer justice according to the laws
here established ; and for want thereof, according to
the rule of the Word of God." It was provided in
Article 4, "that the Governor be always a member of
some congregation." One clause in the oath of office
to be taken by the Governor and the magistrates was :
"I, N. M. . . . do swear, by the great and
dreadful name of the ever-living God, . . . to
further the execution of justice, for the time aforesaid, according to the righteous rule of God's Word ;
so help me God, in the name of the Lord Jesus
Christ."

In accordance with the recommendation of the Commissioners of the United Colonies of New England, the
General Court of Connecticut, October 4, 1656, enacted
that " No town entertain Quakers, Ranters, Adamites,
or such like notorious heretics, or suffer to continue
with them above the space of fourteen days, upon penalty of five pounds per week ; . . . but the towns-
men shall give notice to the two next magistrates or
assistants, who shall have power to send them to prison

for securing them until they can be conveniently sent out of the jurisdiction." [1]

By an Act of 1650 relating to burglary and robbery, the commission of those crimes on the Sabbath day was made an aggravation which called for punishment of increased severity. "He shall for the first offence have one of his ears cut off; for the second offence, in the same kind, he shall lose his other ear in the same manner; and if he fall into the same offence the third time he shall be put to death."

A law almost identical with that of Massachusetts Bay and New Hampshire was enacted against contemptuous carriage towards God's Word and the ordinances and ministers of the gospel: "Forasmuch as that the open contempt of God's Word and messengers thereof is the desolating sin of civil States and churches; and that the preaching of the Word by those whom God hath sent is the chief ordinary means ordered by God for the converting, edifying, and saving of the souls of the elect, through the presence and the power of the Holy Ghost, thereunto promised; and that the ministry of the Word is set up by God in his churches for those holy ends; and according to the respect or contempt of the same, and of those whom God hath set apart for his own work or employment, the weal or woe of all Christian States is much furthered or promoted;

"It is therefore ordered and decreed that if any Christian (so called) within this jurisdiction shall behave himself contemptuously towards the word preached, or the messengers thereof, called to dispense the same in any congregation, when he faithfully executed the service and office therein, according to the will and

---

[1] *The Public Records of the Colony of Connecticut, Prior to the Union with New Haven, May, 1663*, pp. 283, 284.

word of God, either by interrupting him in preaching,
or by charging him falsely with an error which he hath
not taught, in the open face of the church ; or, like a
son of Korah, cast upon his true doctrine or himself
any reproach, to the dishonor of the Lord Jesus, who
hath sent him ; and to the disparagement of that his
holy ordinance, and making God's way contemptible
or ridiculous ; that every such person or persons (whatsoever censure the church may pass), shall for the first
scandal be convented and reproved openly by the
magistrate, at some lecture, and bound to their good
behavior. And if a second time they break forth into
the like contemptuous carriages, they shall either pay
five pounds to the public treasurer, or stand two hours
openly upon a block or stool four feet high upon a
lecture day with a paper fixed upon his breast with
capital letters, *An open and obstinate contemner of God's
holy ordinance*, that others may fear and be ashamed of
breaking out into like wickedness." [1]

"It is ordered and decreed by this Court and the
authority thereof, that wheresoever the ministry of the
Word is established according to the order of the
gospel, throughout this jurisdiction, every person shall
duly resort and attend thereunto, respectively, upon
the Lord's day, and upon such fast days and days of
thanksgiving as are to be generally kept by the appointment of authority. And if any person within this
jurisdiction shall, without just and necessary cause,
withdraw himself from hearing the public ministry of
the Word, after due means of conviction used, he shall
forfeit for his absence from every such public meeting,
five shillings." [2]

[1] *Ibid.*, pp. 523, 524.
[2] *Public Records of the Colony of Connecticut, Prior to 1665*,
pp. 514, 524.

The following was enacted by the General Assembly, October 11, 1666:

"This Court doth conclude and consider of some way or means to bring those ecclesiastical matters that are in difference in several plantations to an issue, by stating some suitable accommodation and expedient thereunto, and do therefore order that a Synod be called to consider and debate those matters; and that the matters and questions to the elders and ministers that are called to this Synod, shall be publicly disputed to an issue. And this Court doth confer power on this Synod, being met and constituted, to order and authorize the disputation so as may most conduce, in their apprehension, to attain a regular issue of their debates. . . . This Court doth order that the questions stated by this Court shall be those that shall be considered and publicly disputed in the Synod next May. . . :

"17. Question 1st. Whether federal holiness or covenant interest be not the proper ground of baptism?

"Whether it be not justifiable, by the Word of God, that the civil authority indulge Congregational and Presbyterian Churches and their discipline in the churches?"

On May 20, 1668, the following was enacted:

"*Whereas,* The sanctification of the Sabbath is a matter of great concernment to the weal of the people, and the profanation thereof is that as pulls down the judgments of God upon that place or people that suffers the same; it is therefore ordered by this court and the authority thereof, that if any person shall profane the Sabbath, by unnecessary travel or playing thereon, in the time of public worship, or before or after, or shall keep out of the meeting-house during the public worship unnecessarily, there being convenient room in the house, he shall pay five shillings for every such offence, or sit in the stocks one hour. And the constables in the several plantations are hereby required to make search after all offenders against this law and make return thereof to the commissioners or assistants." [1]

On May 15, 1676, the following was enacted :

" *Whereas,* Notwithstanding former provisions made for the due sanctification of the Sabbath, it is observed that by sundry abuses the Sabbath is profaned ; the ordinances rendered unprofitable, which threatens the rooting out of the power of godliness and the procuring of the wrath and judgments of God upon us and our posterity ; for preventing whereof, it is ordered by this Court that if any person or persons henceforth, either on the Saturday night or on the Lord's day night, though it be after the sun is set, shall be found sporting in the field of any town in this jurisdiction, or be drinking in houses of public entertainment, or elsewhere, unless for necessity ; every person so found, complained of and proved transgressing, shall pay ten shillings for every such transgression, or suffer corporal punishment for default of due payment. Nor shall any sell or draw any sort of strong drink at any time, or to be used in any such manner, upon the like penalty for every such default.

" It is also further ordered that no servile work shall be done on the Sabbath, viz. : such as are not works of piety, charity, or necessity ; and no profane discourse or talk, rude or unreverent behavior, shall be used on that holy day, upon penalty of ten shillings fine for every transgression hereof ; and in case the offence be

[1] *Public Records of the Colony of Connecticut, 1665–1678,* p. 88.

4

circumstanced with high-handed presumption as well as profaneness, the penalty to be augmented at the discretion of the judges." [1]

The Lords Commissioners, April 8, 1678, ordered that "some particular queries be prepared which may lead to those informations concerning them [the New England colonies] which may give light into their behavior, so as to guide their Lordships in advising his Majesty into such methods for the settlement and regulation thereof as may best conduce to his royal service"; and the answer given to the 26th query by the Colony of Connecticut was :

"Our people in this colony are, some, strict Congregational men ; others, more large, Congregational men, and some moderate Presbyterians ; and take the Congregational men of both sorts, they are the greatest part of the people in this colony. There are four or five Seven Day men in our colony, and about as many more Quakers.

"27. Answer (1) Great care is taken for the instruction of the people in the Christian religion, by ministers catechising of them, and preaching to them twice every Sabbath days, and sometimes lecture days ; and so by masters and families instructing and catechising their children and servants, being so required to do by law.

"(2) In our corporation are twenty-six towns, and there are one and twenty churches in them.

"(3) For the maintenance of the ministers, it is raised upon the people by way of rate ; and it is in some places one hundred pounds per annum, some ninety pounds, some eighty pounds, some sixty pounds, but in no place less than fifty pounds per annum, as we

[1] *Ibid.*, p. 280.

know of, and so the proportion raised is according as the occasion of the minister calls for it, and the people's ability will allow." [1]

These answers were adopted July 15, 1680. On May 12, 1688, the General Court adopted the following :

"This Court, taking into their most serious consideration, of what high importance it is for the glory of God and the welfare of his Majesty's good subjects inhabiting in this colony, that a competent and certain maintenance of the ministers of the gospel be duly stated and settled ; have judged it their duty to order and appoint, and accordingly do by the authority of this Court enact, order, and appoint, that the towns and plantations in this colony pay unto the respective ministers in the said towns or plantations annually the several sums and payments which shall be agreed upon, which sums or payments in each town or society shall be levied and assessed on the persons inhabiting in such towns or plantations, according to their respective estates. . . . And, it is further ordered by this Court and the authority thereof, that if any towns in this colony shall be, in and for any year or years, without a minister, preaching the gospel unto them, such town or towns shall, in the said year or years, notwithstanding, pay such sums or payments as the General Court shall appoint, as if there were a minister there." [2]

On October 12, 1699, it was enacted :

"That in every town, plantation, or society within this colony where the major part of the householders of any the said town, plantation, or society, who in or

[1] *Ibid.,* May, 1676 ; June, 1689, pp. 299, 300.
[2] *Ibid.,* 1688–1704, pp. 198, 199.

by law are an allowed society, are agreeing in calling
and settling a minister, such minister so called and
settled shall be accounted the lawful minister of said
town, plantation, or society ; and that all agreements,
respecting the maintenance and settlement of such
minister, made by the major part of the householders
of said town, plantation, or society, shall be binding
and obliging to the whole and all of said town, plantation, or society, and to their successors, according to
all the true intents and purposes thereof.

" And it is further ordered and enacted, by the
authority aforesaid, that where this Court hath determined the bounds and limits of any society in any town
or plantation in this colony where there are more than
one society, that in every such case, all persons living
within the bounds and limits, and their estates lying
within the same, shall bear their proportion of, and be
rateable according to law for the support and maintenance of the minister of that society, any law, usage, or
custom to the contrary notwithstanding." [1]

Upon the observance of the Sabbath it was enacted
in October, 1709 :

" That if any single persons, being boarders or sojourners, or any young persons whatsoever, under the
government of parents or masters, within this colony,
shall convene or meet together in company or companies, in the street or elsewhere, on the evening after
the Sabbath, or any public day of fast or any lecture
day, and be thereof duly convicted, shall pay a fine of
five shillings, or be set in the stocks, not exceeding
two hours for each such offence." [2]

October, 1715.   " *Whereas*, In the printed law entitled *Sabbath*, p. 104, no provision is made to prevent

[1] *Ibid.*, p. 316.   [2] *Ibid.*, 1706-1716, p. 130.

vessels sailing up and down the great river Connecticut on the Sabbath day, which the masters of vessels,
taking the advantage of, do frequently, and without
restraint, pass up and down said river on said day ; Be
it therefore enacted, that if any vessel shall sail or pass
by any town or parish on said river where the public
worship of God is maintained, or shall weigh anchor
within two miles of said place, unless to get nearer
thereto on the Sabbath day, any time betwixt the morning light and the sun setting, the master of such vessel
shall be liable to the like penalty as if he had departed
out of a harbor." [1]

" Whatsoever person shall not attend the public
worship of God on the Lord's day in some congregation, allowed by law, unless hindered by sickness or
otherwise necessarily detained, and be thereof convicted,
shall incur the penalty of five shillings money for every
such offence." [2]

7. **New Haven.**—The colony of New Haven was
founded in 1638, by a number of English emigrants led
by the Rev. John Davenport, who had been minister
of St. Stephen's Church, London, but was deprived of
his charge and banished on account of his Puritanism ;
and by Mr. Theophillus Eaton, a wealthy merchant of
London, who had been a member of Mr. Davenport's
church, and sympathized with him in his Puritan
views.

On the 4th day of the fourth month, called June,
1639, all the free planters assembled together in a general meeting in " a mighty barn," to consult about
settling a civil government according to God, and about
the nomination of persons who might be found, by consent of all, fittest in all respects for the foundation work

[1] *Ibid.*, p. 525.   [2] *Ibid.*, 1717–1725, p. 248.

of a church, which was intended to be gathered in Quinipiack. It was agreed by vote that "the Scriptures do hold forth a perfect rule for the direction and government of all men in all duties which they are to perform to God and men, as well in the government of families and commonwealths, as in matters of the church. That church members only shall be burgesses, and that they only shall choose magistrates and officers among themselves to have the power of transacting the public civil affairs of this plantation ; of making and repealing laws ; dividing inheritances ; deciding differences that may arise, and doing all things or business of like nature ; and that all that should be hereafter admitted here as planters subscribe their names to the above order."

" That twelve men be chosen, that their fitness for the foundation work may be tried ; however, there may be more named, yet it may be in their power who are chosen, to reduce them to twelve ; and it be in the power of those twelve to choose out of themselves seven that shall be most approved of the major part to begin the church."

Mr. Davenport having preached a sermon at the opening of the meeting from the text, Prov. ix., 1 : " Wisdom hath builded her house, she hath hewn out her seven pillars," the seven men were chosen as pillars of the church, in supposed accordance with the action of Wisdom as set forth in that text.

On October 25, 1639, the Court " consisting of those seven only who were the foundation of the church . . . met, and after solemn prayer unto God, did proceed as follows " :

First. All former power or trust for managing any public affairs in this plantation, into whose hands soever formerly committed, was now abrogated, and from henceforward utterly to cease.

Second. They admitted nine new members, upon their acceptance of the terms propounded in a charge delivered to them.

"This being done the Court proceeded to the choice of a magistrate and four deputies to assist in the public affairs of the plantation, Mr. Davenport first opening two Scriptures, viz. : Deut. i., 13 ; Ex. xviii., 21, wherein a magistrate, according to God's mind is described."[1]

The town of Milford having admitted six men to be free burgesses who were not church-members, and the matter having been brought before the Court, it was agreed, first, that these six are not to be chosen, either deputies or into any public trust for the combination ; second, that they are not to vote for magistrates ; third, none are to be admitted by Milford hereafter to be free burgesses but church-members ; but the six are to be allowed to sit in town business, in which the combination is not interested. Two may vote for deputies to the General Courts for the combination or jurisdiction, which deputies shall always be church-members.[2]

The following enactment was made April 3, 1644 :

"In the beginning of the first foundation of this plantation and jurisdiction, upon a full debate with due and serious consideration, it was agreed, concluded, and settled, as a fundamental law, not to be disputed or questioned hereafter, that the judicial laws of God, as they were delivered by Moses and expounded in other parts of the Scripture, so far as they are a fence to the

[1] *Records of the Colony and Plantation of New Haven,* 1638–1649, pp. 20, 21.

[2] *Ibid.,* pp. 110, 111.

moral law, being neither typical nor ceremonial, nor having a reference to Canaan, shall be accepted as of moral equity, and as God shall help, shall be a constant direction for all proceedings here and a general rule in all courts of this jurisdiction, how to judge between party and party, and how to punish offenders till the same be branched out into particulars hereafter." [1]

The following enactments were made with reference to the observance of the Sabbath and attendance at church, January 31, 1647: "The Court, considering that it is their duty to do the best they can that the law of God may be strictly observed, did therefore order that whosoever in this plantation shall break the Sabbath by doing any of their ordinary outward occasions, from sunset to sunset, either upon the land or upon the water, extraordinary cases, works of necessity and mercy being excepted, he shall be counted an offender and shall suffer such punishment as the particular court shall judge mete according to the nature of the offence." [2]

" Whosoever shall profane the Lord's day or any part of it, either in sinful servile work, or by unlawful sport, or otherwise, whether wilfully or in careless neglect, shall be duly punished by fine, imprisonment, or corporally, according to the nature and measure of the sin and offence. But if the Court upon examination, by clear and satisfying evidence, find that the sin was proudly, presumptuously and with a high hand committed against the known command and authority of the blessed God, such a person, therein despising and reproaching the Lord, shall be put to death, that all

[1] *Revision of Feb. 24, 1644-45,* p. 191.
[2] *Records of the Colony and Plantation of New Haven, 1638-1649,* p. 358.

others may fear and shun such provoking rebellious courses. Num. xv., 30–36.'' [1]

"And it is further ordered that wheresoever the ministry of the Word is established within this jurisdiction, according to the order of the gospel, every person, according to the mind of God, shall duly resort and attend thereunto upon the Lord's days, at least, and also upon days of public fasting or thanksgiving ordered to be generally kept and observed. And if any person within this jurisdiction shall without just and necessary cause absent or withdraw himself from the same, he shall, after due means of conviction used, for every such sinful miscarriage, forfeit five shillings to the plantation, to be levied as other fines.'' [2]

Charles II., on the 23d of April, 1662, gave a charter to John Winthrop and others, constituting them a body-politic under the title, "Governor and Company of the English Colony of Connecticut, in New England, in America.'' Hartford and New Haven, which had hitherto remained separate colonies, accepted this charter, April 20, 1665, and thus became a part of the colony of Connecticut.

One object of the King in granting this charter, as stated therein, was that "our said people inhabiting there may be so religiously, peaceably, and civilly governed, as their good life and orderly conversation may win and invite the natives of the country to the knowledge and obedience of the only true God and Savior of mankind and the Christian faith ; which, in our royal intentions, and the adventurers free profession is the only and principal end of this plantation.''

This expression of the purpose of the plantation, being almost identical with that contained in other

[1] *Ibid.*, 1653–1655, p. 605.   [2] *Ibid.*, p. 588.

charters, may have been on the part of its author or authors an empty form, but it reflects, nevertheless, the public sentiment of the day, and reveals one of the purposes held to be obligatory in all such enterprises.

In 1770, an Act was passed allowing all sober persons who conscientiously differed from the established worship and ministry of the colony, to meet together for worship without incurring the penalties provided in previous laws against such meetings, and against absence from the recognized services.[1]

The Charter of 1662 continued to be the organic law of the State of Connecticut until 1818, with the addition of only four brief articles; and the laws upon the subject of religion made under the charter continued to be in force throughout and beyond the colonial period.

8. The Confederation.—In 1643, Articles of Confederation betwixt the Plantations of Massachusetts, the Plantations under the government of Plymouth, the Plantations under the government of Connecticut, and the government of New Haven were adopted constituting the four colonies a confederation, under the title of "The United Colonies of New England." The government of the confederation was to be entrusted to a body composed of two Commissioners from each of the four colonies.

In the Preamble to the Articles of Agreement, they say : " *Whereas*, All came into these parts with one and the same end and aim, namely, to advance the kingdom of the Lord Jesus Christ and to enjoy the liberties of the gospel in purity and peace : . . ."

It was solemnly and unanimously approved and concluded as a fundamental agreement upon which the combination was formed, " That none shall be admitted

[1] *Acts and Laws of Connecticut, 1750–1772*, p. 351.

freemen or free burgesses within this jurisdiction or any
part of it, but such planters as are members of some
one or other of the approved churches of New England ;
nor shall any but such be chosen to magistracy, or to
carry on any civil judicature, or as deputies or assistants, to have power or vote in establishing laws, or in
making or repealing orders ; or to any military office or
trust ; nor shall any other but church-members have
any vote in any such elections." [1]

" This Court, thus framed, shall, 1st, with all care and
diligence from time to time provide for the maintenance
of the purity of religion and suppress the contrary,
according to their best light and directions from the
Word of God. 2dly, though they humbly acknowledge that the supreme power of making laws and of
repealing belongs to God only, and that by Him this
power is given to Jesus Christ as Mediator, Matt.
xxviii., 19 ; John v., 22 ; and that the laws for holiness
and righteousness are already made and given us
in the Scriptures, which, in matters moral or of moral
equity, may not be altered by any human power or
authority. . . . Yet civil rulers and courts, and
this General Court in particular, (being instructed by
the freemen as before,) are the ministers of God for the
good of the people, and have power to declare, publish,
and establish, for the Plantations within their jurisdiction, the laws He hath made ; and to make and repeal
orders for smaller matters, not particularly determined
in Scriptures, according to the more general rules of
righteousness, and while they stand in force, to require
due execution of them." [2]

" Forasmuch as the Word of God as it is contained

[1] *Code of New Haven, 1656*, pp. 562, 567.
[2] *Ibid.*, 569.

in the Holy Scriptures is a pure and precious light, by
God, in His free and rich mercy, given to His people,
to guide and direct them in safe paths to everlasting
peace. And for that the preaching of the same in the
way of due exposition and explanation, by such as
God doth furnish and send, is, through the presence
and power of the Holy Ghost, the chief ordinary
means appointed by God for conversion, edification,
and salvation ; it is ordered that if any Christian, so
called, shall within this jurisdiction behave himself
contemptuously toward the word preached, or any
minister thereof called and faithfully dispensing the
same in any congregation, either by interrupting him
in his preaching, or falsely charging him with error, to
the disparagement and hindrance of the work of Christ
in his hands, every such person or persons shall be
duly punished, either by the plantation court or court
of magistracy, according to the quality and measure of
the offence, that all others may fear to break out in
such wickedness.'' [1]

''It is ordered that if any Christian within this jurisdiction shall go about to subvert or destroy the Christian faith or religion by broaching, publishing, or
maintaining any dangerous error or heresy, or shall
endeavor to draw or seduce others thereunto, every
such person so offending and continuing obstinate
therein, after due means of conviction, shall be fined,
banished, or otherwise severely punished.'' [2]

On September 5, 1644, the Commissioners of the
United Colonies sent to the colonies the following for
adoption :

'' *Whereas,* The most considerable persons in these
colonies came to these parts of America that they

[1] *Ibid.*, p. 588.   [2] *Ibid.*, p. 590.

might enjoy Christ in his ordinances without disturbance ; and

" *Whereas,* Among many other precious mercies, the ordinances are and have been dispensed among us with much purity and power ; the Commissioners took it into their serious consideration how some due maintenance according to God might be provided and settled, both for the present and future, for the encouragement of the ministers who labor therein, and concluded to propound and commend to each General Court, that those who are taught in the Word in the several plantations be brought together, that every man voluntarily set down what he is willing to allow to that end and use ; and if any may refuse to pay a meet proportion, that then he be rated with authority in some just and equal way ; and if after this any man withhold or delay due payment, the civil power to be exercised as in other just debts." [1]

In September, 1656, the Commissioners of the United Colonies, upon the suggestion of the magistrates of Massachusetts Bay Colony, " Proposed to the several General Courts that all Quakers, Ranters and other notorious heretics be prohibited coming into the United Colonies ; and if any shall hereafter come or arise amongst us that they be forthwith secured and removed out of all the jurisdictions." [2]

9. **Rhode Island.**—Roger Williams, who was ordained a clergyman of the Church of England, became a zealous Puritan soon after his ordination. In 1631, at the age of twenty-five, he emigrated to Massachusetts with his young wife. Arriving in Boston, he

[1] *Records of the Colony of Connecticut Prior to the Union with New Haven,* 1663, p. 112.

[2] *Ibid.,* p. 283.

refused to join the congregation of that town because
they would not make public declaration of their repentance for having been once in connection with the
Church of England, and going to Salem he became
assistant minister at that place, but was soon involved
in controversy with his brethren, which waxed so hot
and so disturbed the peace, that he was finally banished
in 1635. Among the reasons for his banishment was
his denying the right of the civil government to impose
faith and worship, and affirming that the power of the
civil magistrate extends only to the bodies, goods, and
outward state of men, and not to their souls and consciences. He went to what is now Providence, R. I.,
and there established a pure democracy, withholding
from the body-politic all power to interfere in matters
which concern man and his Maker only.

In 1643 the inhabitants of Providence, Portsmouth,
and Newport, upon their petition, were granted "a
free and absolute charter of incorporation, to be known
by the name of The Incorporation of Providence Plantations in the Narragansett Bay in New England, with
full power to rule themselves . . . by such form
of civil government as by voluntary consent of all, or
the greater part of them, they shall find most suitable
to their estate and condition."

The Commonwealth of England, in 1651, claimed
the right to appoint the governor of the Providence
Plantations. In 1663 Charles II. granted a new charter
securing to the people the full freedom of the old one.
In this charter the King says :

" *Whereas*, We have been informed by the humble
petition of our trusty and well-beloved subject, John
Clarke, on the behalf of Benjamin Arnold . . .
(and others), that they, pursuing with peaceable and

loyal minds their sober, serious, and religious intentions of godly edifying themselves and one another in
the holy Christian faith and worship, as they were persuaded ; together with the gaining over and conversion
of the poor ignorant Indian natives in those parts of
America to the sincere profession and obedience of the
same faith and worship ; . . .

"*And Whereas,* In their humble address, they have
freely declared that it is much in their hearts (if they
may be permitted) to hold forth a lively experiment,
that most flourishing civil state may stand and best be
maintained, and that among our English subjects, with
a full liberty in religious concernments ; and that true
piety, rightly grounded upon gospel principles, will
give the best and greatest security to sovereignty, and
will lay in the hearts of men the strongest obligation
to loyalty ;

"*Now know ye* that we, being willing to encourage the
hopeful undertaking of our said loyal and loving subjects, and to secure them in the free exercise and enjoyment of all their civil and religious rights, appertaining to them, as our loving subjects ; and to preserve
unto them that liberty in the true Christian faith and
worship of God which they have sought with so much
travail, and with peaceable minds and loyal subjection
to our royal progenitors and ourselves, to enjoy ; and because some of the people and inhabitants of the same
colonies cannot in their private opinions conform to the
public exercise of religion according to the liturgy, forms
and ceremonies of the Church of England, or take or
subscribe the oaths and articles made and established
in that behalf ; and for that the same, by reason of the
remote distances of those places, will (as we hope) be
no breach of the unity and uniformity established in

this nation ; have therefore thought fit, and do hereby publish, grant, ordain, and declare, that our royal will and pleasure is that no person, within the said colony, at any time hereafter, shall be molested, punished, disquieted, or called in question, for any differences in opinion in matters of religion, that do not actually disturb the civil peace of our said colony ; but that all and every person and persons from time to time, and at all times hereafter, may freely and fully have and enjoy his and their own judgments and consciences in matters of religious concernments, throughout the tract of land hereafter mentioned ; they behaving themselves peaceably and quietly, and not using their liberty to licentiousness and profaneness, nor to the civil injury or outward disturbance of others. . . .''

This charter remained in force as the fundamental law of the colony and also of the State until the adoption of the first State Constitution, Nov. 21–23, 1842.

While the laws of the colony established no denominational church and provided for no compulsory attendance on religious services, yet not only was a profession of Christianity required as a qualification for office, but also of Protestantism. From 1719 to 1783 the following was on the statute book, purported to have been enacted in 1664 : '' That all men professing Christianity, and of competent estates, and of civil conversation, who acknowledge and are obedient to the civil magistrate, though of different judgments in religious affairs (Roman Catholics only excepted) shall be admitted freemen, and shall have liberty to choose and be chosen officers in this colony, both military and civil.'' [1]

There were no laws compelling the people to observe

[1] *Records of the Colony of Rhode Island and Providence Plantations*, vol. ii., p. 36.

the Sabbath religiously, but certain things, allowable on other days of the week, were prohibited on the Sabbath.

On the 2d of September, 1673, it was "Voted this Assembly considering that the King hath granted us that not any in this colony are to be molested in the liberty of their consciences, who are not disturbers of the peace, and we are persuaded that a most flourishing government, with loyalty, may be best propagated where liberty of conscience, by any corporal power, is not obstructed, that is not to any unchasteness of body, and not by a body doing any hurt to a body, neither endeavoring so to do, and although we know, by man not any can be forced to worship God, or for to keep or not to keep holy any day ; but forasmuch as the first days of the weeks, it is usual for parents and masters not to employ their children or servants as upon other days ; and some others also that are not under such government, accounting it as spare time, and so spend it in debaistness or tippling, and unlawful games and wantonness, and most abominally there practised by those that lived with the English, at such times to resort to towns ; therefore, this Assembly, not to oppose or propagate any worship, but as by preventing debaistness, although we know masters or parents cannot, and are not, by violence to endeavor to force any under their government to any worship or from any worship, that is not debaistness or disturbant to the civil peace, but they are to require them, and if that will not prevail, if they can, they should compel them not to do what is debaistness, or uncivil, or inhuman, not to frequent any immodest company or practices.

"Therefore, by his Majesty's authority, it is enacted that on the first days of the weeks, whoever he be that

5

doth let any have any drink, that he or any other is drunk thereby, besides all other forfeitures therefor, for every one so drunk they shall forfeit six shillings ; and for every one that entertains in gaming or tippling upon the first day of the week, he shall forfeit six shillings. And by his Majesty's authority thereby it is enacted, that for to prevent any such misdemeanors, or if any are so guilty, to discover them, that every first day of the week in every town in this colony there shall be a constable's watch, for every inhabitant fit to watch to take his turn that belongeth to the town, or pay for hiring one, so for one or more to watch in a day, as the Town Council judge necessary, to restrain any debaistness, or immodesty, or concourse of people, tippling or gaming, or wantonness, that all modest assemblies may not be interrupted ; especially all such as profess they meet in the worship of God ; if some of them will be most false worshippers, they should only be strove against therefore with spiritual weapons, if they do not disown that they should not be condemned, whoever they be, that be unchaste with their bodies, or with bodies oppress, or do violence to what is mortal of any man, but as they should be subject to such, to suffer for such transgressions, parents may thereof correct their children, and masters their servants ; and magistrates should be a terror to such evil doers." [1]

10. **Vermont.**—Vermont can scarcely be said to have had a colonial existence, but in the towns which were under the jurisdiction of New York the Church of England was favored by the law ; and in the towns that acknowledged the jurisdiction of New Hampshire or Massachusetts, the Congregational Church was the established church.

[1] *Ibid.*, pp. 503, 504.

11. New York.—Under the Dutch West India Company, chartered in 1621, no other religion was to be publicly tolerated or allowed in New Netherland save that then taught and exercised by authority of the Reformed Church in the United Provinces. Under the royal grants to James, Duke of York and Albany, 1664 and 1674, the Church of England became the established church of the Province. In both cases, however, on account of the mixed character of the people and the almost perpetual conflicts of jurisdiction, it was impossible to put the establishment in anything like uniform and rigorous enforcement. It is probable also that the Duke of York was inclined to toleration.

In 1673 each town was empowered to make laws against Sabbath-breaking and other immoralities. In 1695 a law was enacted of which the following was the preamble, viz. :

" *Whereas*, the true and sincere worship of God, according to His holy will and commandments, is often profaned and neglected by many of the inhabitants and sojourners in this Province who do not keep holy the Lord's day, but in a disorderly manner accustom themselves to travel, laboring, working, shooting, fishing, sporting, playing, horse-racing, frequenting tippling-houses, and the using many other unlawful exercises and pastimes, upon the Lord's day, to the great scandal of the holy Christian faith, be it enacted," etc.

A fine of six shillings was imposed by this law upon the offences specified in the preamble ; a justice of the peace might convict on his own sight ; in default of payment of the fine the offender was to sit in the stocks three hours ; if any master refused to pay the fine imposed on a negro or Indian slave or servant, the slave or servant was to be whipped thirteen lashes ; it was

lawful to travel any distance under twenty miles for
the purpose of attending public worship, and to go for
a physician or a nurse.[1]

12. New Jersey.—The Duke of York, whose
charter covered the territory southward to the east side
of the Delaware Bay, granted in 1664 the territory,
now belonging to the State of New Jersey, to Lord
John Berkley and Sir George Carteret. These proprietors divided their holding by a line running from
Barnegat Creek a little north of west to the Rancocas ;
the one taking the southern part, which was called
West Jersey, and the other the northern part, which
was called East Jersey. The line of division was afterwards made to run northward from Little Egg Harbor
in the lower part of Delaware Bay. Berkley sold West
Jersey to a company of Quakers, and in 1682 a society
of Quakers, under the lead of William Penn, bought
East Jersey of the heirs of Carteret. During the proprietary government, there was no uniform church and
State establishment, but the multiplicity of proprietors
and the conflict between diverse interests and opinions
led the proprietors in 1702 to surrender their right of
government to the Crown, when the Church of England became the established church of the province.
Liberty of conscience, however, was permitted to all but
Roman Catholics.

13. Pennsylvania.—Charles II. granted a charter
to William Penn for the Province of Pennsylvania,
March 4, 1681. In 1682 Penn promulgated *The
Frame of Government in Pennsylvania in America*, in
the preface of which he says on the subject of the rise

[1] *Laws of New York*, 1691-1773, vol. i., pp. 23, 24. *New
York*, 1874 : Lewis, pp. 200, 201.

and end of government : " So that government seems to me a part of religion itself, a thing sacred in its institution and end, . . . and is as such (though a lower, yet) an emanation of the same Divine Power that is both author and object of pure religion."

Among the laws agreed upon in England by the Governor and divers freemen of the province, April 20, 1682, are :

" XXXV. That all persons living in this Province who confess and acknowledge the one Almighty and Eternal God to be the Creator, Upholder, and Ruler of the world, and that hold themselves obliged, in conscience, to live peaceably and justly in civil society, shall in no ways be molested or prejudiced for their religious persuasion or practice in matters of faith and worship ; nor shall they be compelled at any time to frequent or maintain any religious worship, place, or ministry whatever.

" XXXVI. That according to the good example of the primitive Christians, and the ease of the creation, every first day of the week, called the Lord's day, people shall abstain from their common daily labor, that they may the better dispose themselves to worship God according to their understandings.

" XXXVII. That, as a careless and corrupt administration of Justice draws the wrath of God upon magistrates, so the wildness and looseness of the people provoke the indignation of God against a country ; therefore, that all such offences against God as swearing, cursing, lying, profane talking, drunkenness, drinking of healths, obscene words, incest, sodomy, rapes, fornication, and other uncleanness (not to be repeated), . . . all prizes, stage players, cards, dice, May-games, gamesters, masques, revels, bull-baitings, cruelty, looseness and irreligion, shall be respectively discouraged and severely punished."

The counties of "New Castle, Kent, Sussex upon Delaware" were purchased of the Duke of York by Penn in 1682, and were added to Pennsylvania, under the title of "The Territories."

William and Mary upon ascending the throne of England took the government of the Provinces and Territories of Pennsylvania into their own hands, but afterwards, August 26, 1695, restored to Penn his former possessions.

In the Charter of Privileges for Pennsylvania, granted by Penn, October 28, 1701, he says :

Article 1. " *Whereas*, no people can be truly happy, though under the greatest enjoyment of civil liberties, if abridged of the freedom of their consciences as to their religious profession and worship ; and Almighty God, being the only Lord of conscience, Father of lights and spirits, and the author, as well as the object of all divine knowledge, faith, and worship, who only doth enlighten the minds and persuade and convince the understandings of people ; I do hereby grant and declare that no person or persons inhabiting this Province or Territories, who shall confess and acknowledge one Almighty God, the Creator, Upholder, and Ruler of the world, and profess him or themselves obliged to live quietly under civil government, shall be in any case molested or prejudiced in his or their person or estate because of his or their conscientious persuasion or practices ; nor be compelled to frequent or maintain any worship, place, or ministry, contrary to his or their mind ; or to do or suffer any other act or thing contrary to their religious persuasion.

" And that all persons who also profess to believe in

Jesus Christ, the Savior of the world, shall be capable (notwithstanding their other persuasions and practices in point of conscience or religion) to serve this government in any capacity, both legislatively and executively. . . .''

This charter remained in force until the formation of the first Constitution in 1776.

While the first legislative acts of the colony recognized the Christian religion, and guaranteed liberty of conscience, yet it was enacted, '' to the end that looseness, irreligion, and atheism may not creep in, under pretence of conscience, whoever shall speak loosely and profanely of Almighty God, Jesus Christ, the Holy Spirit, or Scriptures of truth, and is thereof legally convicted, shall forfeit and pay five pounds, and be imprisoned five days in the house of correction.''

All legislators, judges, and public officers were required to subscribe a declaration of their disbelief in transubstantiation, the adoration of the Virgin Mary and other saints, and the sacrifice of the Romish mass, as superstitious idolatries ; also a declaration of their belief in the Holy Trinity and in the divine inspiration of the Scriptures.

14. Maryland.—Sir George Calvert, who was made Lord Baltimore, in 1625, being much disturbed by the French in the possession of his province of Avalon in New Foundland, and having explored the territory bordering on the Chesapeake Bay in 1628, returned to England and petitioned Charles I. to grant him a charter for a colony to be settled about the head of Chesapeake Bay. This petition was granted, but as he died before the papers were executed, the charter was issued to his son Cecilius Calvert, second Lord Baltimore, June 20, 1632. The charter sets forth as one of the grounds upon which it is granted, the fact that the grantee is "animated with a laudable and pious zeal for extending the Christian religion." It goes on to grant and confirm unto the said Baron of Baltimore, his heirs and assigns, . . . "the patronages and advowsons of all churches which (with the increasing worship and religion of Christ) within the said region, islands, islets, and limits aforesaid, hereafter shall happen to be built ; together with license and faculty of erecting and founding churches, chapels, and places of worship, in convenient and suitable places within the premises ; and of causing the same to be dedicated and consecrated, according to the ecclesiastical laws of our kingdom of England."

Sir George Calvert had become a Roman Catholic in 1624, and in the light of that fact the restriction in the last clause of this paragraph may fairly be interpreted as prohibiting the establishment of the Catholic Church in the colony, and as providing for the establishment of the Church of England.

Cecilius Calvert, second Lord Baltimore, sent his brother Leonard over as manager of an expedition, which consisted of two hundred persons. The expedition sailed from Cowes, in the Isle of Wight, November 22, 1633, and reached its destination, March 27, 1634. The founding of the proprietary colonies was, in a large measure, a business enterprise on the part of the proprietors, and as their interest lay in the speedy settlement of their estates in the new world, they were ready to receive respectable and thrifty emigrants from all countries and of all religious persuasions. Among other inducements they offered religious toleration. Such a consideration, together with the prohibition in the charter as to the establishment of the Roman Catholic Church, may have contributed to the determination of Lord Baltimore to make religious tolerance a prominent feature of the new colony. He instructed his governor and commissioners to cause all acts of the Roman Catholic religion, on shipboard going over, to be done as privately as possible ; that they instruct the Roman Catholics to abstain from discourse on matters of religion ; and that they treat the Protestants with as much mildness and favor as justice will permit. It appears that he promised liberty of conscience, and offered lands to a colony of Puritan refugees from Virginia ; and that he sent a commission to Boston to invite Puritans from Massachusetts Bay to settle in Maryland, offering them lands. There can hardly be a doubt, however, that he was an enlightened and sincere believer in religious toleration, and that he was moved to this determination by principle, as well as policy.

On the 21st day of April, 1649, an Act of Toleration was passed and was confirmed by the Lord Proprietary August 26, 1650. It contained the following provisions, viz. :

"*An Act Concerning Religion.* Forasmuch as in a well governed and Christian Commonwealth, matters concerning religion and the honor of God ought, in the first place, to be taken into serious consideration, and endeavored to be settled ; Be it therefore ordered and enacted, by the Right Honorable Cecilius Lord Baron of Baltimore, absolute Lord and Proprietary of this Province, with the advice and consent of this General Assembly ; that whatsoever person or persons within this Province and islands thereunto belonging shall from henceforth blaspheme God, that is, curse Him or deny our Savior Jesus Christ to be the son of God, or shall deny the Holy Trinity, the Father, Son, and Holy

Ghost, or the Godhead of any of said three persons of the Trinity, or the unity of the Godhead ; or shall use or utter any reproachful speeches, words, or language concerning the said Holy Trinity, or any of the said three persons thereof; shall be punished with death and confiscation or forfeiture of all his or her lands or goods to the Lord Proprietary and his heirs. . . .

" And be it also enacted, by the authority and with the advice and assent aforesaid, that whatsoever person or persons shall from henceforth use or utter any re-proachful words or speeches concerning the blessed Virgin Mary, the mother of our Savior, or the Holy Apostles or Evangelists, or any of them, shall in such case for the first offence forfeit to the said Lord Proprietary the sum of five pound sterling or the value there-of. . . . And that every such offender or offenders for every second offence shall forfeit ten pound sterling or the value thereof. . . . And that every person or persons before mentioned offending herein the third time, shall for such third offence forfeit all his lands and goods, and be forever banished and expelled out of this Province.

" And be it also further enacted, by the same author-ity, advice, and assent, that whatsoever person or persons shall from henceforth, upon any occasion of offence or otherwise, in a reproachful manner or way declare, call, or denominate any person or persons whatsoever inhabiting, residing, trafficking, trading, or commercing within this Province, or within any ports, harbors, creeks, or havens, to the same belonging, an Heretic, Schismatic, Idolator, Puritan, Independent, Presbyterian, Popish priest, Jesuit, Jesuited papist, Lutheran, Calvinist, Anabaptist, Brownist, Antinomian, Barrowist, Roundhead, Separatist, or any other name or term, in a reproachful manner, relating to the matter of religion, shall for every such offence forfeit and lose the sum of ten shillings sterling, or the value thereof, to be levied on the goods and chattels of every such offender or offenders, the one half thereof to be forfeited and paid unto the person and persons of whom such reproachful words were or shall be spoken or uttered ; and the other half thereof to the Lord Proprietary and his heirs, Lords and Proprietaries of this Province. But if such person or persons who shall at any time utter or speak any such reproachful words or language, shall not have goods or chattels sufficient and overt, within this Province, to be taken to satisfy the penalty aforesaid, or that the same be not otherwise speedily satisfied, then the person or persons so offending shall be publicly whipped, and shall suffer imprisonment without bail or mainprise until he, she, or they, respectively, shall satisfy the party so offended or grieved by such reproachful language, by asking him or her respectively for forgiveness publicly, for such his offence, before the magistrate or chief officer or officers of the town or place where such offence shall be given.

" And be it further likewise enacted, by the authority and consent aforesaid, that every person and persons, within this Province, that shall at any time hereafter profane the Sabbath or Lord's day, called Sunday, by frequent swearing, drunkenness, or by any uncivil or disorderly recreation, or by working on that day, when absolute necessity doth not require it, shall for every such offence forfeit 2s. 6d. sterling, or the value thereof, and for the second offence 5s. sterling, or the value thereof; and for the third offence, and so for every time he shall offend in like manner afterwards, 10s. sterling, or the value thereof. . . .

" And whereas, the inforcing of conscience in matters of religion hath frequently fallen out to be of dangerous consequences, in those Commonwealths where it hath been practised ; and for the more quiet and peaceable government of this Province, and the better to preserve mutual love and amity amongst the inhabitants thereof ; Be it therefore, also, by the Lord Proprietary, with the advice and consent of this Assembly, ordained and enacted (except as in this present Act is before declared and set forth) that no person or persons whatsoever, within this Province, or the islands, ports, harbors, creeks, or havens thereunto belonging, professing to believe in Jesus Christ, shall from henceforth be any ways troubled, molested, or discountenanced for, or in respect of his or her religion, nor in the free exercise thereof within this Province or the islands thereunto belonging ; nor any way compelled to the belief or exercise of any other religion against his or her consent, so as they be not unfaithful to the Lord Proprietary, or molest or conspire against the civil government established or to be established in this Province under him or his heirs." [1]

It is said that this Act is the first instance on this continent in which religious liberty was proclaimed by law. It has been disputed whether the Protestants or the Roman Catholics were in the majority in the Province and in the General Assembly at this time, and to which of these parties the credit of this Act belongs. The fact that there were Protestants enough in the colony at the time to make this a disputed question, is itself evidence that the Catholic Proprietary had, from the first, adopted the principle or the rule of toleration.

[1] *Archives of Maryland Assembly*, vol. i., pp. 244–247.

In 1652 the royal government of England having been superseded by the Commonwealth, commissioners were sent over to Maryland, who, co-operating with the Puritans, succeeded in establishing the authority of the Commonwealth in the colony.

"*An Act Concerning Religion.* It is enacted and declared in the name of his Highness, the Lord Protector, with the consent and the authority of the present General Assembly, that none who profess and exercise the popish religion, commonly known by the name of the Roman Catholic religion, can be protected in this Province by the laws of England, formerly established and yet unrepealed ; nor by the government of the Commonwealth of England, Scotland, and Ireland, and the dominions thereunto belonging, published by his Highness the Lord Protector, but are to be restrained from the exercise thereof ; Therefore all and every person or persons concerned in the law aforesaid are required to take notice.

"Such as profess faith in Jesus Christ (though differing in judgment from the doctrine, worship, and discipline publicly held forth), shall not be restrained from, but shall be protected in, the profession of the faith, and exercise of their religion, so as they abuse not this liberty to the injury of others, or the disturbance of the public peace on their part ; provided, that this liberty be not extended to popery or prelacy, nor to such as under the profession of Christ hold forth and practice licentiousness." [1]

"It is enacted that every person or persons within this Province that shall be lawfully convicted of swearing, shall be liable to pay for every oath ten pounds of tobacco. . . ."

[1] *Ibid.*, vol. ii., pp. 340, 341.

No work shall be done on the Sabbath day, but that which is of necessity and charity to be done. No inordinate recreations, as fowling, fishing, hunting, or other, no shooting of guns shall be used on that day except in case of necessity.

Whoever shall be lawfully convicted of the breach of any such law shall be liable to pay one hundred pounds of tobacco, half whereof shall be to the informer and the other half to the public use.[1]

In 1657 the proprietary government was restored, and Lord Baltimore issued the following order :

" His Lordship wills and requires his said Lieutenant and Council that the law in this said Province entitled *An Act Concerning Religion*, and passed heretofore there with his Lordship's assent, whereby all persons who profess to believe in Jesus Christ have liberty of conscience and free exercise of their religion, there be duly observed in the said Province by all the inhabitants thereof ; and that the penalties mentioned in the said Act be duly put in execution upon any offenders against the same or any part thereof." [2]

The members of the Church of England, though a very small minority of the population, made frequent and strenuous efforts to secure the establishment of their church in the colony by the home government, but by the firm and reasonable opposition of Baltimore were defeated. At length, after the close of the English revolution, making occasion of the failure of Lord Baltimore's deputies to proclaim William and Mary, they induced the King and Queen to take the government into their own hands, and the Church of England was made the established church of the Province.

[1] *Ibid.*, pp. 343, 344.   [2] *Ibid.*, Council I., 325.

15. Carolina.—Charles II., on the 24th of March, 1663, granted a charter to Edward, Earl of Clarendon, and others, erecting, ordaining, and incorporating a province to be called the Province of Carolina, extending from 31° to 36° N. latitude, from the mouth of the Satilla River in Georgia to Albemarle Sound. In 1665 a second charter was given extending the limits northward to 36° 30', and southward to 29°, including all the territory between the present northern boundary of North Carolina and a point sixty-five miles south of St. Augustine, Fla.

The first charter sets forth, as one of the grounds upon which it is granted, the fact that the incorporators were "excited with a laudable and pious zeal for the propagation of the Christian faith." Article 3d gives them "the patronage and advowsons of all the churches and chapels which, as Christian religion shall increase within the country, isles, islets, and limits aforesaid, shall happen hereafter to be erected; together with license and power to build and found churches, chapels, and oratories, in convenient and fit places, within the said bounds and limits, and to cause them to be dedicated and consecrated according to the ecclesiastical laws of our kingdom of England."

18th. "And because it may happen that some of the people and inhabitants of the said Province cannot, in their private opinions, conform to the public exercises of religion according to the liturgies, forms, and ceremonies of the Church of England, or take and subscribe the oaths and articles made and established in that behalf; and for that the same, by reason of the remote distances of these places, will, we hope, be no breach of the unity and uniformity established in this nation; our will and pleasure therefore is, and we do by these presents, for us, our heirs and successors, give and grant unto the said Edward, Earl of Clarendon . . . full and free license, liberty, and authority by such legal ways and means as they shall think fit to give and to grant unto such person or persons inhabiting and being within the said Province, or any part thereof, who really in their judgments, and for conscience sake cannot, or shall not conform to the said liturgy and ceremonies, and take and subscribe the oaths and articles aforesaid, or any of them, indulgencies and dispensations in that behalf, for and during such time and times, and with such limitations and restrictions as they, the said . . . shall in their discretion think fit and reasonable ; and with this express proviso and limitation, also, that such person or persons . . . do not in any wise . . . scandalize or reproach the said liturgy, forms, and ceremonies, or anything relating thereunto, or any person or persons whatsoever, for or in respect of his or their use or exercise thereof, or his or their obedience and conformity thereunto.''

This Article was included in the second charter, excepting that after the words '' think fit and reasonable,'' and in place of what follows thereafter, the following provision is added, viz. :

''And that no person or persons unto whom such liberty shall be given shall be any way molested, punished, disquieted, or called in question for any differences in opinion or practice, in matters of religious concernments, who do not actually disturb the civil peace of the Province, county, or colony that they shall make their abode in. But all and every such person and persons may from time to time, and at all times, freely and quietly have and enjoy his and their judgments and consciences in matters of religion, throughout all the said Province or colony, they behaving themselves peaceably and not using this liberty to licentiousness, nor to the civil injury or outward disturbance of others."

In the *Fundamental Constitutions of Carolina*, prepared by John Locke in 1669, and amended by the Earl of Shaftesbury, are the following provisions and requirements, viz. :

"96. As the country comes to be sufficiently planted and distributed into fit divisions, it shall belong to the Parliament, to take care for the building of churches and the public maintenance of divines to be employed in the exercise of religion according to the Church of England, which being the only true and orthodox and the national religion of all the King's dominions, is so also of Carolina ; and therefore it alone shall be allowed to receive public maintenance by grant of Parliament.[1]

"97. . . . And seven or more persons agreeing in any religion shall constitute a church or profession, to which they shall give some name to distinguish it from others.

"98. The terms of admittance and communion with any church or profession shall be written in a book, and therein be subscribed by all the members of said church or profession ; which book shall be kept by the public register of the precinct wherein they reside.

"100. In the terms of communion of any church or profession, these following shall be three ; without

---

[1] It is said that this article was drawn up and inserted in the *Fundamental Constitutions* by some of the Proprietors against the judgment of Mr. Locke.

which no agreement or assembly of men, upon pretence of religion, shall be counted a church or profession, within these rules : 1st. That there is a God. 2d. That God is publicly to be worshipped. 3d. That it is lawful and the duty of every man, being thereunto called by those that govern, to bear witness to truth. . . .

" 101. No person, above seventeen years of age, shall have any benefit or protection of the law, or be capable of any place of profit or honor, who is not a member of some church or profession, having his name recorded in some one, and but one, religious record at once.''

These *Fundamental Constitutions* were abrogated by the Lords Proprietors in April, 1693, and the government was carried on again under the provisions of the charter. The charter was not consistent in its provisions relating to religion. One part of it guarantees religious toleration to the settlers ; another furnishes a basis for the establishment of the Church of England. It was the interest of the proprietors, and their purpose, as a body, to faithfully observe the guaranty of religious freedom, but the " Society for the Propagation of the Gospel in Foreign Parts," incorporated June 16, 1701, construed its mission to the colonies in America to be the establishment of the Church of England, and pursued that mission in Carolina with almost fanatical zeal, basing their action on the provisions of the charter, which gave to the proprietors license and power to build churches and to cause them to be dedicated according to the ecclesiastical laws of England. The movement was finally successful, and the Church of England became the established church of both the Carolinas, and continued to be so throughout the colonial period.

16. Georgia.– General James Oglethorpe, having been appointed a trustee for the relief of insolvent debtors in England, conceived a plan for the formation of a colony in America, to improve their condition, and to afford a refuge for the persecuted Protestants of Europe. He organized a company for colonization, to which a charter was granted by George II., June 9, 1732. The King says in the charter : " *Whereas*, We are credibly informed that many of our poor subjects are, through misfortunes and want of employment, reduced to great necessity, inasmuch as by their labor they are not able to provide a maintenance for themselves and families ; and if they had means to defray their charges of passage and other expenses incident to new settlements, they would be glad to settle in any of our provinces in America ; . . . *And whereas* we think it highly becoming our crown and royal dignity . . . to extend our fatherly compassion even to the meanest and most infatuated of our people, and to relieve the wants of our above-mentioned poor subjects ; and that it will be highly conducive for accomplishing those ends that a regular colony of said poor people be settled and established in the southern territories of Carolina ; . . . Know ye, therefore, for the considerations aforesaid . . . ordained, constituted, and appointed . . . be and shall be one body politic and corporate in deed and in name, by the name of the Trustees for establishing the colony of Georgia in America. . . ."

" And for the greater ease and encouragement of our loving subjects and such others as shall come to inhabit in our said colony, we do by these presents . . . grant, establish, and ordain that, forever hereafter, there shall be a liberty of conscience allowed in the worship of God to all persons inhabiting, or which shall inhabit or be resident within our said Province ; and that all such persons, except papists, shall have a free exercise of religion, so they be content with the quiet and peaceable enjoyment of the same, not giving offence or scandal to the government. . . . And we do hereby grant and ordain that such person or persons, for the time being, as shall be thereunto appointed by the said corporation . . . shall have full power and authority to administer and give the oaths, appointed by an Act of Parliament, made in the first year of the reign of our late royal father, to be taken, instead of the oaths of allegiance and supremacy, and also the oath of abjuration, . . . and, in like cases, to administer the solemn affirmation to any of the persons commonly called Quakers in such manner as by the laws of our realm of Great Britain the same may be administered. . . ."

The Trustees of the new colony regarded themselves as charged with responsibility for the spiritual condition of the inhabitants and for the conversion of the Indians, and they engaged Rev. John Wesley to go out as a missionary. Wesley went out in 1735, accompanied by his brother Charles and two others, but notwithstanding that he was at the time a high churchman, and notwithstanding that he had not yet experienced what he afterwards regarded as Christian conversion, yet it appears that he was more zealous to turn the people from their wicked ways than to secure the establishment of the Church of England. His public rebukes and the exercise of his ecclesiastical authority in denying the privileges of the communion to persons who in his opinion had rendered themselves unworthy by wrongdoing unrepented of, brought upon him a persecution which was intended to drive him from the colony, and did cause him to return to England in 1738.

CHAPTER III.

DEDUCTIONS FROM THE HISTORY.

It appears from the historical survey we have made, that up to the time of the colonization of America the union of civil and religious institutions had been universal. It appears also that in the various colonial governments founded in America, toleration, when secured, was only the separation of some particular sect of Christians, not of Christianity itself, from the civil institutions. Even in the fundamental law of the Province of Rhode Island, a Christian purpose is expressly stated and a particular form of Christianity (Protestantism) was required as a qualification for office.

In the frame of government of Pennsylvania, prepared by the proprietor, William Penn, while the principle of toleration was most firmly established, the Christian character of the government was at the same time most positively asserted, and the most rigid provisions made for its establishment. In the colonial governments, of larger religious freedom, no discrimination was made between the various divisions of Protestantism, but they were Protestant as against Roman Catholicism. In those of largest freedom, no discrimination was made between the various divisions of the Christian church, but they were Christian as against all other forms of religion, and against unbelief. Not one was negative, or neutral, on the subject of Christianity.

Thus far, the union of the religion of a people with their civil institutions is a universal fact. Two different interpretations may be put upon the fact :

1st. The universal fact may be taken as revealing a law of nature. Man is by the constitution of his nature religious, as well as social ; therefore, his religious and social sentiments will be necessarily blended in all their manifestations. Man will be religious in his social institutions, just as he is social in his religious institutions. No antecedent purpose or effort has been required to bring about a union of the civil and religious institutions of mankind, for the reason that such union is the primordial and natural state of things. Purpose and effort have been necessary to effect a separation between them, for the reason that the separation is a secondary and adventitious state of things. Therefore, any effort to accomplish a complete separation will be an effort against nature, and will prove to be either futile or destructive.

2d. The union of civil and religious institutions, although primordial, is to be regarded as a low condition which is destined to be abolished by the operation of the forces of progress, which are ever present in nature, either as latent or potential energy. Conflict has been necessary to convert the one form of energy into the other. The striking of the steel on the flint is necessary to bring out the spark ; so has conflict been necessary to kindle the light of liberty. When any party becomes so strong as to have no fear of the opposition, it will assume paternal prerogatives, no matter what may be the form of government or the character of the constitutional restraints. An equal division of the people into parties is a providential provision, as necessary to the perpetuation of liberty, as a like division into sexes is necessary for the perpetuation of the species. As a matter of fact, where there has been no party strong enough to maintain a conflict, which, if it were in the military world, would be entitled to recognition as a state of war, paternalism has reigned. It was the conflict between Protestantism and the Church of Rome, and between the various divisions of the Protestant Church which brought out the principles and kindled the fires of religious liberty in these later centuries. And during this period the flame has gone out where it once burned brightly, when one party became so predominant as to suppress all conflict. The Congregationalists of Massachusetts Bay banished dissenters, and with them banished religious liberty from the colony ; and liberty returned not until conflict came again. The Puritans of all New England and of Maryland looked to the absence of conflict as the ideal condition of the Commonwealth, and hesitated not to use the most despotic measures to bring about that condition. When they were given toleration, they accepted it as a piece of good fortune or as a providential favor to the truth they espoused, not as a right belonging to all men. When in power, they felt bound by principle to deny the boon to all those whom they regarded as advocates of false doctrine. Nevertheless the forces of progress, working constantly against all resistance, made steady advancement, till now in this country the principle of toleration is universally accepted.

May we not expect this righteous evolution to continue, until toleration shall be rejected as a lingering vestige of spiritual despotism, and the era of true religious liberty shall be ushered in, by the removal of all religious character from our civil institutions?

We shall not now enter upon the consideration of the merits of these two interpretations of the facts of history, but shall proceed to take up our second subject of inquiry,—The question of fact.

PART II.

A question of fact. What is the relation of the Christian religion to civil government, in the United States, at the present time?

CHAPTER I.

In entering upon the inquiry, What is the relation of the Christian religion to civil government in these United States? let us bear in mind that it is simply one of *fact*, and not of theory or opinion ;—what *is* ; not what *ought to be*. The caution is needed ; for there are unmistakable indications in some quarters that opinion as to what ought to be has established a foregone conclusion as to what *is*. On the part of many it is assumed that in this country there is an entire separation between religion and civil government ; or, if there be not in fact such a separation, the connection, whatever it may be, is in violation of the fundamental principles of our institutions, and is a wrong to a number of our fellow-citizens which a proper sense of justice would speedily remove. It is assumed that the underlying principles of our political institutions require that they should be entirely destitute of religious character,—that they should be no more Christian than they are Mohammedan or pagan. We speak of this as an assumption for the reason that while it is often uttered as an opinion, or taken for granted as a truth, there is seldom any attempt made to sustain it

91

by proof. If any such attempt is made, it is usually but little more than the assertion that the whole history and genius of our institutions are directly against the contrary assumption. The history, as we have shown, and shall still farther show, instead of furnishing ground for the assumption in question, furnishes ground for the very opposite. As to the *genius* of our institutions, it may properly be regarded as too indefinable a thing to be made the basis of a definite proposition; especially, if there are facts, as we shall show that there are, which have a bearing in the opposite direction.

CHAPTER II.

THE CONSTITUTION OF THE UNITED STATES.

We shall begin this part of our investigation, with an effort to ascertain the bearing of the Constitution of the United States on the question.

We find that very little is said in the Constitution on the subject of religion, and that what little is said is of a prohibitory character. There is in the body of it no mention of the name of the Divine Being; nor any recognition of His existence, not even in the form of oath prescribed to be administered to the President at his induction into office.

It may be said that this negative and prohibitory character of the Constitution is ground for a very strong presumption as to the intent of its framers. It may be said, also, that this presumption is supported by the fact that there were influential members of the Constitutional Convention, who might be supposed to be averse to giving the Constitution the slightest religious character. It is to be remarked, however, that the persons referred to were a very small part of the membership of the convention. It is to be remarked, also, that there are facts which indicate that even they would not be disposed to divest the civil institutions of the land of all religious character. It was Benjamin Franklin who introduced the resolution proposing that the sessions of the convention be opened with prayer. In making the motion he said, "The longer I live, the more convincing proofs I see of this truth, that God governs the affairs of men." Surely if Franklin was not averse to opening with prayer the body that framed the Constitution, he would not be averse to a provision for opening, with prayer, the legislative bodies, acting under the Constitution. Thomas Jefferson, whose influence may have been felt in the convention, said, in his first message as president, "Can the liberties of a nation be thought secure when we have removed their only firm basis, a conviction in the minds of the people that their liberties are the gift of God." Surely, when he was not averse to reminding the people officially of this fact, he would not be averse to a recognition of the fact in the system of institutions under which he held his office.[1]

[1] In a letter to Dr. Joseph Priestley, dated at Washington, June 19, 1802, Mr. Jefferson writes : "One passage in the paper you enclosed me, must be corrected. It is the following, 'And all say it was yourself more than any other individual that planned and established it,' *i. e.* the Constitution. I was in Europe when the Constitution was planned, and never saw it until after it was established. On receiving it, I wrote strongly to Mr. Madison, urging the want of provision for the freedom of religion, freedom of the press, trial by jury, habeas corpus, the substitution of militia for a standing army, and an express reservation to the States of all rights not specifically

Now turning to the Constitution itself, we find the following provisions :

Article VI. "No religious test shall ever be required as a qualification to any office or public trust under the United States."

Amendment I., Article the First. " Congress shall make no law respecting an establishment of religion, or prohibiting the free exercise thereof."

If it be admitted that these two Articles are a sufficient ground for the assumption in question, yet it is to be remembered that they are expressly made to apply to the general government alone. They do not apply to the States. It may have been the intent in framing the Constitution to assign the matter of religion to the domain of the States, rather than to accomplish an elimination of all religious character from our civil institutions. It may be said that this conjecture needs proof before it can be accepted as true. Of that we are well aware, and we shall now proceed to give the proof.

In Article 1, Section 10, of the Constitution, the States are prohibited doing certain specified things, and the establishment of religion is not one of those things. According, therefore, to the accepted maxim of interpretation, *Designatio unius est exclusio alterius ; et expressum facit cessare tacitum*, the subject of religion is left to the jurisdiction of the States. But the Constitution expressly declares (Amendment 1, Article the Ninth) that " The enumeration in the Constitution of certain rights shall not be construed to

granted to the Union. He accordingly moved in the first Congress for these amendments, which were agreed to and ratified by the States as they now stand. This is all the hand I had— related to the Constitution." *Works*, vol. iv., pp. 440, 441.

deny, or disparage others, retained by the people."
And Article the Tenth says that "The powers, not
delegated to the United States by the Constitution, nor
prohibited by it to the States, are reserved to the States,
respectively, or to the people."

By a fair interpretation of the Constitution, the right
to recognize Christianity, and even to make a law respecting an establishment of religion, is to be held as
one of the rights reserved to the States. We would not
presume to offer our mere interpretation of the Constitution, as conclusive on the question, but we have to
say—

1st. That our interpretation is sustained by high authority. Judge Story, in his *Commentary on the Constitution of the United States*, pp. 702, 703. says, " Thus,
the whole power over the subject of religion was left
exclusively to the State governments, to be acted on
according to their own sense of justice, and the State
Constitutions."

2d. The Circuit Court of the United States, W. D.,
Tennessee, *In re King*, August 1, 1891, decided that
"The fourteenth amendment of the Constitution of the
United States has not abrogated the Sunday laws of the
States, and established religious freedom therein. The
States may establish a Church or Creed, and maintain
them, so far as the Federal Constitution is concerned."
The Court said, " As a matter of fact they (the founders
of our government) left the States the most absolute
power on the subject, and any of them might, if they
chose, establish a creed and a church and maintain
them." [1]

3d. This interpretation of the Constitution is made
conclusive by the fact that nearly all of the original

[1] *The Federal Reporter*, vol. 46, p. 912.

States either by express provision, by the disqualifications for office specified, or by the oaths of office prescribed in their Constitutions, have at some time in their history established either Protestantism or Christianity as the religion of the State ; while one of them established a particular Protestant denomination as the Church of the State—all maintaining these several relations of religion to the State, unchallenged under the Constitution of the United States.

CHAPTER III.

THE STATES.

1. **Connecticut.**—The Constitution of 1818, Article VII., entitled *Of Religion*, is as follows, viz. :

Section 1. "It being the duty of all men to worship the Supreme Being, the great Creator and Preserver of the Universe, and their right to render that worship in the mode most consistent with the dictates of their consciences ; no person shall, by law, be compelled to join or support, or be classed with or associated with any congregation, church, or religious association ; but every person now belonging to such congregation, church, or religious association shall remain a member thereof until he shall have separated himself therefrom in the manner hereinafter provided. And each and every society or denomination of Christians in this State shall have and enjoy the same and equal powers, rights, and privileges ; and shall have power and authority to maintain the ministers or teachers of their respective denominations, and to build and repair houses of public worship, by a tax on the members of any such society only, to be laid by a major vote of the legal voters assembled at any society meeting, warned and held according to law, or in any other manner.''

Section 2. '' If any person shall choose to separate himself from the society or denomination of Christians to which he may belong, and shall leave a written notice thereof with the clerk of such society, he shall thereupon be no longer liable for any future expenses which may be incurred by said society.''

The following continued in force in Connecticut after the adoption of the Constitution of the United States :

"Be it enacted by the Governor, Council, and Representatives, in General Court assembled, and by the authority of the same, that all and every person and persons in this State shall, and they are hereby required, on the Lord's day carefully to apply themselves to the duties of religion and piety, publicly and privately. And whatsoever person shall not duly attend the public worship of God on the Lord's day in some congregation allowed by law, provided there be any which he can conscientiously and conveniently attend, unless hindered by sickness, or otherwise necessarily prevented, shall for every such offence pay a fine of three shillings.'' [1]

A statute of 1791 imposed a fine, not exceeding twelve shillings nor less than six shillings, for not abstaining from any kind of servile labor and recreation, works of necessity and mercy excepted, on Fast and Thanksgiving days.

2. **Vermont.**—Constitution of 1777, Chapter I. *Section 3.* "Nor can any man who professes the Protestant religion be justly deprived or abridged of

---

[1] Revised and approved, Jan. 8, 1784.

7

any civil right as a citizen, on account of his religious sentiment or peculiar mode of religious worship.
. . . Nevertheless, every sect or denomination ought
to observe the Sabbath or the Lord's day, and keep up
and support some sort of religious worship which to
them shall seem most agreeable to the revealed will
of God."

Chapter II. *Section 9.* "And each member (of the
House of Representatives) before he takes his seat,
shall make and subscribe to the following declaration,
viz. : 'I do believe in one God, the creator and governor of the universe, the rewarder of the good and the
punisher of the wicked ; and I do acknowledge the
Scriptures of the Old and New Testaments to be given
by divine inspiration ; and own and profess the Protestant religion.' And no further or other religious test
shall ever hereafter be required of any civil officer or
magistrate of this State." This requirement continued in force until the adoption of the Constitution
of 1793.

3. **New Hampshire.**—Constitution of 1784. Bill
of Rights. Article VI. "As morality and piety,
rightly grounded on evangelical principles, will give
the best and greatest security to government, and will
lay in the hearts of men the strongest obligation to
due subjection, and as the knowledge of these is most
likely to be propagated through a society by the institution of the public worship of the Deity, and of public
instruction in morality and religion ; therefore, to promote these important purposes, the people of this State
have a right to impower, and hereby do fully impower,
the Legislature to authorize from time to time the
several towns, parishes, bodies politic, or religious
societies within this State, to make adequate provision,

at their own expense, for the support and maintenance of public Protestant teachers of piety, religion,
and morality."

Part II. *Section 14.* " Every member of the House
of Representatives . . . shall be of the Protestant
religion."

Section 29. " Provided, nevertheless, that no person
shall be capable of being elected a Senator who is not
of the Protestant religion. . . ."

Section 42. " And no person shall be eligible to this
office . . unless he shall be of the Protestant
religion."

These provisions continued in force until 1877.

4. New Jersey.—Constitution of 1776. Article
XIX. " . . . And that no Protestant inhabitant
of this colony shall be denied the enjoyment of any
civil right merely on account of his religious principles, but that all persons professing a belief in the faith
of any Protestant sect who shall demean himself peaceably under the government, as hereby established, shall
be capable of being elected to any office of profit or
trust, or of being a member of either branch of the
Legislature. . . ."

This article continued in force until 1844.

5. Pennsylvania.—Constitution of 1776. Bill of
Rights. Article II. " . . . Nor can any man
who acknowledges the being of a God be justly deprived, or abridged, of any civil right as a citizen on
account of his religious sentiments or peculiar mode
of religious worship."

Frame of Government. Section 10. " And each member (of the House of Representatives) before he takes
his seat shall make and subscribe the following declaration, viz. :

"I do believe in one God, the creator and governor of the universe, the rewarder of the good, and the punisher of the wicked. And I do acknowledge the Scriptures of the Old and New Testament to be given by Divine inspiration.

"And no further, or other, religious tests shall ever hereafter be required of any civil officer or magistrate in this State."

This test remained in force until the adoption of the Constitution in 1790.

Constitution of 1790. Article IX. *Section 4.* "That no person who acknowledges the being of a God and a future state of rewards and punishments, shall on account of his religious sentiments be disqualified to hold any office or place of trust or profit under this Commonwealth."

This article was incorporated in the Constitution of 1838, as Article IX., Sec. 4; and in the Constitution of 1873 as Article I., Sec. 4.

6. **Delaware.**—Constitution of 1776. Article XXII. "Every person who shall be chosen a member of either House, or appointed to any office or place of trust, before taking his seat or entering upon the execution of his office, shall take the following oath or affirmation, if conscientiously scrupulous of taking an oath, to wit:

"'I, A. B., do profess faith in God the Father, and in Jesus Christ his only Son, and in the Holy Ghost, one God, blessed forevermore; and I do acknowledge the Holy Scriptures of the Old and New Testaments to be given by Divine inspiration.'"

This Article was part of the organic law of the State until 1792.

7. **Maryland.**—Constitution of 1776. Declaration

of Rights. Article XXXIII. "That it is the duty of every man to worship God in such manner as he thinks most acceptable to him ; all persons professing the Christian religion are equally entitled to protection in their religious liberty ; . . . yet the Legislature may, in their discretion, lay a general and equal tax for the support of the Christian religion, leaving to each individual the power of appointing the payment over the money, collected from him, to the support of any particular place of worship or minister, or for the benefit of the poor of his own denomination, or the poor in general, of any particular county."

This power given to the Legislature was revoked by an amendment which was adopted in 1810.

8. North Carolina. Constitution of 1776. Article XXXII. "That no person who shall deny the being of God, or the truth of the Protestant religion, or the divine authority either of the Old or New Testaments, or shall hold religious principles incompatible with the freedom and safety of the State, shall be capable of holding any office, or place of trust or profit, in the civil department within this State.

This Article was amended in 1835 by the substitution of the words "Christian religion" for the word "Protestant religion."

Constitution of 1876. Article VI. *Section 5*. "The following persons shall be disqualified for office : First, all persons who shall deny the being of Almighty God. . . ."

9. South Carolina. Constitution of 1778. Article XXXVIII. ". . . The Christian Protestant religion shall be deemed, and is hereby constituted and declared to be, the established religion of this State. That all denominations of Christian Protestants in this

State, demeaning themselves peaceably and faithfully,
shall enjoy equal religious and civil privileges   .   .   . ;
and that when fifteen or more male persons, not under twenty-one years of age, professing the Christian
Protestant religion, and agreeing to unite themselves
in a society for religious worship, they shall (on com-
plying with the terms hereinafter mentioned) be, and
be constituted a church ; and be esteemed and regarded,
in law, as of the established religion of the State ; and
on a petition to the Legislature shall be entitled to be
incorporated, and to enjoy equal privileges.   .   .   .
But that previous to the establishment and incorporation of the respective societies of every denomination,
as aforesaid, and in order to entitle them thereto,
every society so petitioning shall have agreed to
and subscribed in a book, the following five articles,
without which no agreement or union of men, upon
pretence of religion, shall entitle them to be incorporated and esteemed as a church of the established religion of this State : 1st. That there is one eternal
God, and a future state of rewards and punishments.
2d. That God is publicly to be worshipped. 3d.
That the Christian religion is the true religion. 4th.
That the Holy Scriptures of the Old and New Testaments are of divine inspiration, and are the rule of faith
and practice. 5th. That it is lawful, and the duty of
every man, being thereunto called by those that govern,
to bear witness to the truth. And that every inhabitant of this State when called upon to make appeal to
God as a witness to truth shall be permitted to do it, in
that way which is most agreeable to the dictates of his
own conscience. And that the people of this State
may forever enjoy the right of electing their own pastors or clergy, and that at the same time the State may

have sufficient security for the discharge of the pastoral office by those who shall be admitted to be clergymen, no person shall officiate as minister of any established church who shall not have been chosen by a majority of the society to which he shall minister, or by persons appointed by the said majority to choose and procure a minister for them ; nor, until the minister so chosen and appointed shall have made and subscribed to the following declaration, over and above the aforesaid five articles, viz. : ' That he is determined by God's grace, out of the Holy Scriptures, to instruct the people committed to his charge, and to teach nothing, as required of necessity to salvation, but that which he shall be persuaded may be concluded and proved from the Scripture ; that he will use both public and private admonitions, as well to the sick as to the whole within his cure, as need shall require and occasion shall be given ; and that he will be diligent in prayers, and in reading of the Holy Scriptures, and in such studies as help to the knowledge of the same ; that he will be diligent to frame and fashion his own self and his family according to the doctrine of Christ, and to make both himself and them, as much as in him lieth, wholesome examples and patterns to the flock of Christ ; that he will maintain and set forward, as much as he can, quietness, peace, and love among all people, and especially among those that are or shall be committed to his charge. . . .''

It was provided in this Constitution that no person should be eligible to the office of Governor and Lieutenant Governor, membership in the Privy Council, in the Senate, and House of Representatives, who was not of the Protestant religion ; also that no person should be an elector who does not acknowledge the being of a

God, and believe in a future state of rewards and punishments.

This Constitution continued to be the fundamental law of the State until June 3, 1790, two years after the Constitution of the United States had become the supreme law of the land, and two years after the State had ratified that Constitution.

10. **Massachusetts.**—Constitution of 1780. Part First. Declaration of Rights. Article III. " As the happiness of a people, and the good order and preservation of civil government, essentially depend upon piety, religion, and morality ; and as these cannot be generally diffused through a community but by the institution of the public worship of God, and of public instructions in piety, religion, and morality ; Therefore, to promote their happiness, and to secure the good order and preservation of their government, the people of this Commonwealth have a right to invest their legislature with power to authorize and require, and the legislature shall from time to time authorize and require, the several towns, parishes, precincts, and other bodies-politic or religious societies, to make suitable provision at their own expense for the institution of the public worship of God, and for the support and maintenance of public Protestant teachers of piety, religion and morality, in all cases in which such provision shall not be made voluntarily.

" And the people of this Commonwealth have also a right to, and do, invest their legislature with authority to enjoin upon all the subjects an attendance upon the institutions of the public teachers aforesaid, at stated times and seasons, if there be any on whose instructions they can conscientiously and conveniently attend. *Provided notwithstanding*, that the several towns, parishes, precincts, and other bodies-politic, or religious societies shall at all times have the exclusive right of electing their public teachers, and of contracting with them for their support and maintenance.

"And all moneys, paid by the subject to the support of public worship and of the public teachers aforesaid, shall, if he require it, be uniformly applied to the support of the public teacher or teachers of his own religious sect or denomination, provided there be any on whose instructions he attends ; otherwise it may be paid toward the support of the teacher or teachers of the parish or precinct in which the said moneys are raised. And every denomination of Christians, demeaning themselves peaceably, and as good subjects of the Commonwealth, shall be equally under the protection of the law ; and no subordination of any one sect or denomination to another shall ever be established by law."

Chapter VI. Article I. "Any person, chosen governor, lieutenant-governor, councillor, senator, or representative, and accepting the trust, shall before he proceed to execute the duties of his place or office, make and subscribe the following declaration, viz. :

"'I, A. B., do declare that I believe the Christian religion, and have a firm persuasion of its truth,'" etc.

The former article remained in force until 1833 ; the latter until 1822.

Under this Constitution, the Legislature adopted the following statute, March 4, 1800, viz. :

Section 2. "*Be it further enacted*, that every corporate town, parish, precinct, district, or other body-politic, or religious society, aforesaid, is hereby required to be constantly provided with a public Protestant teacher of piety, religion and morality ; and in default of being so provided and supplied for the term of three months in every six months, such town, parish, precinct, district, and other body-politic, or religious society, which shall in the judgment of the court of general sessions of the peace for the same county, be adjudged of sufficient ability to be so provided, shall pay a fine, for a first offence, of a sum not exceeding *sixty* dollars, nor less than *thirty*; and for each and every like offence after the first a fine not exceeding *one hundred dollars*, nor less than *sixty* dollars, together with costs of prosecution; such fine to be recovered by indictment in the court of general sessions of the peace in the county where such delinquency may happen, and levied on the inhabitants comprising such town, parish, precinct, district, and other body-politic and religious society, so delinquent, in the same manner as other fines are levied on the inhabitants of towns.

Section 3. " *Be it further enacted,* . . . And in order that all the citizens of this Commonwealth may, according to the wise and reasonable provision of the constitution, be alike required to contribute to the support of their public teachers aforesaid.

Section 4. " *Be it further enacted,* that every town, parish, precinct, district and other body-politic and religious society, aforesaid, is hereby authorized to cause all sums of money, by them respectively voted to be raised from time to time in any legal meeting duly assembled or holden for the settlement or support of any public teacher or teachers aforesaid, or the building or repair of any house or houses of public worship, to be assessed upon all the ratable polls of each particular corporation or religious society aforesaid (the polls and estates of Quakers excepted) in the same proportion as state and town taxes are by law assessed. . . . *Provided*, however, that when any person taxed in any such tax or assessment voted to be raised as aforesaid, being, at the time of voting or raising any such tax or assessment, of a different sect or denomination from that of the corporation, body-politic or religious society, by which said tax was so assessed, shall request that the tax set against him or her in the assessment made for the purpose aforesaid may be applied to the support of the public teacher of his own religious sect or denomination ; such person procuring a certificate, signed by the public teacher on whose instruction he usually attends, and by two other persons of the society of which he is a member (having been especially chosen as a committee to sign such a certificate) in substance as follows, viz. : 'We, the subscribers, A. B., public teacher of a society for the religious sect or denomination called   in the town, district, precinct, or parish of   and C, D, E, F, committee of said society, do hereby certify that   doth belong to said society ; and that he (or she as the case may be) frequently and usually, when able, attends with us in our stated meeting for religious worship.' Which certificate having been produced to the selectmen, committee or assessors, (as the case may require) of the town, district, parish, precinct, or other body-politic or religious society, by whom he or she has been taxed, as aforesaid, it shall be sufficient to require them, respectively, to order and direct the treasurer of such corporation or religious society to pay over the amount of such taxes, so applied for, to the use of the public teacher of the religious sect or denomination to which such applicant belongs ; and such public teacher shall thereby be entitled to receive the same.' It required in one instance fourteen suits at law before a town treas-

[1] Buck's *Ecclesiastical Law of Massachusetts*, pp. 253–255.

urer yielded the taxes, and in another an expense of one hundred dollars and four years' time to get four dollars out of his hands for the use of a Baptist minister.[1]

In 1832 Nathaniel P. Fisher of Walpole was arrested for refusing to pay the tax of $2.38 levied on him at the town meeting for the support of the gospel.

Towns and Parishes—the latter being territorial subdivisions of the Town, as the Towns were of the County—were the only religious organizations known to the law ; they embraced all the inhabitants within their boundaries, and were obliged to maintain and support public religious worship. The Supreme Court of Massachusetts has made the following decisions :

" But when no part of a town is included in or constitutes a parish, the duties of a parish are required of the town, which is obliged to maintain and support public religious worship, and perform all parish duties."[2]

" Every town is considered to be a parish until a separate parish is formed within it, and then the inhabitants and territory not included in this separate parish constitute the first parish, in pursuance of the statute of 1786, C. x., S. 4."[3]

" A town may, by its town officers, assess a tax for parochial purposes upon the members of the first parish, though there be a second parish in the town."[4]

" Liability to taxation is the criterion of membership (in a parish) so far as relates to voting, and whoever is a member of a parish has a right to vote ; and

---

[1] Buck's *Ecclesiastical Law of Massachusetts*, p 43.

[2] Dillingham *v.* Snow, 5 Massachusetts, 554, 1809 ; and Cochran *v.* Camden, 15 Massachusetts, 302 ; 1818.

[3] Brunswick *v.* Dunning, 7 Mass., 445 ; 1811.

[4] Ashley *v.* Wellington, 8 Pick.. 524 ; 1829.

the officer who refuses the vote of a member is liable to an action." [1]

Ministers, " by the constitution and laws of the commonwealth, are to receive their maintenance from the parish and not from the church." [2]

" This body (the church) has no power to contract with or settle a minister ; that power residing wholly in the parish, of which the members of the church, who are inhabitants, are a part. The church nominates the minister. A contract of settlement is made wholly between the parish and the minister, and is obligatory only on them." [3]

" A Congregational Church, connected with a parish, is not a corporation, nor a *quasi*-corporation, for the purpose of holding property ; although, like a corporation, in respect to its power to act by vote and majorities." [4]

" Nor are the deacons of such a church made a corporation by the statute of 1785, C. 51, for receiving and managing a fund for the support of a minister." [5]

Chief-Justice Parsons held that, whatever the usage in settling ministers, the Bill of Rights of 1780 secures to towns, not to churches, the right to elect the minister in the last resort. [6]

Every citizen being taxed for the support of the

[1] Sparrow *v.* Wood, 16 Mass., 457 ; 1820. Oakes *v.* Hill, 14 Pick., 442 ; 1833.

[2] Boutell *v.* Cowdin, 9 Mass., 253 ; 1812. General Statutes, C. xxxi. S. 1.

[3] Burr *v.* 1st Parish in Sandwich, 9 Mass., 296 ; 1812.

[4] Stebbins *v.* Jennings, 10 Pick., 172 ; 1830. Parker *v.* May, 5 Cush., 345 ; 1850. Weld *v.* May, 9 Cush., 181 ; 1852. Jefts *v.* York, 10 Cush., 392 ; 1852.

[5] Boutell *v.* Cowdin, 9 Mass., 254 ; 1812. General Statutes, C. xxxi., S. 1.

[6] Avery *v.* Tyringham, 3 Mass., 181.

church had a right to vote in the administration of the affairs of the church. This right did not produce any serious trouble until the rise of the Unitarian controversy in 1820. The non-communicants of the town or parish in some cases united with a Unitarian minority in the church and elected a Unitarian pastor, against the protest of the Orthodox majority of the communicants. The town of Dedham in 1818 chose Mr. Lamson, a Unitarian, as pastor. Two thirds of the communicants, being opposed to him, went across the street to worship ; and holding that they were the church, brought suit for the possession of the property. The case went to the Supreme Court of the State, and the court decided, Justice Parker giving the decision, that the Orthodox majority had no right to the property, and further decided that " that body (the church) could not take fee or succession because it was not a body-politic, and could neither take nor hold a legal interest in land." [1] Upon this decision about half of the towns of Eastern Massachusetts elected Unitarian pastors ; thus, in effect, ejecting the Orthodox communicants from their church property. The Orthodox were now willing to consent to the separation of the church, as a religious organization, from the town and parish, as civil organizations, which was effected in the amended Bill of Rights of 1834. The Bill of Rights was so amended as to simply recognize "the public worship of God and instruction in piety, as promoting the happiness and prosperity of a people, and the security of a republican form of government." Up to this time it was the duty of the Commonwealth, not only to recognize the value of such worship and instruction, but to provide for it and enforce attendance upon it.

[1] Baker *et al. v.* Fales, 16 Mass., 487 ; 1820.

As late as 1835 a fine might have been collected in Massachusetts from any able-bodied citizen who absented himself from preaching for three months.[1]

It appears to be conclusive, therefore—

1st. From a fair interpretation of the Constitution itself;

2d. From the opinions of jurists ; and

3d. From the fact that States made laws respecting an establishment of religion, and maintained such an establishment under the Constitution unquestioned, that the authority in relation to religion, which was prohibited by the Constitution to congress, was reserved to the States ; and that the Constitution of the United States was not intended to, and did not, effect a total separation between the religious and civil institutions of the people.

CHAPTER IV.

THE ORDINANCE OF 1787.

WE turn now to the Ordinance of 1787 as bearing upon the question of fact.

On the 1st of March, 1784, Virginia ceded to the United States the territory northwest of the Ohio River. The cession was accepted, and on the 13th of July, 1787, Congress passed an ordinance for the government of that territory. Article III. of that ordinance is in part : " Religion, morality, and knowledge, being necessary to good government and the happiness of mankind, schools and the means of education shall forever be encouraged." The ordinance declares itself to be a compact, and was adopted by the United States as

[1] Buck's *Ecclesiastical Law of Massachusetts*, p. 27.

such.   Article VI. which says "There shall be neither
slavery nor involuntary servitude in the said territory,
otherwise than in punishment of crimes, whereof
the party shall have been duly convicted," has been
repeatedly interpreted as a compact.   Upon a motion
to repeal it, in 1803, in the interests of the slave-
holding States, John Randolph reported adversely on
the ground that it was a part of a compact.   This
ordinance was adopted before the adoption of the Constitution of the United States, but it was re-affirmed
after the adoption of the Constitution, on May 7,
1800, in providing for the government of Indiana territory ; on February 3, 1809, in providing for the government of Illinois territory ; on April 18, 1818, in the act
enabling the people of Illinois to form a State Constitution.   The ordinance, excepting Article VI. prohibiting
slavery, was re-adopted, under the Constitution, April
24, 1802, in accepting the cession of territory from
Georgia.   In the act of March 2, 1819, authorizing the
people of Alabama to form a Constitution and State
government, it was required that the Constitution
should not be "repugnant to the ordinance of the 13th
of July, 1787, between the people of the United States
and the people of the territory northwest of the Ohio
river."

There can be no doubt that it was the intention of
the framers of the ordinance to make its articles perpetually binding.   On this question the ordinance itself is conclusive, the 14th section being as follows :
" It is hereby ordained and declared, by the authority
aforesaid, that the following articles shall be considered as articles of compact between the original
States and the people and States in said territory, and
forever remain unalterable unless by common consent."

In two of the articles the words " forever " are applied to the stipulations therein contained, viz.: Article III., to the encouragement of schools and the means of education for the promotion of religion, morality and knowledge ; Article IV., to the prohibition of " tax, impost or duty " upon the use of " the navigable waters leading into the Mississippi and St. Lawrence, and the carrying places between the same."

For a long time it was the prevailing public opinion that the articles of the ordinance were perpetually binding on the States formed out of the Northwestern and Southwestern Territories, but the courts have differed in opinion on the subject. It has been held by the courts that when Congress by act extended the provisions of the ordinance to territory outside of that described in the ordinance, those provisions were not binding on the States formed out of such territory. This view, which is obviously correct, was held by the Supreme Court of the United States in Permoli *v.* the Municipality of New Orleans, 3 How., 589, and in Williamette Iron Bridge Co. *v.* Hatch, Oct., 1887, 125, U. S., 1.

It has been held by the courts that the terms of the ordinance were perpetually binding on the States formed out of the territory described therein, and that when the State Constitution departed in any particular from the terms of the ordinance, and the Constitution was approved by Congress, that approval completed the assent of the original parties to the alteration thus made in the terms of the compact. The first part of Article VI. of the ordinance, that prohibiting slavery, was incorporated in the State Constitution of Ohio, but the last part, that allowing the slave escaping into the territory from any of the original States to be " reclaimed and conveyed to the person claiming his or her labor or service," was omitted, and it was held by the Supreme Court of the United States in Strader *et al. v.* Graham, Dec., 1850, 10 How., 82, that the act of Congress admitting the State into the Union with that omission in her Constitution was a modification of the terms of the compact, in accordance with the provisions made in the ordinance for the purpose. Three slaves valued at $3000 had escaped by the steamer *Pike* from Louisville, Ky., to Cincinnati, O., and thence to Canada, and the owners of them brought suit against the owners and the master of the steamer, citizens of Ohio, to recover value. The plaintiffs argued that their claim was made good by the provision in the last part of Article VI. of the Ordinance of 1787. The court decided against the claim on the ground that the Constitution of Ohio, having received the sanction of Congress, that part of Article VI. stood suspended or altered by consent. In rendering the decision the Court said : " For thirty years the State courts within the territory ceded by Virginia have held this part of Article IV. (relating to free navigation of the waters) to be in force and binding on them respectively, and I feel unwilling to disturb this wholesome decision which is so conservative of the rights of others, in a case in which the 4th Article is in no wise involved, and when our opinion might be disregarded by the State courts as *obiter* and a *dictum* uncalled for."

The Legislature of Ohio incorporated the Zanesville Canal and Manufacturing Company, authorizing them to make a dam and lock in the Muskingum River. In a freshet the lock became so filled with driftwood and sand that it could not be used. Williams and Hogg had loaded a boat for the New Orleans market, and being unable to go through the lock employed skilful pilots to take the boat over the dam ; the boat became unmanageable in the passage, and striking against a pier below the dam was wrecked. The owners brought suit for damages, basing their claim on the last part of Article IV. of the Ordinance of 1787, which is as follows :

" The navigable waters leading into the Mississippi and St. Lawrence and the carrying places between them shall be common highways, and forever free, as well to the inhabitants of the said Territory, as to the citizens of the United States, and those of any other States that may be admitted into the confederacy, without any tax, impost or duty therefor."

The Supreme Court of Ohio, in giving its decision in the case, said : " This part of the Ordinance is as much obligatory upon the State of Ohio as our own Constitution. In truth, it is more, for the Constitution may be altered by the people of the State, while this cannot be altered without the assent both of the people of this State and of the United States, through their representatives. It is an article of compact, and until we assume the principle that the sovereign power of the State is not bound by compact, this clause must be considered obligatory. . . . Every citizen of the United States has a perfect right to its (the Muskingum River) free navigation ; a right, derived not from the Legislature of Ohio, but from a superior source. With this right the Legislature cannot interfere ; in other words, cannot by any law which they may pass impede or obstruct the navigation of the river ; but it does not follow that laws may not be enacted to improve the navigation of these rivers. In passing laws to improve the navigation, care must be taken that that which was intended as an improvement shall not operate as an obstruction. The court are unanimous in the opinion that the plaintiffs have a right of action." [1]

In Hutchinson *et al. v.* Thompson *et al.*, 9 Ohio, 66, the Supreme Court said, "The conclusion to which I have come is that the clause in the Ordinance (relating to 'navigable waters') contains a limitation on the power of the general government, as well as a prohibition on the States."

In the case of Lessees of Thomas Cochran's Heirs *v.* David Loring, 17 Ohio, 409, the Supreme Court said : "The principles declared in these articles (of the Ordinance of 1787) are to prevail not only during the territorial government, but for all remaining time."

The Supreme Court of the United States in Huse *v.* Glover, 119 U. S., 543, held that the tolls collected at the Henry and Copperas Creek locks in the Illinois River were not violations of the Ordinance of 1787, in that they were taken simply as compensation for the use of artificial facilities constructed to improve the navigation of the river, and not as an impost ; seeming to imply that any exaction amounting to an impost would be in violation of the ordinance, and would be prohibited.

In Escanaba Co. *v.* Chicago, 107 U. S., 678, however, that court said : "Whatever limitation upon her powers (the State of Illinois) as a government, whilst in the Territorial condition, whether from the Ordinance of 1787, or the legislation of Congress, it ceased to have any operative force except as voluntarily adopted by her, after she became a State of the Union. On her admission she at once became entitled to and possessed

---

[1] Williams and Hogg *v.* Zanesville Canal and Manufacturing Co., 5 Ohio, 410.

all the rights of dominion and sovereignty which belonged to the original States. She was admitted, and could be admitted, only on the same footing with them."

In Sands *v.* Manistee River Improvement Co., Nov., 1887, 123 U. S., 288 the court said : "There was no contract in the 4th article of the Ordinance of 1787 . . . which bound the people of the Territory, or of any portion of it when subsequently formed into a State and admitted into the Union."

This view has been held with almost complete uniformity by that court. Besides the decisions already referred to as setting it forth, it is affirmed in the cases of Permoli *v.* the Municipality of New Orleans, 3 How., 589 ; in Huse *v.* Glover, 119 U. S., 543, and in Pollard's Lessee *v.* Hagan, 3 How., 391.

It may be that the principle of the sovereignty of the State in its domestic affairs, subject to the Constitution of the United States, does necessarily render the Ordinance of 1787 void in the States formed out of the Northwestern and Southwestern Territories. It may be that the States formed out of the Northwestern Territory might after admission into the Union have altered their constitutions, and established the institution of slavery had they so willed. The decision of the Supreme Court of the United States in the case of Menard *v.* Aspasia, 5 Peters, 504 ; Jan., 1831, giving a slave her freedom, implies as much, for if the terms of the ordinance in § 2, "saving, however, to the French and Canadian inhabitants and other settlers of the Kaskaskies, St. Vincent's, and the neighboring villages, who have heretofore professed themselves citizens of Virginia, their laws and customs now in force among them, relative to the descent and conveyance of property," are void in a

State, all the terms of the ordinance are void in the like case. [1]

There can be no doubt, however, that the overwhelming public sentiment of the country would have regarded the establishment of the institution of slavery, by any State formed out of the Northwestern Territory, as a violation of a compact, which the founders of our government intended to be of perpetual obligation.

It may be that the article of the ordinance requiring that "schools and the means of instruction shall be forever encouraged" for the purpose of promoting "religion, morality and knowledge," is void in the

[1] The mother of Aspasia, a colored woman, was born a slave and was held as such by a French inhabitant of Kaskaskia, Illinois, previous to the year 1787, and after that year was held as a slave by the same individual, who was a citizen of that country before its conquest by Virginia, and before the passage of the ordinance for the government of the territory northwest of the river Ohio, and who continued to be such afterwards and was such at the time of Aspasia's birth. Aspasia was born in the year 1787, and from the time of her birth she was raised and held as a slave till some time in the year 1821, when she was purchased by the plaintiff in error, who immediately after gave her to his son-in-law, Francis Chouteau, then residing in St. Louis, Mo., who held her as his slave until October 10, 1827, when he returned her to the plaintiff in error, in consequence of the claim she set up for her freedom.

The Circuit Court of St. Louis and the Supreme Court of Missouri sustained her claim for freedom, whereupon appeal was taken to the Supreme Court of the United States.

The plea set up in court against her claim was, that the case was protected by the contract made with the State of Virginia, contained in the Ordinance of 1787 above cited. When Gen. Gage in 1764 took possession of the country in behalf of Great Britain, he promised in his proclamation to the subjects of France then in the territory, that they should enjoy the same rights and privileges and the same security for their persons

States formed out of the Northwestern and Southwestern Territories, and that the prohibition of all religious exercises in the public schools of those States would not be a violation of any fundamental law of the land, but there can be no doubt that it was the intention of the founders of our government to make a fundamental law requiring that schools and the means of instruction should forever be encouraged for the purpose specified, and that but for the unforeseen effect of the principle of State sovereignty and State equality such would have been the law.

and property as under their former sovereign. The treaty made with France also gave the same guaranty.

In 1778 the territory was conquered by the troops of Virginia under Gen. George Rogers Clarke, and by an act of Virginia erecting it into a county it was declared that the inhabitants shall enjoy their own religion, "together with all their civil rights and property." The cession of this territory by Virginia to the United States was made with a full knowledge of the existence of property in slaves therein, and of the guaranties previously made. Congress recognized the existence of such property in the act of May 7, 1800, which provided that the division of the territory of the United States northwest of the river Ohio into two separate governments should take place " when satisfactory evidence shall be given to the Governor thereof that such is the wish of a majority of the *free* male inhabitants of the age of 21 years and upwards " ; and also provided that the representatives in the General Assembly are to be apportioned to the several counties " agreeably to the number of *free* males of the age of 21 and upward." It was pleaded also that the case was protected by Article 11 of the Ordinance of 1787, which provided that "No person shall be deprived of his liberty or property but by the judgment of his peers or the law of the land."

The Supreme Court of the United States dismissed the case for want of jurisdiction, which, in the circumstances, was equivalent to a confirmation of the decision of the lower court.

There can be no doubt that the United States Government was bound by the compact of 1787 to promote "religion, morality and knowledge," by encouraging "schools and the means of education" within the territory received by cession from Virginia and Georgia while the local governments therein were of the territorial form.

And there can be no doubt that the religion which it was under obligation to promote was the Christian religion, and not the religion of the Winnebago and Choctaw Indians.

In view of these facts, it can hardly be held that the founders of our government intended to produce an entire separation of the religion of the people from their civil institutions, and it would be preposterous to assume that they had done what they intended not to do.

CHAPTER V.

THE COMMON LAW.

IN the investigation of the question of fact, it is to be observed that some connection between the religious and civil institutions of a people is an inevitable result of the conditions of all social and political organization.

So far, we have not undertaken to define our civil institutions, or to obtain any precise idea of what they are. Very important constituent elements of them we have, thus far, left entirely out of view. It would be a very great error to suppose that so brief a document as the Constitution of the United States embraced in its provisions the whole compass of our civil institutions. True, it is the supreme law of the land; but there was a vast body of law which existed long before it was framed, and which continued in force under it, either by express provision or necessary implication. The common law, and that body of law which we may say has been made by equity decisions, form a very large and important part of our civil institutions. Lord Stair says that "equity is the body of the law; the statutes of men are but as the ornament and vestiture thereof." The order in the development of the civil institutions of a people, as given by Sir Henry Maine in his work on ancient law, has been, not first, the laying down of principles and then building thereon, but, first, a single judgment on a particular case; second, custom or common law; third, equity; fourth, legislation and constitutions. Constitutions came last of all and were super-added to a great body of law which had previously existed,—they *modified*, but did not *displace* the pre-existent law. Amendment VIII. of the Constitution of the United States says, "And no fact tried by a jury shall be, otherwise, re-examined in any court of the United States than according to the rules of the common law," and all the courts have affirmed the common law to be a part of the law of the land. The common law is not sufficiently defined as the *Lex non scripta*, in distinction from the *Lex scripta*. Nor is it sufficiently defined as composed of customs, "whereof the memory of man runneth not to the contrary." It is in great part written, and it also gives force to customs that are not of immemorial origin. Sir Matthew Hale says: "When I call those parts of our laws *Leges non scripta*, I do not mean as if these laws were only oral, or communicated from former ages to the latter merely by word.

For all these laws have their several monuments in writing, whereby they are transferred from one age to another, and without which they would soon lose all kind of certainty. They are for the most part extant in records of pleas, proceedings, and judgments, in books of reports, and judicial decisions, in tractates of learned men's arguments and opinions, preserved from ancient times and still extant in writing." The authority of the common law is therefore not the feeble and uncertain authority of a shadowy tradition, but the fixed and vigorous authority of a written law. It has a close connection with, if it does not derive a large part of its contents from, equity decisions.

CHAPTER VI.

EQUITY.

A CERTAIN writer has said that "It is impossible, in the nature of things, that any code of laws should provide a remedy suited to every particular case. It has therefore been found necessary in every civilized nation to establish some form of authority which should control the rigor and remedy the deficiency of positive law." Another has said that "Some contrivance must be provided to meet those cases in which the application of existing laws would, in the manifold complications of human affairs, work injustice." In these cases the judge must decide in accordance with reason and right, governing his decision by moral rather than by legal considerations. "Courts of equity or chancery were supposed to proceed from those principles which affect the moral sense, and on this account the presid-

ing judge or chancellor was in the early days an ecclesiastic. In the old law abridgments chancery law is
found under the title Conscience." [1] In England it was
said that " Equity flowed from the king's conscience." [2]

Equity decisions form an important part of the law
of almost every civilized people. Now it is very plain
that the decision of the judge in these cases will be
governed by the moral code which prevails among the
people, and thus the principles of that moral code,
whatever it may be, will enter into the law of the land.

The Romans found it to be necessary, in administering
justice among the subjugated Italian nations to allow
the judges to be governed in their decisions by the rules
of law which were common to the Romans and those
nations ; whence sprang up what was called the *jus
gentium.* [3]

The speculative Greeks regarded the general principles of justice, which were applicable to all nations, as
having their basis in nature ; and by nature they meant a
something which was manifested, not only in the forms
of the material world, in the life of plants and animals,
but also in the thoughts, feelings, and volitions of man.
This mystic, primal, all-pervading something, called
nature, was the standard of perfection. As man was
not perfect, he had fallen ; and the great work set
before him was the return to nature. To live according to nature was to live right. [4] Upon the conquest
of Greece by the Romans this philosophy made instan-
taneous progress in Rome, and passed into the *jus
gentium.* It has been remarked that the Roman law
was constantly and powerfully influenced by the Stoic
and Academic philosophy, and that they were the main

[1] *Ancient Law*, p. xii.
[2] *Ibid.*, xxvii., 68.
[3] *Ibid.*, xxii.
[4] *Ibid.*, xviii., 57–62.

sources of those doctrines of universal justice which were quietly and constantly passing into the civil law, through their incorporation with judicial decisions.[1]

All nations who are ruled by laws and customs are governed partly by their own particular laws (civil law), and partly by those laws which are common to all mankind. "Equity claims to supersede the civil law by virtue of superior sanctity in its principles." "Its claim to authority is grounded, not on the prerogative of any external person or body; not even on that of the magistrate who enunciates it; but on the special nature of its principles to which, it is alleged, that all law ought to conform." "The rules of Equity pretend to a paramount sacredness, entitling them at once to the recognition of courts, even without the concurrence of prince or parliamentary assembly."[2]

Through Equity, the moral code of a people enters into the laws by which they are governed, and becomes a part of the law of the land. If that code rests upon the teachings of the Zend Avesta, then Zoroastrianism will become a part of the law of the land; if on the Koran, then Mohammedanism; if on the Scriptures of the Old and New Testaments, then Christianity will become part of the law of the land. It is, in the nature of things, inevitable; no disbelief of the basis of the code, or desire to have it otherwise on the part of particular individuals, can prevent it. The cup of water taken from the spring or well contains various mineral and organic matters in solution, and though one should prefer that it were otherwise, or believe that the water would be more wholesome if it did not contain these substances, yet it is plainly impossible that it should be otherwise, coming, as the water does, through beds

[1] *Ibid.*, 52-4.   [2] *Ibid.*, xvii, 27, 28, 44.

of clay and gravel and crevices in rocks that are full
of these substances. There might, perhaps, be no objection to a man's preference or his opinions on this subject, but it would be a great mistake to take these as
exponents of the fact, and point to the clearness of the
water as a proof of the fact. The question—What is,
and of necessity must be the fact in such a case? it
would seem that any reasonable person could answer
without a moment's hesitation.

The question before us is a similar one, and it would
seem that whatever one's preference or opinion might
be, there could hardly be a doubt as to the fact, that
Christianity does, and of necessity must, hold some
real and valid connection with the civil institutions of
a Christian people.

CHAPTER VII.

THE OPINIONS OF JURISTS.

BLACKSTONE says in section 2 of the Introduction to
his Commentaries, " Upon these two foundations, the
law of nature and the law of revelation, depend all
human laws ;—that is to say, no human laws should
be suffered to contradict these."

Sir Matthew Hale, in a decision he gave, said that
" Christianity is part of the law of England." Lord
Mansfield said : " The true principles of natural religion
are part of the common law ; the essential parts of revealed religion are part of the common law : so that a
person vilifying, subverting, or ridiculing them may be
prosecuted at common law ; but temporal punishments
ought not to be inflicted for mere opinions."

James Wilson, of Pennsylvania, who was a member
of the Constitutional convention of the United States,
and who was afterwards judge of the Supreme Court
of the United States, states that profaneness and blasphemy are offences punishable by fine and imprisonment, and that Christianity is part of the common
law. [1]

The late Theodore W. Dwight, LL. D., President
of the Columbia College Law School, New York, says :
" It is well settled by decisions in the courts of the
leading States of the Union, that Christianity is a part
of the common law of the State. . . . The American
states adopted these principles from the common law
of England, rejecting such portions of the English law
on this subject as were not suited to their customs and
institutions.   Our national development has, in it, the
best and purest elements of historic Christianity, as related to the government of States.   Should we tear
Christianity out of our law we would rob our law of
its fairest jewels ; we would deprive it of its richest
treasures ; we would arrest its growth ; and bereave it
of its capability to adapt itself to the progress in culture,
refinement, and morality of those for whose benefit it
properly exists." [2]

Judge Story, in his *Commentaries on the Constitution of the United States*, (p. 698) says : " The right of
a society or government to interfere in matters of religion will hardly be contested by any persons who believe that piety, religion, and morality, are intimately
connected with the well-being of the State, and indispensable to the administration of civil justice.   The
promulgation of the great doctrines of religion, the
being, and attributes, and providence of one Almighty

[1] *Works*, vol. iii., p. 112.   [2] *Church and State*, Schaff, p. 61.

God ; the responsibility to him for all our actions, founded on moral freedom and accountability ; a future state of rewards and punishments ; the cultivation of all personal, social, and benevolent virtues,—these never can be a matter of indifference to a well-ordered community. It is, indeed, difficult to conceive how any civilized society can exist without them. And, at all events, it is impossible for those who believe in the truth of christianity as a divine revelation to doubt that it is the special duty of the government to foster and encourage it among all citizens and subjects. This is a point wholly distinct from that of private judgment, in matters of religion, and of freedom of public worship, according to the dictates of one's own conscience. . . . Probably at the time of the adoption of the Constitution, and of the amendment of it now under consideration (Amendment I. ' Congress shall make no law respecting an establishment of religion or prohibiting the free exercise thereof.') the general, if not the universal, sentiment in America was that Christianity ought to receive encouragement from the State, so far as it is not incompatible with the private rights of conscience and the freedom of religious worship. An attempt to level all religions, and to make it a matter of State policy to hold all in utter indifference, would have created universal disapprobation, if not universal indignation.''

CHAPTER VIII.

DECISIONS OF THE STATE SUPREME COURTS.

The Supreme Court of New York in the case of the People *v.* Ruggles, August 1811, the indictment being for blasphemous utterances against Christ,—Kent, Chief

Justice, delivering the opinion, said : " The very idea of jurisprudence with the ancient lawgivers and philosophers embraced the religion of the country. . . . The free and undisturbed enjoyment of religious opinion, whatever it may be, and free, decent discussions on any religious subject is granted and secured ; but to revile with malicious and blasphemous contempt the religion professed by almost the whole community is an abuse of right. Nor are we bound by any expressions in the Constitution, as some have strangely supposed, either not to punish at all, or to punish indiscriminately, the like attacks upon the religion of Mahomet or of the grand Lama ; and for this plain reason that the case assumes that we are a Christian people, and the morality of the country is deeply engrafted upon Christianity, and not upon the doctrines or worship of those impostors. . . . The object of the 38th article of the constitution was to 'guard against spiritual oppression and intolerance,' by declaring that ' the free exercise and enjoyment of religious profession and worship, without discrimination or preference, should forever thereafter be allowed within this state to all mankind.' This declaration, (noble and magnanimous as it is, when duly understood,) never meant to withdraw religion in general, and with it the best sanctions of moral and social obligation, from all consideration and notice of the law." [1]

In the decision of the Supreme Court of New York in the case of Lindenmuller *v.* the People, Feb. 4, 1861, Judge J. Allen, delivering the opinion, said : " Religious tolerance is entirely consistent with a recognized religion. Christianity may be conceded to be the established religion, to the qualified extent mentioned,

[1] 8 Johnson, 290.

while perfect civil and political equality with freedom
of conscience and religious preference is secured to
individuals of every other creed and profession. It is
not disputed that Christianity is a part of the common
law of England, and in Rex *v.* Woolston Str. 834, the
court of King's bench would not suffer it to be debated, whether to write against Christianity in general
was not an offence punishable in the temporal courts at
common law. The common law, as it was in force on
the 20th day of April, 1777, subject to such alterations
as have been made from time to time by the Legislature, and except such parts of it as are repugnant to
the Constitution is, and ever has been, a part of the
law of the State." The Court goes on to say that : " It
was conceded in the convention of 1821 that the court
in People *v.* Ruggles did decide that the christian religion was the law of the land, in the sense that it was
preferred over all other religions, and entitled to the
recognition and protection of the temporal courts by the
common law of the State. Mr. Root proposed an
amendment to obviate that decision . . . to the
effect that the judiciary should not declare any particular religion to be the law of the land. The decision
was vindicated as a just exponent of the Constitution,
and the relation of the Christian religion to the State ;
and the amendment was opposed by Chancellor Kent,
Daniel D. Tompkins, Col. Young, Mr. Van Buren,
Rufus King, and Chief-Justice Spencer, and rejected
by a large majority ; and the former provision retained,
with the judicial construction in People *v.* Ruggles
fully recognized. *New York State Convention of 1821,
462–571.* It is true that the gentlemen differed in
their views as to the effect and extent of the decision,
and as to the legal status of the Christian religion in

9

the State. One class, including Chief-Justice Spencer
and Mr. King, regarded Christianity—the Christian
religion—as distinguished from Mohammedanism, etc.,
as a part of the common law, adopted by the Constitution ; while another class, including Chancellor
Kent and Mr. Van Buren, were of the opinion that the
decision was right, not because christianity was established by law, but because christianity was in fact
the religion of the country, the rule of our faith and
practice, and the basis of public morals. According to
their views, as the recognized religion of the country,
'the duties and injunctions of the Christian religion'
were interwoven with the law of the land and were
part and parcel of the common law, and that maliciously to revile it is a public grievance, and as much
so as any other outrage upon common decency and
decorum. This difference in views is in no sense material, as it leads to no difference in practical results
and conclusions. All agreed that the Christian religion was engrafted upon the law and entitled to protection as a basis of our morals and the strength of
our government, but for reasons differing in terms
and in words, rather than in substance. .   .   .   The
conviction was right, and judgment must be affirmed."[1]

One Updegraph was indicted in Pennsylvania for
blasphemy in saying that " The Holy Scriptures were
a mere fable ; that they were a contradiction, and that
although they contained a number of good things, yet
they contained a great many lies," and was charged
with "contriving and intending to scandalize and bring
into disrepute and vilify the Christian religion and
the Scriptures of Truth .   .   .   to great dishonor of

[1] 33 Barbour, 560–578. (Judgment for violation of the law
against Sunday theatres).

Almighty God, to the great scandal of the profession
of the Christian religion, to the evil example of all
others in like case, offending and against the form of
the Act of Assembly in such case made and provided."
The plea in defence was, 1st, That the Act of 1700
("An act to prevent the grievous sins of cursing
and swearing," etc.) was virtually repealed by the
adoption of the Constitution of 1776. 2d, If the Constitution of 1776 repealed the Act of 1700 it also
repealed the common law upon the subject. 3d. Such
expression only becomes criminal when it interferes
with the order of government, disturbs the peace of
society. 4th, This State was a British province at the
time the law of 1700 had its birth, a part of the British empire, when it was necessary, as the Christian
religion formed part of the laws of the land, that laws
should be enacted for its support and protection. It
was then consistent with the system of despotism
under which the country groaned ; it formed a necessary part of the whole machine.

The case went to the Supreme Court of Pennsylvania
and that Court, (Duncan, Justice, delivering the opinion,) said : " The assertion is once more made that
Christianity never was received as part of the common
law of this Christian land, and it is added that if it was,
it was virtually repealed by the Constitution of the
United States, as inconsistent with the liberty of the
people, the freedom of religious worship, and hostile
to the genius and spirit of our government. . . . We
will first dispose of what is considered the grand objection, the Constitutionality of christianity ; for in effect
that is the question. Christianity, general christianity,
is, and always has been, a part of the common law of
Pennsylvania ; christianity, without the spiritual artil-

lery of European countries, for this christianity was one of the considerations of the royal charter, and the very basis of its great founder William Penn ; not christianity founded on any particular religious tenets ; not christianity with an established church and tithes and spiritual courts ; but christianity with liberty of conscience to all men. . . . It is liberty run mad to declaim against the punishment of these offences, or to assert that the punishment is hostile to the spirit and genius of our government. . . . No free government now exists in the world unless where christianity is acknowledged and is the religion of the country. So far from christianity, as the counsel contends, being part of the machinery necessary to despotism, the reverse is the fact. Christianity is part of the common law of this state. It is not proclaimed by the commanding voice of any opinion, but expressed in the calm and mild accents of customary law. Its foundations are broad, and strong, and deep ; they are laid in the authority, the interest, the affections of the people." [1]

In the case of Johnson *v.* Commonwealth, being a complaint for running an omnibus into the city of Pittsburgh on Sunday, the Supreme Court of the same State said, Woodward delivering the opinion, Black and Lewis dissenting, " The common law adopted it (Sunday) along with Christianity, of which it is one of the bulwarks." [2]

In the case of the State *v.* Ambs, the indictment being for keeping open an alehouse on Sunday, on appeal to the Supreme Court of Missouri, the plea was made in

[1] Updergraph *v.* the Commonwealth, 11 Sergeant and Rawle, 398 ; 1822.
[2] 10 Harris, 102, 115.

defence, " that the whole system of laws, designed to enforce the observance of the Christian Sabbath, is unconstitutional : 1st. They interfere with the rights of conscience. 2d. They impose a religious form of worship. 3d. They give a preference to one religious sect over all others." The Court said, Scott, J., delivering the opinion, and all concurring: " Those who question the constitutionality of our Sunday laws seem to imagine that the Constitution is to be regarded as an instrument framed for a State, composed of strangers, collected from all quarters of the globe, each with a religion of his own, bound by no previous social ties, nor sympathizing in any common reminiscences of the past ; that, unlike ordinary laws, it is not to be construed in reference to the state and condition of those for whom it was intended. . . . It is apprehended that such is not the mode by which our organic law is to be interpreted. We must regard the people for whom it was ordained. It appears to have been made by Christian men. The Constitution on the face of it shows that the Christian religion was the religion of its framers. . . . The convention sat under a law exacting a cessation of labor on Sunday. The journal of the convention will show that this law was obeyed by its members, as such, by adjourning from Saturday until Monday. . . . They then who engrafted on our constitution the principles of religious freedom, therein contained, did not regard the compulsory observance of Sunday as a day of rest a violation of those principles. They deemed a statute compelling the observance of Sunday necessary to secure the full enjoyment of the rights of conscience." [1]

[1] 20 Missouri, Bennett, v., pp., 214, 221.

In the case of Shover *v.* the State, the Supreme Court of Arkansas said : " This system of religion (the Christian) is recognized as constituting part and parcel of the common law, and as such all of the institutions growing out of it, or in any way connected with it, in case they shall not be found to interfere with the rights of conscience, are entitled to the most profound respect and can rightfully claim the protection of the law-making power of the State." Indictment for keeping a dram shop open on Sunday.[1]

In the case of Richmond *v.* Moore,[2] the Supreme Court of Illinois, Walker, J. delivering the opinion, said, " Although it is no part of the functions of our system of government to propagate religion and enforce its tenets, yet when the great body of the people are Christians, in fact, or in sentiment, our laws and our institutions must necessarily be based upon and embody the teachings of the Redeemer of mankind. It is impossible that it should be otherwise. And, in this sense, and to this extent, our civilization and our institutions are emphatically Christian."

In the case of the State *v.* Chandler,[3] the Supreme Court of Delaware rendered a decision distinguished for its learning and its clear enunciation of principles. The indictment " was for blasphemy, and charged that Thomas J. Chandler on the 10th day of May in the year of our Lord 1836, with force and arms, and not having the fear of the Lord before his eyes, but being moved and seduced by the instigation of the devil, and contriving and intending to scandalize and vilify the Christian religion, and to blaspheme God and our Lord Jesus Christ, the Savior of the world, *unlawfully*, wick-

---

[1] 5 Arkansas, English, 260.   [2] 107 Illinois, p. 429.
[3] 2 Harrington, 553.

edly, and *blasphemously*, in the presence and hearing of divers citizens of this State, spoke, pronounced and with a loud voice *published* these profane and *blasphemous* words, viz. : *That the Virgin Mary was a whore and Jesus Christ was a bastard ;* to the great dishonor of Almighty God, in contempt, and to the great scandal of the christian religion, against the form of an act of the General Assembly, in such case made and provided; and against the peace and dignity of the State."

M'Beth, of counsel for the defendant, relied mainly on the alleged unconstitutionality of the statute against blasphemy, as being a law preferring Christianity to other modes of worship.

"After verdict, the defendant's counsel moved in arrest of judgment in each case (he had been tried and convicted in another case, in which he had simply transposed the terms of the statement, saying that *Jesus Christ was a   and the Virgin Mary was a   ,*) and the question of the constitutionality of the statute against blasphemy was again discussed, Rogers, deputy Attorney General for the State, and M'Beth for the defendant. . . . The court held both cases under advisement until the November term, 1837, (The first hearing having been at the May term proceeding) when the following opinion was delivered by the Chief Justice, J. M. Clayton."

The Court said, "It is true that the maxim of the English law that ' Christianity is part of the common law,' may be liable to misconstruction, and has been misunderstood. It is a current phrase among the special pleaders, ' that the Almanac is a part of the law of the land.' By this it is meant that the court will judicially notice the days of the week, month, and other things properly belonging to an almanac, without pleading or proving them. In the same sense it is sometimes said that the *lex parliamentaria* is a part of the law of the land. So, too, we apprehend, every court in a civilized country is bound to notice in the same way what is the prevailing religion of the people.

. . . It (the common law) took cognizance of and gave faith and credit to the religion of Christ as the religion of the common people. It acknowledged their right voluntarily to prefer that religion, and to be protected in the enjoyment of it ; and it carried that protection to the full length of punishing any man who outraged the feelings of the people, and insulted civil society, by wantonly and maliciously reviling or ridiculing the religion which they had freely preferred, and upon which they had staked all their hopes and happiness, both here and hereafter. . . . The distinction is a sound one between a religion preferred by law and a religion preferred by the people, without the coercion of law. . . . We hold that the people of Delaware have a full and perfect constitutional right to change their religion as often as they see fit. They may tomorrow, if they think it right, profess Mahometanism or Judaism, or adopt any other religious creed they please ; and so far from any court having power to punish them for such an exercise of right, all their judges are bound to notice their free choice and religious preference, and to protect them in the exercise of their right. Put the case then that they repudiate the religion of their fathers and adopt Judaism ; and that their legislature in obedience to their wishes ordains that to deride or ridicule the Jewish creed shall be blasphemy, and punishable, as blasphemy is now punished. On an indictment against any man for maliciously reviling Moses in public, in the language of this defendant, and publishing the Jewish religion as a villainous imposture, are we, or are we not bound to sentence him according to the statute ? Suppose the people then abjure Judaism, adopt the Koran and profess the religion of Mahomet. If their legislature enact that to revile or ridicule the prophet shall be blasphemy, may we, or may we not against him who shall go in to their public places and with a loud voice, maliciously revile and ridicule Mahomet, denounce the penalties of their statute? . . . It will be seen that in our judgment, by the Constitution and laws of Delaware, the Christian religion is a part of those laws ; so far that blasphemy against it is punishable, while the people prefer it as their religion, and no longer. The moment they change it and adopt any other, as they may do, the new religion becomes in the same sense a part of the law, for their courts are bound to yield it faith and credit, and respect it as their religion. . . . But it may, and will be objected, by some (for the question has excited deep interest among the writers of the day) that this mode of considering the subject is open to the remark that the law may forever change with the religion and customs of the people. Then it may be said, that the Christian himself may live to see the day when he shall not dare to proclaim publicly that the religion of Mahomet, or the impostures of Joe Smith, are the just topics of his ridicule and contempt. We answer that when that day shall arrive, (if come it must) in which the people shall forsake the faith of their forefathers for such miserable delusions, no human power can restrain them from compelling every man, who lives among them, to respect their feelings. A new code of laws, and a new Constitution, would at once spring into existence, if they found that those under which we live did not protect them from such insults. But in that event no man could justify himself under the *present* civil institutions of the State in endangering the public peace. He might feel himself impelled by a stern sense of religious duty to brave public opinion and become a martyr for his zeal. All this he might do and justify himself in his own opinion for it before God. So too that resistance to government, which would be rebellion or treason in a court of law, may be patriotism and virtue *in foro consciencia.* He who forcibly resists a bad religion is thus far like him who resists a bad government : if successful in his resistance he may become a reformer of men or a hero : if unsuccessful, a martyr or a traitor. But a court of law is not merely the *forum consciencia.* When human justice is rightly administered according to our common law and our Constitution, it refuses all jurisdiction over crimes against God, unless they are by necessary consequence crimes against civil society, and known and defined as such by the law of man. It assumes that for sin against our Creator, vengeance is his, and he will repay. It adapts itself to the condition of man as he is. . . . So far from its being true that it (the common law) cannot suit itself to the religious and moral code, and the ever varying conditions of the people, whenever they voluntarily prefer to change them, it tolerates every change in either, prohibits no reformation ; and, keeping constantly in view that its great object is to preserve the public peace and good order of society, without dictating what religion will best sustain it, or prohibiting any reformation in religious matters, it tolerates under all circumstances every attempt to change which does not by some overt act endanger the public peace and safety. It is emphatically a law for the protection of religious liberty, and no law can be such which does not protect the public peace from insults and outrages upon public opinion, when freely established and known to be so, whether the protection be for Christian, Infidel, Jew, or Turk.''

CHAPTER IX.

DECISIONS OF THE UNITED STATES SUPREME COURT.

THE question was in issue before that court in 1844 in the case of Vidal and others *v.* the Executors of Stephen Girard.

Stephen Girard, who died in Philadelphia, Pa., in 1831, left by his will forty-five acres of land and two millions of dollars to found and endow a college, in which poor white male orphans between six and ten years of age were to be received, educated, and maintained until they were between fourteen and eighteen years of age. One of the provisions of the will was as follows, viz. : '' I enjoin and require that no ecclesiastic, missionary, or minister of any sect whatever shall ever hold or exercise any station or duty whatever in the said college; nor shall any such person ever be admitted for any purpose within the premises appropriated to the purposes of said college.'' The will was contested on three grounds : 1st, on account of the uncertainty in the description of those who are intended to receive its benefits ; 2d, on account of the incompetence of the city of Philadelphia to receive the trust ; 3d, because the plan proposed by Mr. Girard was derogatory to the Christian religion. Mr. Webster, the great expounder of the Constitution, appeared for the contestants, and made in the case one of his notable legal arguments. Upon the last ground of contest the substance of his argument was: 1st. Our civil institutions are Christian. 2d. Any bequest which is made purposely hostile to Christianity cannot receive the protection of the law as a charity. 3d. The hostility manifested in the provisions of the will against the agents employed in the promotion of Christianity must be construed as hostility to christianity itself. He argues that while there is in this land perfect freedom of opinion, of speech, and worship, yet the law cannot use its power to establish and perpetuate anything that is directly and avowedly hostile to Christianity. He says: "Any man may go into that State [Pennsylvania] and speak or write as much as he pleases against a popular form of government, freedom of suffrage, trial by jury; he may decry civil liberty, and assert the divine right of kings, still he does nothing criminal; but if to give success to such efforts special powers from a court of justice is required it will not be given. . . . If Mr. Girard in his life time had founded schools and employed teachers to preach and teach infidelity, or against popular government, free suffrage, trial by jury, or the alienability of property, there was nothing to stop him or prevent him from doing so; but where any one or all of these come to be provided for a school or system, as a charity, and come before the courts for favor, then in neither one, nor all, nor any, can they be favored, because they are opposed to the general public policy and public law of the State." He says: "There can be found no such thing as a school of instruction, in a Christian land, from which the Christian religion has been, of intent and purpose, rigorously and opprobriously excluded, and yet such school regarded as a charitable trust, a foundation. I do not say that there may not be charity schools in which religious instruction is not provided. I need not go that length, although I take that to be the rule of the English law, but what I do say and repeat is that a school for the instruction of the young, which sedulously and reproachfully excludes Christian knowledge, is no charity, either on principle or authority, and is not therefore entitled to the character of a charity in a court of Equity. I have considered this proposition, and am ready to stand by it. I am willing that inquiry should be prosecuted to any extent of research to controvert this position." "There is nothing we look for with more certainty than this general principle, that Christianity is part of the law of the land. This was the case among the Puritans of England, the Episcopalians of the Southern States, the Pennsylvania Quakers, the Baptists, the mass of the followers of Whitefield and Wesley, and the Presbyterians,—all brought and adopted this great truth, and all have sustained it. And where there is any religious sentiment among men at all, this sentiment incorporates itself with the law. Every thing declares it,—the massive cathedral of the Catholic, the Episcopal church with its lofty spire pointing heavenward, the plain temple of the Quaker, the log church of the hardy pioneer of the wilderness, the mementos and memorials around us, the graveyards, their tombstones and epitaphs, the silent vaults, the mouldering contents,—all attest it. The dead prove it, as well as the living. All, all proclaim that Christianity, general, tolerant Christianity, Christianity independent of sects and parties, that Christianity to which the sword and fagot are unknown, general, tolerant Christianity, is the law of the land."'

---

[1] *Works*, vol. vi., pp. 133, 177.

The will was sustained by the court. Not, however, because the validity of the first two propositions in Mr. Webster's argument was questioned, their validity being expressly affirmed by the court, but because the construction of the will set forth in the third proposition, which was that the hostility manifested in the will against the agents employed in promoting Christianity must be construed as hostility against Christianity itself, was held by the court not to be a necessary construction, and not in accordance with the facts in the case. Justice Story delivered the opinion of the court, which was unanimous. The Court says : " It is also said, and truly, that the Christian religion is a part of the common law of Pennsylvania ; . . . yet it is so in this qualified sense, that its divine origin and truth are admitted, and, therefore, that it is not to be maliciously and openly reviled and blasphemed against, to the annoyance of believers, or the injury of the public. . . . There must be plain, positive, and express provisions demonstrating, not only that Christianity is not to be taught, but that it is to be impugned or repudiated. Now in the present case there is no pretence to say that any such positive or express provisions exist, or are even shadowed forth in the will. The testator does not say that Christianity shall not be taught in the college, but only that no ecclesiastic of any sect shall hold or exercise any station in the college. Suppose, instead of this, he had said that no person but a layman shall be an instructor, or officer, or visitor in the college. What legal objection could be made to such restriction, and yet the actual prohibition is in effect the same in substance. But it is asked, why are ecclesiastics excluded if it is not because they are the stated and appropriate preachers of Christianity ? The

answer may be given in the very words of the testator :
' In making this restriction I do not mean to cast any
reflection on any sect or person whatsoever ; but I desire to keep the tender minds of the orphans who are
to derive advantage from this bequest free from the
excitement which clashing doctrine and sectarian controversy are so apt to produce.' . . . But the objection itself assumes the proposition that Christianity
is not to be taught because ecclesiastics are not to be
instructors or officers. Why may not laymen instruct
in the general principles of Christianity as well as
ecclesiastics ? There is no restriction as to the religious
opinions of the instructors or officers—why may not
the Bible, and especially the New Testament, without
note or comment, be read and taught as a divine revelation, in the college, its general precepts expounded,
its evidences explained, and its glorious principles of
morality inculcated ? What is there to prevent a work,
not sectarian, upon the general evidences of Christianity
from being read and taught by lay teachers ? Certainly
there is nothing in the will that proscribes such studies.
Above all, the testator positively enjoins, ' that all the
instructors and teachers in the college shall take pains
to instill into the minds of the scholars the purest principles of morality, so that on their entrance into active
life they may, from inclination and habit, evince benevolence towards their fellow-creatures, and a love for
truth, sobriety, and industry, adopting, at the same
time, such religious tenets as their matured reason may
enable them to prefer.' Now, it may well be asked,
what is there in all this which is positively enjoined
inconsistent with the spirit or truth of Christianity ?
Are not these truths all taught by Christianity, although it teaches much more ? Where can the purest

principles of morality be learned so clearly or so perfectly as from the New Testament? Where are benevolence, the love of truth, sobriety, and industry so powerfully and irresistibly inculcated as in the sacred volume? The testator has not said how these great principles are to be taught, or by whom, except it be by laymen; nor what books are to be used to explain or enforce them. All that we can gather from his language is that he desires to exclude sectarians and sectarianism from the college, leaving the instructors and officers free to teach the purest morality, the love of truth, sobriety, and industry by all proper means, and of course including the best, the surest, and the most impressive. We are satisfied that there is nothing in the devise establishing a college, nor in the regulations and restrictions contained therein, which are inconsistent with the Christian religion, or are opposed to any known policy of the State of Pennsylvania." [1]

In this decision it is expressly asserted that Christianity is a part of the common law of the State of Pennsylvania, and it is distinctly implied that the Christian religion is so connected with our civil institutions that, if the will in question had required anything to be taught, or if there had been anything in the regulations and restrictions contained therein which was inconsistent with the Christian religion, the devise would not have been protected by the power of the United States.

In the case of Rector, etc., of Holy Trinity Church, *v.* United States, on "Construction of Statutes," "Alien Contract Labor Law," Mr. Justice Brewer, delivering the opinion of the court, said: ". . . But

---

[1] *Reports of Decisions in the Supreme Courts of the United States*, vol. xv., 2; 3 Howard, pp. 83–87.

beyond all these matters, no purpose of action against religion can be imputed to any legislation, State or National, because this is a religious people." After reviewing the commission to Columbus, the colonial grants and charters, various State constitutions, the cases of Updegraph *v.* Commonwealth, The People *v.* Ruggles, and Vidal *v.* Executors of Stephen Girard, as official declarations of the fact that Christianity is part of the common law, he says : " If we pass beyond these matters to a view of American life, as expressed by its laws, its business, its customs, and its society, we find everywhere a recognition of the same truth. . . . These and many other matters which might be noticed, add volumes of unofficial declarations to the mass of organic utterances, that this is a Christian nation." The summary of the decision is in part as follows :

" 4. It being historically true that the American people are a religious people, as shown by the religious objects expressed in the original grants and charters of the colonies, and the recognition of religion in the most solemn acts of their history, as well as in the Constitutions of the States and the Nation, the courts, in construing statutes, should not impute to any legislature a purpose of action against religion.

" 5. Although the Alien Contract Labor law (23 St., p. 332) prohibits the importation of 'any' foreigners under contract to perform 'labor or service of any kind,' yet it does not apply to one who comes to this country under contract to enter the service of a church as its rector. 36 Fed., Rep., 303. Reversed." [1]

[1] Decision rendered February 29, 1892. *The Supreme Court Reporter*, vol. xii., p. 511.

10

CHAPTER X.

JEFFERSON'S ARGUMENT.

WHILE the great legal authorities of England and the United States agree in the opinion that Christianity is a part of the common law, at least one very eminent man has held, and with apparent learning has endeavored to maintain, the opposite opinion.

Mr. Thomas Jefferson, shortly after the decision of the Supreme Court of New York in the case of The People *v.* Ruggles, and of the Supreme Court of Pennsylvania in the case of Updegraph *v.* The Commonwealth, wrote a letter to Major John Cartwright, then of London, controverting the principles laid down in these decisions. The letter is dated at Monticello, June 5, 1824. In it he says: " I am much indebted for your kind letter of February 29th, and for your valuable volume on the English Constitution. . . . I was glad to find in your book a formal contradiction at length of the judiciary usurpation of legislative powers; for such the judges have usurped in their repeated decisions that Christianity is a part of the common law. The proof of the contrary which you have adduced is incontrovertible. . . . But it may amuse you to learn when and by what means they stole this in upon us. In a case of *quare impedit*. . . Here I might defy the best read lawyer to produce one scrip of authority for this judiciary forgery : and I might go on further to show how some of the Anglo-Saxon priests interpolated into the text of Alfred's laws the 20th, 21st, 22nd and 23d chapters of Exodus, and the 15th of the Acts of the Apostles, from the 23d to the 29th verses. But this would lead my pen and your patience too far. What a conspiracy between Church

and State ! Sing Tantarara, rogues all, rogues all.
Tantarara, rogues all." [1]

The argument of this letter, revised and amplified,
is an Appendix to Jefferson's *Reports of Cases Determined in the General Court of Virginia from 1730–
1740, and from 1768–1772* Published at Charlottes-
ville, Va., by F. Carr & Co. 1829, the Appendix having no connection whatever with the subject-matter of
the work to which it is appended. It is as follows :

" In *Quare impedit* in C. B. H. 6, fo. 38, the defendant Bishop of Lincoln pleads that the church of the
plaintiff became vacant by the death of the incumbent ;
that the plaintiff and I. S. each pretending a right,
presented two clerks ; that the church being thus rendered litigious, he was not obliged by the ecclesiastical
law to admit either until an inquisition *de jure patrona-
tus* in the ecclesiastical court ; that by the same law
this inquisition was to be at the suit of either claimant,
and was not *ex-officio* to be instituted by the Bishop
and at his proper costs ; that neither party had desired
such an inquisition ; that six months passed, wherein
it belonged to him of right to present, as on a lapse,
which he had done. The plaintiff demurred. A question was, how far the ecclesiastical law was to be respected in this matter by the common law court. And
Prisot (c. 5.) in the course of his argument uses this expression : ' A tels leis que ils de seint eglise ont en
ancien scripture, covient à nous à donner credence ;
car ceo common ley sur quel touts manners leis sont
fonde s. Et auxy, Sir, nous sumus obligés de conustre
lour ley de saint eglise : et semblablement ils sont obligés
de conustre nostre ley, et, Sir, si poit apperer or a nous
que l'evesque ad fait come un Ordinary fera en teil cas,

adonq nous devous ceo adjurer bon, ou auterment
nemy,' etc. It does not appear what judgment was
given. Y. B. ubi supra 3. c. Fitzh. Abr. Qu. imp. 89.
Bro. Abr. Qu. imp. 12. Finch mis-states this in the
following manner : ' To such laws of the church as have
warrant in *Holy Scripture* our law giveth credence,'
and cites the above case and the words of Prisot in the
margin. (Finch's law. B. I. c. 3. published 1613.)
Here we find *ancien scripture* converted into *Holy Scripture*, whereas it can only mean the ancient written laws
of the church. It cannot mean the Scriptures : 1st.
Because the term *ancient* scripture must then be understood as meaning the *Old* Testament in contra-distinc-
tion to the *New*, and to the exclusion of that, which would
be absurd and contrary to the wish of those who cited
this passage to prove that the scriptures, or *Christianity*,
is a part of the common law. 2nd. Because Prisot says
' ceo (est) Common ley sur quel tonts manners leis sont
fondes.' Now it is true that the ecclesiastical law, so
far as admitted in England, derives its authority from
the common law. But it would not be true that the
Scriptures so derive their authority. 3rd. The whole
case and arguments show that the question was, how
far the ecclesiastical law in general should be respected
in a common law court. And in Bro's Abr. of this case
Littleton says, ' les juges del Common ley prendra con-
usans quid est lex ecclesiæ vel admiralitates et hujus
modi ? ' 4th. Because the particular part of the ecclesiastical law then in question, viz. : the right of the
patron to present to his advowson, was not founded on
the law of God, but subject to the modification of the
law-giver, and so could not introduce any such general
position as Finch pretends. Yet Wingate (in 1658)
thinks proper to erect this false quotation into a maxim

of the common law, expressing it in the very words of
Finch but citing Prisot. Wingate, Max. 3. Next
comes Sheppard (in 1675) who states it in the same
words of Finch and quotes Y. B., Finch and Wingate.
3. Shep. Arb. tit. Religion.

"In the case of King and Taylor, Sir Matthew Hale
lays it down in these words : ' Christianity is parcel of
the laws of England.' (I. Ventr. 293. 3. Keb. 607.)
But he quotes no authority. It was from this part of
the supposed common law that he derived his authority
for burning witches. So strong was this doctrine become in 1728 by additions and repetitions from one another that in the case of The King *v.* Woolston the court
would not suffer it to be debated, whether to write
against Christianity was punishable in the temporal
courts at common law, saying it had been settled in
Taylor's case, ante, 2 stra. 834. Therefore Wood in his
Institutes, lays it down that all blasphemy and profaneness are offences by the common law, and cites Strange,
ubi supra, Wood, 409. And Blackstone (about 1763)
repeats, in the words of Sir Matthew Hale, that ' Christianity is part of the laws of England,' citing Ventr. and
Stra. ubi supra, 4. Bl. 59. Lord Mansfield qualified a
little by saying, in the case of the Chamberlain of London *v.* Evans, 1767, that ' The essential principles of revealed religion are part of the common law.' But he
cites no authority and leaves us at our peril to find out
what in the opinion of the judge, and according to the
measure of his foot or his faith, are those *essential* principles of revealed religion, obligatory on us as a part of
the common law. Thus we find this string of authorities, when examined to the beginning, all hanging on
the same hook, a perverted expression of Prisot's, or on
nothing, for they all quote Prisot, or one another, or

nobody. Thus Finch quotes Prisot ; Wingate also ; Sheppard quotes Prisot, Finch, and Wingate. Hale cites nobody ; the court in Wollston's case cites Hale. Wood cites Wollston's case ; Blackstone that and Hale ; and Lord Mansfield, like Hale, ventures it on his own authority. In the earlier ages of the law, as in the Year Books, for instance, we do not expect much recurrence to authorities by the judges, because in those days there were few or none such made public. But in later times we take no judge's word for what the law is further than he is warranted by the authorities he appeals to. His decision may bind the unfortunate individual who happens to be the particular subject of it, but it cannot alter the law. Although the common law be termed the *Lex non scripta*, yet the same Hale tells us : ' When I call those parts of our laws *Leges non scriptæ*, I do not mean as if all those laws were only oral, or communicated from the former ages to the latter merely by word. For all these laws have their several monuments in writing whereby they are transferred from one age to another, and without which they would soon lose all kind of certainty. They are for the most part extant in records of pleas, proceedings and judgments, in books of reports and judicial decisions, in tractates of learned men's arguments and opinions, preserved from ancient times and extant in writing.' (Hale's Common Law, 22.) Authorities for what is common law may, therefore, be as well cited as for any part of the *lex scripta*. And there is no better instance of the necessity of holding the judges and writers to a declaration of their authorities than the present, where we detect them endeavoring to make law where they found none and to submit us, at one stroke, to a whole system no particle of which has its foundation in common law, or has re-

ceived the '*esto*' of the legislator. For we know that
the common law is that system of law which was introduced by the Saxons on their settlement in England, and
altered from time to time by proper legislative authority
from that to the date of the *Magna Charta*, which termi-
nates the period of the common law or *lex non scripta* and
commences that of the statute law or *lex scripta*. This
settlement took place about the middle of the fifth century, the conversion of the first Christian king of the
Heptarchy having taken place about the year 598, and
that of the last about 686. Here then was a space of
two hundred years during which the common law was
in existence and Christianity no part of it. If it ever,
therefore, was adopted into the common law it must
have been between the introduction of Christianity and
the date of the *Magna Charta*. But of the laws of this
period we have a tolerable collection by Lambard and
Wilkins ; probably not perfect, but neither very defective ; and if any one chooses to build a doctrine on any
law of that period, supposed to have been lost, it is incumbent on him to prove it to have existed and what
were its contents. These were so far alterations of the
common law and became themselves a part of it, but
none of these adopt Christianity as a part of the common law. If therefore from the settlement of the Saxons to the introduction of Christianity among them
that system of religion could not be a part of the common
law, because they were not yet Christians ; and if having
their laws from that period to the close of the common
law we are able to find among them no such act of adoption, we may safely affirm (though contradicted by all
the judges and writers on earth) that Christianity
neither is nor ever was a part of the common law.

"Another cogent proof of this truth is drawn from the

silence of certain writers on the common law. Bracton gives us a very complete and scientific treatise of the whole body of the common law. He wrote this about the close of the reign of Henry III., a very few years after the date of the *Magna Charta.* We consider this book as the more valuable as it was written about the time that divides the common and statute law ; and therefore gives us the former in its ultimate state. Bracton too was an ecclesiastic, and would certainly not have failed to inform us of the adoption of Christianity as a part of the common law had any such adoption ever taken place. But no word of his which indicates anything like it has ever been cited. Fleta and Britton, who wrote in the succeeding reign of E. I., are equally silent. So also is Glanvil, an earlier writer than any of them ; to wit, temp. H. 2, but his subject might not perhaps have led him to mention it. It was reserved then for Finch five hundred years after in the time of Charles II. by a falsification of a phrase in the Year Book to open this new doctrine, and for his successors to have joined full mouthed in the cry, and give to the fiction the sound of fact. Justice Fortescue Aland, who professed more Saxon learning than all the judges and writers before mentioned put together, places this subject on more limited ground. Speaking of the laws of the Saxon kings he says : ' The ten commandments were made part of their law, and consequently were *once* part of the law of England ; so that to break any of the ten commandments was then esteemed a breach of the common law of England, and why it is not so now perhaps it may be difficult to give a good reason.' (Preface to Fortescue's *Reports*, xvii.) The good reason is found in the denial of the fact.

" Houard in his Contumes Anglo-Normaudes I. 87.

notices the falsification of the laws of Alfred, by pre-
fixing to them four chapters of the Jewish law, to wit,
the 20th, 21st, 22nd, and 23rd chapters of Exodus ; to
which he might have added the 15th of the Acts of the
Apostles, verse 23 to 29, and precepts from other parts
of the scripture. These he calls *Hors d'oeuvre* of some
pious copyist. This awkward monkish fabrication
makes the preface to Alfred's genuine laws stand in
the body of the work. And the very words of Alfred
himself prove the fraud, for he declares in that preface
that he has collected these laws from the laws of Ina,
of Offa, Aethelbert and his ancestors, saying nothing
of any of them being taken from the scripture. It is
still more proved by the inconsistencies it occasions.
For example, the Jewish legislator, Exodus xxi, 12,
13, 14, (copied by the pseudo Alfred 13) makes murder
death. But Alfred himself Ll. xxvi, punishes it with
a fine only, called a weregild, proportioned to the condition of the person killed. It is remarkable that Hume
(Appendix I. to his *History*), examining this law of
Alfred without perceiving the fraud, puzzles himself
with accounting for the inconsistency it had introduced. To strike a pregnant woman so that she die
is death by Exodus xxi, 22, 23, and Pseudo Alfred
S. 18, but by the Ll. Alfred ix, the offender pays a
weregild for both the woman and the child. To
smite out an eye or a tooth, Exodus xxi, 24–27,
Pseudo Alfred S. 19, 20, if of a servant by his master
is freedom to the servant ; in every other case retaliation ; but by Alfred Ll. xl, a fixed indemnification is
paid. Theft of an ox or a sheep by the Jewish law,
Exodus xxii, 1, was repaid fivefold for the ox and
fourfold for the sheep ; but by Alfred Ll. xvi, he who
stole a cow and calf was to repay the worth of the

cow and 40 s. for the calf. Goring by an ox was
the death of the ox, and the flesh was not to be
eaten, Exodus xxi, 28, Pseudo Alfred S. 21. By Ll.
Alfred xxiv the wounded person had the ox. This
Pseudograph makes municipal laws of the ten commandments ; S. 1-10 regulates concubinage ; S. 12
makes it death to strike, or to curse father or mother ;
S. 14, 15 give an eye for an eye, tooth for tooth, hand
for hand, foot for foot, burning for burning, wound for
wound, stripe for stripe ; S. 19 sells the thief to repay
his theft ; S. 24 obliges the fornicator to marry the
woman he has lain with ; S. 29 forbids interest on
money ; S. 28, 35 make the laws of bailment, and very
different from what Lord Holt delivers in Coggs *v.*
Bernard, and what Sir William Jones tells us they
were ; and punishes witchcraft with death, S. 30,
which Sir Matthew Hale I. P. C. ch. 33, declares was
not a felony before the stat. I. Jac. c. 12. It was under
that statute he hung Rose Callender and Amy Duny 16.
Car. 2. (1662) on whose trial he declared that there were
such creatures as witches, he made no doubt at all ;
for, first, the scriptures had affirmed so much ; second,
the wisdom of all nations had provided laws against
such persons, . . . and such hath been the judgment of this kingdom, as appears by that act of parliament which hath provided punishments proportionable
to the quality of the offence. And we must certainly
allow greater weight to this position, 'that it was no
felony till James' statutes' deliberately laid down in
his H. P. C., a work which he wrote to be printed and
transcribed in his lifetime, than to the hasty *scriptum*,
that 'At common law witchcraft was punished with
death as heresy, by writ *de heretico comburendo*' in his
methodical summary of the P. C. p. 6 ; a work 'not

intended for the press, nor fitted for it, and which he declared he had never read over since it was written.' Preface. Unless we understand his meaning in that to be that witchcraft could not be punished at *common law as witchcraft*, but as *heresy*. In either sense however it is a denial of this pretended law of Alfred. Now all men of reading know that these pretended laws of homicide, concubinage, theft, retaliation, compulsory marriage, usury, bailment, and others which might have been cited from this pseudograph were never the laws of England, not even in Alfred's time ; and of course that it is a forgery. Yet, palpable as it must be to a lawyer, our judges have piously avoided lifting the veil under which it was shrouded. In truth, the alliance between Church and State in England has ever made their judges accomplices in the frauds of the clergy, and even bolder than they are, for instead of being content with the surreptitious introduction of these four chapters of Exodus, they have taken the whole leap, and declared at once that the whole Bible and Testament in a lump make a part of the common law of the land, the first judicial declaration of which was by this Sir Matthew Hale. And thus they incorporate into the English code laws made for the Jews alone, and the precepts of the gospel, intended by their benevolent author as obligatory only in *foro conscientiæ*, and they arm the whole with the coercions of municipal law. They do this too, in a case where the question was not at all, whether Christianity was a part of the law of England, but simply how far the *ecclesiastical law* was to be respected by the common law courts of England, in the special case of a right of presentment ; thus identifying Christianity with the ecclesiastical law of England." [1]   Th. Jefferson.

[1] Jefferson's *Reports*, Appendix, pp 137–142.

Clayton's Answer.—Chief-Justice Clayton, of Delaware, in the decision in the case of the State *v.* Chandler, November, 1837, already referred to, makes the following reply to the argument of Mr. Jefferson :

"The defendent's counsel in the progress of the argument on this subject referred to a letter written by Thomas Jefferson to Major Cartwright, dated June 5, 1824, and published in the fourth volume of his posthumus works. This letter we notice because respectable counsel have cited it. It is phrased in terms more becoming to the newspaper paragraphs of the day than the opinion of a grave jurist who feels respect for the memory of the eminent lawyers of England, because he knows and can appreciate their worth. The opinion of Lord Mansfield, who was one of the brightest luminaries of the common law, palpably misunderstood by this writer, is by him denounced as a '*judicial forgery.*' He considers, and so states, that by this maxim mentioned by Lord Mansfield which recognizes revealed religion as a part of the common law, his lordship has 'engulped Bible, Testament and all into the common law' ; whereas this mode of garbling a remark and then replying to it has done gross injustice to that great man, whose celebrated argument for religious toleration in the English house of lords in the case of Evans, does by no means justify the imputation cast upon him. So far from meaning that Bible and Testament were part of the common law for other purposes than that of punishing subversion, reviling and ridiculing them ; so far from pretending that any man could be punished by the common law for mere infidelity or for worshipping God as he pleases, or for any violation of any divine precept, not expressly adopted by man as human law, which would make courts and juries the regulators of every man's conscience, Lord Mansfield expressly says : ' Conscience is not controllable by human laws, nor amendable to human tribunals. Persecution or attempts to force conscience will never produce conviction, and are only calculated to make hypocrites or martyrs.' ' There is nothing,' he adds, ' more unreasonable, more contrary to the spirit and precept of the Christian religion, more iniquitous or unjust, more impolitic, than persecution. It is against natural religion, revealed religion, and sound policy.'

" Mr. Jefferson endeavors to show that the maxim that Christianity is a part of the common law of England is entirely derived from an opinion of Prisot in the *Year Book*, 34 H., 6, folio 38., (145-8). In a case *quare impedit* a question was made, how far the ecclesiastical law was to be respected in a common law court, and Prisot gives his opinion in these words : ' Prisot . . . a tiels Leys. . . .' The whole of Mr. Jefferson's complaint is that Finch has mistaken this passage by translating ' *auncient scripture*,' *holy scripture*. Mr. Jefferson translates Priscot's Norman French so as to make him decide ' that to such laws of holy church as have warrant in *ancient writing*, it is proper for us to give credence' ; while, says he, Finch interprets the passage, ' to such laws of the church as have warrant in holy scripture our law giveth credence.' Now the question which the judge was considering, when he delivered this opinion, was, whether the sentence of the bishop or ecclesiastical court should have faith and credit at common law. He made the same decision which was afterwards made in 11 H., 7, 9, and again in Caudrey's case reported in Sir Edward Coke, 5 Rep. 1. In Caudrey's case, ' it was resolved by the whole court that the sentence given by the Bishop by the con-

sent of his colleagues was such as the judges of the
common law ought to allow to be given, according to
the ecclesiastical laws : for seeing that their authority
is to proceed and give sentence in a cause ecclesiastical,
upon their proceedings by force of that law, *the judge
of the common law ought to give faith and credit to their
sentence and to allow it to be done according to the ecclesiastical law.* For *Cuilibet in sua arte perito credendum
est.* 'And this,' says Lord Coke, 'is the common
received opinion of all our books'; for which he then
cites the very case, 34 H., 6, 14, where the opinion is
given by Prisot. The point decided was the legal principle that the sentence of a competent court, of exclusive and peculiar jurisdiction, is conclusive, where that
sentence comes incidentally in question in another court.
The judge therefore concluded that 'If it should appear to us (the common law judges) that the Bishop
has done as an ordinary may do in such a case (that is,
has not exceeded his jurisdiction) then we ought to adjudge these good or otherwise.' According to what
Mr. Jefferson calls Finch's interpretation, the judges
decided that the sentence of the ecclesiastical tribunal
when warranted by the *holy scriptures* shall be credited
in a common law court as the decision of a competent
tribunal, provided the ecclesiastical tribunal did not ex-
ceed its jurisdiction. According to Mr. Jefferson's version, the judges decided that the same sentence when
warranted by 'the ancient written laws' should be so
acknowledged and credited. What these written laws
were Mr. Jefferson does not inform us ; but the common
law was emphatically the *lex non scripta* or unwritten
law, as contra-distinguished from the statute law, and
Mr. Jefferson probably knew that ; he must have intended either statutes of parliament or the written laws

of the church. The statutes of parliament could not have been intended, for they did not regulate the ecclesiastical jurisdiction ; and the words ' *car cco est common ley sur que touts manner leys sont fondens*' when applied to them would be nonsense. For how could they be said to be the foundation of all human laws. If by written laws Mr. Jefferson meant the written laws of the church at that day, they at that day credited the holy scriptures and professed to be built upon them. The ecclesiastical tribunals, as we know from Caudrey's case, assumed jurisdiction of all offences purely against God and the Holy Scriptures, *pro salute animæ*, without reference to the mere effect of such offences on the peace of society, which the common law never did. But the common law judges, by yielding up that jurisdiction to the ecclesiastical courts, refusing to reverse or revise their decisions when incidently or collaterally presented in a common law court, thus simply recognizing those decisions as ecclesiastical and not as common law, did no more intend by that to acknowledge the laws of holy church as *common law*, than they intended to acknowledge admiralty law as common law when they gave faith and credit to an admiralty decision.

"It is not within our knowledge that any common law judge has cited the case in the *Year Book* or referred to it in any manner, to prove his opinion in citing a case of blasphemy, with the malicious reviling of Christianity, was punishable at common law. The labor with which Mr. Jefferson has searched the *Year Book* to convict Finch of a mistranslation would have been saved had he been aware that he was only proving, by his own construction of the passage, that the ecclesiastical law was founded in the written laws of the church,

and not in the scriptures alone.   As friends of religious
liberty, we would prefer that the common law should
have 'engulphed Bible and Testament' rather than
the laws of the church, as understood at that day,
which not only professed to comprise the Bible and
Testament, but usurped entire control over the consciences of men, or burnt the body under pretext of
saving the soul.

"Having thus seen Mr. Jefferson's premises, let us
next consider the argument built upon them to convict
Mansfield of judicial forgery.   He says that Hale decided that Christianity was parcel of the laws of England, but quoted no authority ; that by such echoings
and re-echoings from one to another, in 1728, the court
(composed of Lord C. J. Raymond, and Page, Reynolds,
and Probyn, justices) in the case of the King *v.* Woolston, for blasphemy, 2 Str., 834, would not suffer it to be
debated whether writing against Christianity *in general*
was punishable in the temporal courts at common law ;
that Justice Blackstone adopts Hale's opinion and cites
the adjudged cases ; and finally, that Lord Mansfield
had used the words before quoted as delivered by him
in Evans' case, 'that the essential parts of revealed
religion are parts of the common law,' thus, says
Mr. Jefferson, engulfing Bible, Testament, and all
into the common law without citing any authority.
'And thus far,' he adds, 'we find this chain of authorities hanging link by link one upon another, *and
all ultimately upon one and the same book* [*hook ?*] *and
that a mistranslation of the words auncient scripture used
by Prisot.*'   He concludes that he ' might defy the
best read lawyer to produce another scrip of authority
for this judicial forgery.'   This letter-writer then first
admits expressly that neither Hale nor Mansfield had

cited any authority for their opinions, and immediately after charges the principles for which their great names are cited with hanging on what he calls a mistranslation of the words of Prisot. He thought that his erudition had enabled him to detect the very source from which their ignorance and folly, or their knavery, had sprung. Had Hale or Mansfield quoted the passage from Prisot which Mr. Jefferson has thus plumed himself on the translation of, as the foundation for a judicial opinion, then they would have been responsible for the translation of the passage, but neither of them quoted the *Year Book* ; they had no occasion to quote any authority. Long before Lord Hale decided that Christianity was a part of the laws of England, the Court of King's Bench, 34 Eliz., in Ratcliff's case, 3 Coke Rep., 40 b., had gone so far as to declare that 'in almost all cases the common law was grounded on the law of God which it was said was the *causa causans*,' and the court cited the 27th chapter of Numbers to show that their judgment on a common law principle in regard to the law of inheritance was founded on God's revelation of that law to Moses. Mr. Hargrave, in his note on Co. Lit. 11 b., observes that 'this inference from God's precepts to Moses is unwarranted, unless it can be shown that it was promulgated as a law for mankind in general, instead of being like many other parts of the Mosaical law, a rule for the direction of the Jewish nation only.' The author of the reports and the commentary on Littleton was a professor of Christianity, as is visible in all his writings. That Hale, with such an authority before him, should have deemed it necessary to cite Coke, familiar as his writings were to the profession at a time when his works were the principal text-book of every

11

lawyer, cannot be the subject of much wonder; and
we know, notwithstanding Mr. Jefferson's defiance,
that even Finch himself quoted 8 H., 8, '*Ley de Dieu
est Ley de terre*'—the law of God is the law of the land.
Doc. and Stud., lib. i., c. 6. Plowd, 265, to sustain his
position that the holy scripture is of sovereign authority, and to show the extent and meaning of the maxim.
But independent of Lord Coke, or any other judge, Sir
Matthew Hale was an authority of himself, and is considered as a sufficient authority for a common law principle in every case when there is no contrary authority.
What sources of legal knowledge his great erudition
may have consulted on this subject, we have no means
of certainly knowing, nor is it necessary to inquire.

" As for the alleged translation of Finch, we have examined the whole passage and are well satisfied that
if Finch construed '*auncient scripture*' to mean *holy
scripture*, such a translation of the Norman French would
be the true translation. But in fact Finch has not ven-
tured any translation of the passage whatever, notwithstanding Mr. Jefferson professes to copy the *very words*
in which he has translated it. We speak with the
work of Henry Finch of Gray's Inn, book 1, chapter
iii., published in London, 1759, before us. Mr. Jefferson has made a translation for Finch in words with
inverted commas, then attempted to prove his translation false, and failed to do it. Finch evidently believed
that Prisot spoke of the holy scripture, and therefore
cited the *Year Book*, with other authorities, to sustain
a general position in the text, that the scriptures were
of sovereign authority,—a position which, like that of
every other compiler, was good to the full extent of
his authority, and no further; and it is sustained by
the *Year Book* so far as to show that the common law

did recognize the decisions of ecclesiastical courts which were founded on the scriptures *as conclusive when brought collaterally in question in a common law court.* Lord Mansfield's judicial forgery stood, as the cases we have cited prove, upon other and many other authorities than Mr. Jefferson appears ever to have read." [1]

CHAPTER XI.

THE TREATY WITH TRIPOLI.

ARTICLE XI. of the Treaty with Tripoli, ratified by the United States, February 10, 1797, is as follows:

"As the government of the United States of America is not, in any sense, founded on the Christian religion; as it has in itself no character of enmity against the laws, religion, or tranquillity of Musselmen; and as the said States never have entered into any war or act of hostility against any Mahometan nation, it is declared by the parties that no pretext arising from religious opinion shall ever produce an interruption of the harmony existing between the two countries."

The Constitution of the United States, Article VI., declares that "All Treaties made, or which shall be made, under the authority of the United States, shall be the supreme law of the land, and the judges in every State shall be bound thereby."

There can be no doubt that the stipulations of a treaty have the character of a supreme law, but nobody pretends that all the arguments used therein have such a character. The first clause of Article XI. in this Treaty alleges a supposed fact as an argument, bearing

[1] 2 Harrington, pp. 558–562.

upon a conclusion, afterwards stated, and has no more than an argumentative force. That allegation has been regarded as of so little authority that a majority of the courts which have been called upon to adjudicate on the question, whether " The government of the United States of America is, in any sense founded, on the Christian religion," do not even mention it.

Furthermore, whatever may have been the authority of that Treaty, it was superseded by the Treaty of June 4, 1815, in which the clause in question is omitted. Article XIV. of that Treaty is as follows :

" As the government of the United States of America has in itself no character of enmity against the laws, religion, or tranquillity of Musselmen," etc.

This omission in the second Treaty of the statement made in the first, that " The government of the United States of America is not, in any sense, founded on the Christian religion," may fairly be construed as a retraction of that statement, and as an authoritative denial of its truth. Such construction is especially warranted by the fact that Chancellor Kent had rendered his famous decision in the case of People *v.* Ruggles only three years before the negotiation of this treaty.

In summing up the results of this part of our investigation we may take it as established, by the charters and acts of the colonies, by the constitutions and acts of the States, by the intent, and the temporary force, of the Ordinance of 1787, by the necesssities of the case as expressed in the common law, by the principles of equity, by the decisions of the Supreme Courts of the States, and by the decisions of the Supreme Court of the United States, that the civil institutions of this land are necessarily, legally, and rightly Christian.

PART III.

A question of theory. What ought to be the relation of the Christian religion to the civil government, in the United States?

CHAPTER I.

THE large amount of thought which men in all times
have been compelled to bestow upon the subject under
consideration, together with the native impulse of the
human mind to find a principle whereby individual
facts may be brought into a comprehensive unity, has
very naturally led to the formation of various theories
of the State and the Church, and of the relation of each
to the other.

1st. The first we shall mention may be called the Mediæval Ecclesiastical Theory. According to this theory
the civil organization is comprehended in the Church.
The temporal powers derive their authority from the
Church and are responsible to it. Pope Gregory VII.,
the illustrious reformer of his time, who made the
first distinct enunciation of theory and the first demand
for its universal acceptance, compared the Church to
the sun, and the State to the moon, and contended that
as the moon is subject to the sun, and shines only with
a light derived from the sun, so the State is subject to
the Church, and derives all its powers from the Church.
He likened the temporal and spiritual powers belonging to the Church to the two eyes belonging to one
head. The commission our Lord gave to his disciples,
to go into all the world and teach all nations to observe

all things whatsoever he had commanded them, was interpreted as establishing but one authority in the world,—the authority of Christ, which was to be exercised by his representatives. His expression, "It is enough," when in answer to his direction "He that hath no sword let him sell his garment and buy one," they said "Lord, behold here are two swords," was interpreted as meaning that two swords were sufficient for all the purposes of His kingdom on earth ; the one being the symbol of the spiritual, and the other the symbol of the temporal power. It was assumed that he delivered both swords to Peter, and that Peter delivered them into the hands of his successors in the primacy, the bishops of Rome. If the sword of the temporal power is found in the hands of civil rulers, it has been placed there by the supreme pontiff. They hold it at his will and are to be responsible to him for all the use they make of it. Any temporal power that is independent of the Church is to be regarded as an usurpation established by violence and maintained by iniquity, the fruit of which cannot be otherwise than evil.

This theory was not conceived and promulgated in its full form at any particular date. It was the result of the interaction of all historical forces, social, political, and religious, throughout a long period ; from the time of Pope Zacharias (752), or before till the time of Pope Boniface VIII. (1303), a period of nearly six hundred years. It was not the fabrication of any particular man, but was rather a growth. Neither was it like the mould, a growth from corruption. It was rather in its beginning like the mustard seed, the smallest of all seeds, which became a great tree wherein the fowls of the air lodged. It derived its life from the highest conception of the mission of the Church, the noblest aims and the purest intentions. The times seemed to have prepared the way for it, and the voice of God, in his providence, seemed to be calling the Church to enter upon her high mission. The evils following upon the dissolution of the Roman empire were appalling. The temporal powers in their weakness, distraction, and barbarism, seemed to aggravate rather than cure these evils. The Church seemed to be endowed with all the powers necessary to bring in a universal reign of righteousness and peace. The temporal powers were divided ; the Church was united ; the temporal powers were weak, patriotism being almost extinct, tribes and nations being little else than marauding hordes. The Church was strong, deriving its strength from the religious sentiments and the superstitious fears of the people, which at the time exerted a powerful influence upon the conduct of men ; and its power seemed to be all pervasive, penetrating all the nations of Europe. Why should she not avail herself of the opportunity thus offered to realize the highest conception of her character, and fulfil her appointed mission in the world ? It is no matter of wonder that Pope Zacharias, by his legate, anointed and crowned Pepin le Bref, King of the Franks (752) ; that Leo III. placed the imperial crown on the head of Charles the Great, bestowed on him the title of " Augustus Emperor," and upon his kingdom the title of " The Holy Roman Empire " (800) ; that Hadrian II. when Lothair, king of Lotharingia, died without issue, bestowed the crown upon Louis, in preference to his brother Charles the Bald, who had seized the kingdom ; that Pope John VIII. five years later bestowed the imperial crown upon Charles (875) ; that John XII. anointed Otho I. of Ger-

many as emperor (962) ; that Gregory VII. excommunicated and deposed Henry IV., emperor of Germany,
and compelled him to stand without the castle gates of
Canossa, bareheaded and clothed with hair cloth, exposed for three days in January to the inclemency of
the weather, before he would remove the ban of excommunication (1076) ; and that Innocent III. deposed John
(Lackland) King of England and gave his kingdom to
Philip II., Augustus of France (1213).

This theory, plausible as it was at the time, was
never without its opponents. Many learned and able
men asserted the divine ordinance both of Church and
State, and maintained that each was independent of
the other in its own sphere. Political complications
tended constantly to keep up and strengthen this opposition. The popes who attempted to carry out the
theory were in perpetual conflict with the political
powers, and often also with the clergy residing in the
territory of the opposing powers. The theory was
affirmed in its fullest form and its acceptance demanded
in the most peremptory manner by Boniface VIII. in
his quarrel with Philip IV., the Fair, of France. The
Pope sent haughty letters to the King, in which he asserted that the kings of France, with all other kings
and princes whatsoever, were obliged by a divine command to submit to the authority of the popes, as well
in all political and civil matters, as in those of a religious nature. The King answered with contempt. The
Pope rejoined with greater arrogance, and finally issued
the famous Bull "Unam Sanctam Ecclesiam," November 18, 1302, in which he asserted that Christ had
subjected the whole human race to the authority of the
Roman pontiff ; that the Church could have but one
head ; that a two-headed Church would be a monstros-

ity ; that Christ had granted a two-fold power to his Church, the spiritual and the temporal swords, and that the temporal sword wielded by the monarch was borne only at the will and by the permission of the pontiff. The Pope excommunicated the King and absolved his subjects from their allegiance. The King called a council to depose the Pope and sent an agent to seize his person, who executed his commission in such an insulting and brutal manner that the Pope soon after died of an illness brought on or aggravated by his anguish and mortification (1303).

Since the downfall of Boniface VIII. scarcely any attempt has been made to put this theory in practice.

2d. Erastianism. This theory takes its name from Thomas Erastus, a Zwinglian Protestant, who was born at Baden in Switzerland, September 7, 1524, but spent the most of his life at Heidelberg, as court physician and professor of medicine in the university of that city. Having studied philosophy and theology in his early life at the university of Basel, he took an interest in the theological controversies of the day. He was strenuously opposed to the exercise of rigid discipline in the Church, and wrote against what he called the excommunicatory fever of the Protestant Church, affirming that exclusion from the sacraments was not a legitimate punishment for any offences whatever. In his opposition to the rigidity of discipline he came at last to deny the right of the Church to exercise discipline at all. He held that the Jewish Church, in which there were no traces of two diverse jurisdictions, the one civil, the other ecclesiastical, was the divinely appointed model for all time. He said that there was no reason why the Christian magistrate at the present day should not possess the same power which God commanded the magistrate to exercise in the Jewish commonwealth. He contended that excommunication was not a divine ordinance, but a device of man ; that the Church has no power to make laws and decrees, still less to inflict pains and penalties of any kind, the punishment of all offences belonging to the civil magistrate exclusively ; that the sacraments being means of grace ought not to be withheld from any citizen desiring to receive them ; that the sins of professing Christians, like the sins of all other persons, are to be punished by the civil magistrate with civil penalties, and not by pastors and elders with ecclesiastical penalties.

This theory is the opposite of the Mediæval Ecclesiastical theory. According to this theory, the State is the only divine institution, and is possessed of all the powers commonly supposed to belong to the Church. According to the other, the Church is the only divine institution and is possessed of all the powers commonly supposed to belong to the State. According to the one theory, the State, and according to the other, the Church, is charged with the care of both the temporal and spiritual interests of mankind.

3d. The third theory may be called the theory of Paternalism. According to this theory, Church and State are not distinct institutions, which may be in union, or may be co-ordinate and independent of each other, or may be in subordination the one to the other, but are identical. While this theory does not concern itself specially with the relation of the Church and State to each other, yet fully carried out, it necessarily involves a Church and State system. Dr. Thomas Arnold, one of the propounders and advocates of this theory, held that the State is a moral person and responsible for the whole well-being of the citizen. He argued that the right of the State to take life in capital punishment, and to require the sacrifice of life in defensive war, involves as a necessary co-relative the right and duty of the State to care for the whole life of the citizen. It is under obligation, therefore, to provide for his physical, social, mental, moral, and spiritual welfare. Persons who reject the first two theories, the one merging the State in the Church, the other merging the Church in the State, may yet upon this theory hold to a union of Church and State. Mr. Gladstone in a book published in his early life, entitled *The State in its Relations with the Church*, says : " Wherever there is power in the universe, that power is the property of God, the King of that universe ; his property of right, however, for a time withholden or abused. . . . The powers, therefore, that dwell in individuals, acting as a government, as well as those that dwell in individuals acting for themselves, can only be secured for right uses by applying to them a religion."

These theories may be regarded as now antiquated. The first may still be held in the Church of Rome, as a theory, but there is now no place in the civilized world where the assertion of it would not be deemed absurd, and the attempt to carry it out preposterous.

The second was ably espoused in the Westminster Assembly of Divines, but it was almost unanimously rejected, only one member, (Lightfoot), voting against the proposition, that "The Lord Jesus, as King and head of his Church, hath therein appointed a government in the hand of church officers distinct from the civil magistrates." And now it is held only by a Presbyterian body in Scotland and in the United States, the Reformed Presbyterian Church, which in both countries is insignificant in numbers.

The third theory has nowhere met with any general acceptance. The small amount of attention given to it, Mr. Walter Bagehot,—in his *Physics and Politics*, explains by saying that Dr. Arnold "spoke to ears filled with other sounds, and minds filled with other thoughts," which, though true, falls short of being an adequate explanation of the fact. The true explanation is, that the political world had passed far beyond the point in its development at which such a theory could command any serious attention. Mr. Bagehot hints at this explanation when he says, "Dr. Arnold himself, fresh from the study of Greek thought and Roman history, used to preach that this identity was the great cure for the misguided modern world. . . . . But though the teaching was wrong, for the modern world, to which it was applied, it was excellent for the old world from which it was learned."

Mr. Macaulay in his review of Gladstone's book, *The State in its Relations with the Church*, says : " Mr. Gladstone conceives that the duties of governments are paternal ; a doctrine which we shall not believe till he can show us some government which loves its subjects as a father loves his child, and which is as superior in intelligence to its subjects as a father is to a child. He tells in lofty, though somewhat indistinct language, that 'Government occupies in moral the place of τὸ πᾶν (the all) in physical science.' If government be indeed τὸ πᾶν in moral science, we do not understand why rulers should not assume all the functions which Plato assigned to them. Why should they not take away the child from the mother, select the nurse, regulate the school, overlook the playground, fix the hours of labor and recreation, prescribe what ballads shall be sung, what tunes shall be played, what books shall be read, what physic shall be swallowed? Why should they not choose our wives, limit our expenses, and stint us to a certain number of dishes of meat, of glasses of wine, and cups of tea?"

The currents of modern progress have been tending so strongly away from the whole theory of paternalism that it has been, everywhere, losing instead of gaining in acceptance. Mr. Gladstone long since secured the disestablishment of the Irish Church, and now in his old age has devoted his great powers to the establishment of a policy which is entirely out of harmony with the theory he espoused in early life.

CHAPTER II.

NO THEORY TO BE OFFERED. ONLY JUSTICE TO BE SOUGHT.

IT is not our purpose to discuss the merits of the foregoing theories ; neither is it our purpose to propound any theory of our own. The task before us is not that of constructing theories, but of discovering and removing injustice, a less fascinating task perhaps, but a more worthy one. Indeed it will be no small part of our work to guard against the subtle influence of false theories, ill-digested and unformulated, anti-Christian as well as Christian, which in the confusion of thought that now prevails upon the subject are likely to pervert the judgment and lead to injustice on the one hand or the other.

Two well-established facts must, we think, be accepted as having their foundation in nature : *1st.* The fact that the civil institutions of a Christian people are necessarily Christian. *2d.* That the forces of progress have not only caused the several theories we have just mentioned to be now antiquated but have been tending towards a still further restriction of the religious function of civil government. These facts must both be taken account of in any proper determination of the questions relating to the subject. Upon each of them when looked at alone, a false theory may be built, the inevitable outcome of which will be injustice. The problem before us therefore is the finding of the proper adjustment,—the co-ordination of these two facts. Our work will therefore be empirical rather than speculative in its character. Confining ourselves, in the main, to particular cases, we shall endeavor to define the limits of these two facts, so that the one shall not be made the means of inflicting injustice upon non-Christian or anti-Christian people ; and the other shall not be made the means of inflicting injustice upon Christian people. The principles of judgment adopted ought, as a general rule, to be able to bear the test of substitution ; that is, they ought to be equally applicable to Buddhism, Mohammedanism, or Atheism, were any one of those systems of belief to become as prevalent in our land as Christianity now is—a rule which would suggest the expediency of reducing the religious functions of the government to the last degree compatible with the rights of its Christian people.   •

Although the fact is indisputable that the civil institutions of this country are necessarily, rightly, and lawfully Christian, yet it must be admitted that the boundaries of the fact and its legitimate effect have not as yet been well defined. Indeed, legislation has in some cases been framed apparently upon the assumption that our government has, and can have, no Christian character whatever. Jurists and courts have gone so far as to affirm that the government can of right base no determination or requirement upon Christian principles ; that, when it happens to require the observance of a Christian institution, such as the Lord's day, it must be for reasons purely secular, and not in the least degree religious. In this legislation and these affirmations appears very clearly the influence of an ill-digested, tacitly assumed, anti-Christian theory, a theory based exclusively on the first of the facts above mentioned.

It is assumed that the progress begun in these modern times is thus only continued towards its proper terminus in perfect freedom,—a goal which cannot be reached until the government shall have been divested of all Christian character.

The question still remains, therefore, to be answered : What may the government do, and what ought it to do in its Christian character ?—How far are its determinations and requirements to be governed by the principles of Christianity? This question we now propose to answer ; and seeing that the three theories just mentioned, which are all extreme on the Christian side of the question, are rejected by all (no one now believing that it is the duty of the government to take upon itself all forms of Christian work) our answer will have to be in a measure negative, a fixing of limitations.

CHAPTER III.

LIMITATIONS.

It is no part of the proper function of the government to inculcate, or propagate, or even foster, Christianity, (certain special cases excepted, which we shall

12

presently mention). We cannot agree with Judge Story when in the passage before quoted from his *Commentary on the Constitution of the United States* he says : " It is impossible for those who believe in the truth of Christianity to doubt that it is the especial duty of the government to foster and encourage it among all citizens and subjects," if by that statement he means to say that it is the duty of the government not only to give favor and preference to Christianity when called upon to take action in its courts on questions pertaining thereto, but to go further and adopt positive measures for the fostering and encouragement of Christianity. It seems to us that the exercise of such a function by the government would defeat its own end,—would be detrimental to both Church and State. It cannot be doubted that the advancement which has been thus far made in the science of government, has been marked by a progressive elimination of this function from the power of the government ; nor can it be doubted that this elimination has been the product of the true law of progress, differentiation in form, and specialization of function.

The living creature which is nothing but a globular sack, using the whole body in turns, as mouth, stomach, legs, and arms, is lower in the scale of being, than the animal which is completely furnished with organs and members, each of which has its special work to do. Man with only two hands is higher in the scale of being and has more manual skill than the Simians, which are quadrumana, using their feet also as hands. The right-handed man has more dexterity than the man who uses both hands alike. The woodman clearing away the forest may use his axe, if need be, as a mattock, a beetle, or a wedge, but by using it

as a mattock he would dull its edge, and by using as
a beetle or a wedge he would batter its head or bulge
its eye, thereby rendering it less efficient, if not altogether unfitted, for its own appropriate work. If he
would do the most work with the least expenditure of
force and the least injury to his tools, he must furnish
himself with the four implements ; and use the axe
only for chopping, the mattock only for grubbing, the
wedge only for splitting, and the beetle only for driv-
ing the wedge. Even the fact that the axe is essentially a wedge will not justify him in using it in the
the place of a wedge after that implement has been
provided. The same rule holds good for human society. The life of man is one, and if the State and the
Church both are organs of that life it is to be presumed
that each will perform its appropriate special function
best when it confines itself exclusively to that one function. Especially ought this distribution of function to
be precise and exclusive in a republican form of government, for it can be done without violation of the rights
of any supposed paternal prerogative. In a republic
there is no rational basis for such prerogative. The
claim of superior prerogative, without the possession
of the appropriate superior gifts, is absurd. The authority of the father over his children has ample basis
in his superior gifts ; but in a republic the rulers can
lay claim to no such gifts. There has been no such
special communication to them by the divine Spirit as
that which was symbolized by the anointing of the
kings of Israel. There is no lingering shadow of such
a communication in the plea of transmission by heredity, as there is in the monarchies of Europe. In a
republic, therefore, the citizen may justly claim the
utmost freedom in the care of his varied interests ; and

in that form of government the organs of his life ought
to be brought to the highest degree of specialization,
since that is the condition of their attaining the highest degree of efficiency.   It must be presumed therefore that human society will be in its highest condition
when civil government confines itself exclusively to
the secular work of protecting the person and property
of the citizen ; leaving to the Church the care of his
spiritual interests.   It must be presumed that Christianity will be purer, have more vital energy, and make
more rapid advancement, when the government does
not engage in its propagation.

The great founder of Christianity we think had this
law of progress in his mind when he bade his impetu-
ous disciple put up his sword, saying, " They that take
the sword shall perish by the sword " ; when he said
to the Pharisees and Herodians " Render therefore
unto Cæsar the things that are Cæsar's, and unto God
the things that are God's " ; when he said to Pilate,
" My kingdom is not of this world, else would my servants fight, that I should not be delivered to the Jews."
Nothing is more marked in his life than the little concern he manifested to secure the aid of governmental
power for the advancement of his cause ; nothing more
striking than the calm assurance with which he sent
forth his handful of followers to make the conquest of
the world, not only without the aid of secular power,
but against the most determined opposition of the
mightiest secular power on earth.   The watchword
God gave to his church was, " Not by might, nor by
power, but by my Spirit, saith the Lord of Hosts."

CHAPTER IV.

MYSTICAL THEORIES OF THE STATE.

1. Personality of the State.—There are mystical theories of the State, in accordance with which it is held that the care of the life of man, in all its departments, is inherent in, and inseparable from, the State; the theory that the State is a personality having all the attributes of the personalities composing it and standing in authority over all. Plato held that the State was a living body; Mr. Herbert Spencer regards it as a vital organism; the late Rev. Elisha Mulford, D. D., argues in his work entitled *The Nation*, that it is a moral personality; Prof. J. K. Bluntschli asserts in his work entitled *The Theory of the State*, that it is a masculine moral personality. Bluntschli says: "Whilst history explains the organic nature of the State, we learn from it at the same time that the State . . . is a moral and spiritual organism, a great body, which is capable of taking up into itself the feelings and thoughts of the nation, of uttering them in laws, and realizing them in acts; we are informed of the moral qualities and of the character of each State. History ascribes to the State a personality which, having spirit and body, possesses and manifests a will of its own.

"The glory and honor of the State have always elevated the hearts of its sons and animated them to sacrifice. For freedom and independence, for the rights of the State, the noblest and best have in all times and all nations expended their goods and their lives. To extend the reputation and the power of the State, to further its welfare and its happiness, has universally been regarded as one of the most honorable duties of gifted men. The joys and sorrows of the State have always been shared by all its citizens. The whole idea of Fatherland and love of country would be inconceivable if the State did not possess this high moral and personal character. . . .

" The personality of the State is, however, only recognized by free people ; and only in a civilized nation-State has it attained to full efficacy. In the earlier stages of politics only the Prince is prominent ; he alone is a person, and the State is merely the realm of his personal rule. The same is true with regard to the masculine character of the modern State. This becomes first apparent in contrast with the feminine character of the Church. A religious community may have all the other characteristics of a political community, yet she does not wish to be a State, and is not a State just because she does not consciously rule herself like a man and act freely in her external life ; but wishes only to serve God and perform her religious duties. To put together the results of this historical consideration, the general conception of the State may be determined as follows : the State is a combination or association (*Gesammtheit*) of men, in the form of government and governed, on a definite territory, united together into a moral, organized, masculine personality ; or, more shortly, the State is the politically organized national person of a definite country." [1]

It is very evident that according to this theory the care for the religious interests of the people cannot be separated from civil government without detriment to the life of the whole body, for—to use an illustration of Bluntschli given in another place—" The head cannot be separated from the body and made equal to it without killing the man."

[1] *The Theory of the State*, Oxford, 1892, pp. 22, 23.

This theory, if it be anything more than a dream of mysticism, if it be admitted to have a speculative validity, can have very little bearing upon practical politics ; not more than cosmogony, geology, and chemistry have upon practical agriculture. As yet, success in farming is attained by empirical, rather than by scientific methods. As in the one case, so in the other, the question is usually one of results, rather than of principles, allowing, of course, some influence to scientific principles in the determination, but not allowing them to overbalance the practical judgment, as applied to existing conditions. Providence, by the ordering the conditions, historical and local, builds the State ; not man, by the application of his theories.

It is to be noticed that Bluntschli, while holding formally the theory of the moral personality of the State, makes very little further reference to it in the learned and scientific treatise from which we have quoted. Notwithstanding that his theory implies the ultimate supremacy of the State over all human interests, yet he seems to have come, practically, to the position we have just taken. He says : " The idea that the objective difference of political function requires a corresponding subjective separation in the organs to which these functions belong, has been produced by the course of modern politics. . . . Excessive power united in one hand certainly endangers personal freedom. If the different branches of power are separated, they are all mutually limited. Nevertheless the decisive reason for such specialization is not the practical security of civil liberty, but the organic reason that every function will be better fulfilled if its organ is specially directed to this particular end, than if quite different functions are assigned to the same organ. The

statesman only follows the example of nature ;—the eye
is adapted for sight, the ear for hearing, the mouth for
speaking, the hand for seizing. The body-politic should
in the same way have a separate organ for each function." Yet to save the theory, and tempted by the illustration employed, he goes on to say, "The favorite
expression ' separation (*Trennung*) of powers' leads to
false applications of a true principle. A complete separation or sundering of powers would be a dissolution
of the unity of the State. Just as in the body natural,
all the limbs are connected together, so in the body-
politic, the connection of the organs is not less important than their difference. In the State there must be
unity of power, and so the powers, though distinguished
according to their functions, must not be absolutely
separated." He criticises the exactness and compre-
prehensiveness of the threefold distinction made by
Montesquieu in the powers of the State,—Legislative,
Executive, and Judicial,—observing that it has been
"adopted by English political theorists," and "has
been carried out with rigor, but not without exaggeration, in the United States of North America, and has
been sanctioned by a whole series of modern European
constitutions " ; and goes on to say : "The function of
sovereignty may appear to be exhausted by this threefold distinction, and we can easily understand how recent constitutions have commonly limited themselves
to these. But on closer examination we find that there
are two other groups of organs and functions, both of
which are indeed subordinate to that of government,
but may still be distinguished from it, having much less
the character of authority and command, which in government is essential. These are :

"*IV.* The superintendence and care of the intellectual elements of civilization (*Statscultur.*)

" *V.* The administration and care of material interests (*Statswirthshaft*), Political economy in the original
sense.

" In these two groups there is no question of governing. The great factors of civilization,—religion, science,
art,—do not belong to the organism of the State. Thus
the relation of the State, even to the external institutions of religion, science, and art, to the Church and
the school, is fundamentally different from the relation
between government and subjects, in its own proper
sphere. Such matters cannot be subjected to the dominion of the State ; its functions are therefore limited
to superintendence and fostering care (*Aufsicht und
Pflege*). . . .

" This distinction in the functions of the State has
only in recent times come to be gradually recognized.
We still suffer from a confusion of commanding and
fostering. Sometimes things are commanded or forbidden, which should only be managed or controlled ;
sometimes there is a timid assistance or control, where
there ought to be energetic and authoritative action.
But matters are better than they were a hundred, or
even fifty years ago. Many institutions have been already separated from the direct administration of government, and are managed without the employment of
force in a spirit of scientific and technical care, and in
the interests, at once, of the welfare and the freedom
of the community." [1]

If we should accept this theory of the State as true,
and accept also the illustration used—the human body
—as fully analogous, we might still question the correctness of the application of the illustration to the
truth it was intended to illustrate, viz. : that as the
head holds in subjection to itself and governs every

[1] *Ibid.*, pp. 518, 519, 524, 555.

other part of the body, so the civil government must hold in subjection to itself and govern every department of man's social life. We may maintain that the soul, mind, spirit, or whatever that may be called which constitutes the personality of man, resides, not in the head alone, but in the whole body, and varies its manifestations as the organs through which it acts are varied. As in the electrical system of the city, the electricity, fluid, vibrating medium, or whatever it may be, pervades the whole, and is manifested, here, as the dazzling light of the arc lamp, there, as the soft light of the incandescent lamp, and in another place as motive power ; so that which constitutes human personality pervades the whole body, and is manifested in the living cell as vital principle, in muscular fibre as contractile energy, and in the nervous tissue as sensation, feeling, will, and thought. The brain is only one of the organs through which this all-pervading something acts, and has no superiority to the rest, excepting that it may be conceded to be primary while the others are secondary, just as the crank of the machine in the hands of the man who turns it may be said to be primary. So if we should concede this theory of the State to be true, we might still maintain that the people constitute the personality of the State ; that the civil government and the Church are both alike organs through which the people act ; and that while both are united with and dependent upon the same people, they are yet, as organs, separate from and independent of each other. While the civil government is Christian, it is no part of its proper function to inculcate, propagate, or even to foster Christianity, as it is no part of the function of the eye to hear, or of the ear to see.

The distinction Bluntschli makes between the State as a masculine personality and the Church as a feminine personality involves the separation we are contending for. Whatever may have been the union of function in the earlier stages of man's development, it is very plain that now the man cannot exercise the specific functions of the woman, nor can the woman exercise those of the man. No one would ever think of trying to maintain that the fields on which the members of the husbandman's family are working and the house in which they dwell are two persons, the one masculine and the other feminine. There is nothing more in the case than the simple fact that in the fields the one family is engaged in one department of work for the common good, and in the dwelling house it is engaged in another department of work for the same end. So, in the State and the Church, there is nothing more than the fact that the one nation is engaged in different departments of work for the common good. There is as much reason for saying that there is a masculine and feminine personality in the former case as in the latter ; and to make the theory complete, we should have to affirm that the mart constitutes a third personality, a neuter perhaps. Mere increase of dimension may excite the imagination, but it cannot make any difference in principles.

Mr. Gladstone in the work before referred to advanced this theory. He says : " National will and agency are indisputably one, binding either a dissenting minority or the subject-body in a manner that nothing but the recognition of the doctrine of national personality can justify. National honor and good faith are words that are in every one's mouth. How do they less imply a personality in nations than the duty

towards God for which we now contend? They are
strictly and essentially distinct from the honor and
good faith of the individuals composing the nation.
France is a person to us, and we to her. A wilful injury done to her is a moral act, and a moral act quite
distinct from the acts of all the individuals composing
the nation. Upon broad facts like these we may rest
without resorting to the more technical proof which the
laws afford in their manner of dealing with corporations. If, then, a nation have unity of will, have per-
vading sympathies, have capability of reward and
suffering, contingent upon its acts, shall we deny its
responsibility; its need of religion to meet that responsibility? . . . A nation, then, having a personality,
lies under the obligation, like the individuals composing its governing body, of sanctifying the acts of that
personality by the offices of religion, and thus we have
a new and imperative ground for the existence of a
State religion." It is to be observed that this theory
is employed by Mr. Gladstone to justify the union of
Church and State, for if the State be a person it is
bound like every other person to be religious. This
theory, we feel warranted in saying, belongs to the re-
actionary rather than to the progressive tendencies of
the times, an indication of which is to be found in the
fact that Mr. Gladstone himself has abandoned it.
Having long since descended from the heights of
speculative, to the arena of practical politics, he was
compelled to leave his theories behind and deal with
existing evils separately and empirically, or rather to
accept with more confidence the general theory of
freedom.

It is interesting to observe how his large experience
and practical wisdom have confirmed his faith in natural

forces, operating in a state of freedom, for the remedy
of existing evils and the establishment of justice. Upon
the merits of the theory in question as propounded by
him in his early days, it will suffice to quote Mr.
Macaulay's criticism :

"Is it not perfectly clear that this argument applies
with exactly as much force to every combination of
human beings for a common purpose, as to governments? Is there any such combination in the world,
whether technically a corporation or not, which has
not this collective personality from which Mr. Gladstone deduces such extraordinary consequences? Look
at banks, insurance offices, dock companies, canal companies, gas companies. . . . Is there a single one
of these combinations to which Mr. Gladstone's argument will not apply as well as to the State? In all
these combinations, in the Bank of England, for example, or in the Athenæum Club, the will and agency
of the society are one and bind the dissentient minority.
The Bank and the Athenæum have a good faith and
a justice different from the good faith and justice of the
individual members. The Bank is a person to those
who deposit bullion in it. The Athenæum is a person
to the butcher and the wine merchant. If the Athenæum keeps money at the Bank, the two societies are
as much persons to each other as France and England.
Either society may pay its debts honestly ; either may
try to defraud its creditors ; either may increase in prosperity ; either may fall into difficulties. If then they
have this unity of will ; if they are capable of suffering
good and evil, can we, to use Mr. Gladstone's words,
'deny their responsibility or their need of a religion to
meet that responsibility?' Joint-stock banks, therefore, and clubs, 'having a personality, lie under the

necessity of sanctifying that personality by the offices of religion' ; and thus we have 'a new and imperative ground' for requiring all the directors and clerks of joint-stock banks, and all the members of clubs, to qualify by taking the sacraments."

There is no agreement among the advocates of the mystical theory upon the organic unit, which on account of its possessing functions of its own, is to be regarded as a person. With some it is the Nation, with others the State, and with others society. The last are the most philosophical as society is the larger generalization. Society is the genus ; the Nation and State are species : society is primary ; the Nation and State are secondary : society is the source from which the Nation and State derive all their functions. In some scientific treatises on those functions which are supposed to constitute the personality of the State, society alone is spoken of as the subject of them. Society is the person against whom all socialists, anarchists, and vagabonds, charge their grievances. They growl and threaten alike in all civilized Nations and States, for they find that while the Nations and States differ, society and the great body of law are essentially the same in them all. The anarchist may plead—and his plea cannot be gainsaid—that he has no malice aforethought or personal hatred against the man he has killed with his bomb, and therefore that the essential element of the crime of murder is wanting in his act. It is another person he hates and desires to kill. If it were only men he had to deal with he would reason with them ; he would never think of doing anything so preposterous as attempting to bring about the reform he desires by killing off all the men who differed from him in opinion. He has no hope, however, of persuading that mystical person with whom he imagines he has to deal ; there is nothing left for him but to kill that person. He throws his bomb at a shadow which he mistakes for a person, but, unfortunately, it always kills a man when it kills anybody. This theory, therefore, which seemed to be nothing but a harmless dream, has become, in some cases, a very mischievous thing,— a deadly thing to many innocent persons.

2. Sovereignty.—There is another mystical theory of the State, not so distinct in its outline, nor so highly developed in its form, as the foregoing, which has arisen from a supposed necessity of hypostatizing a something to serve as the residence of that essential attribute of all government, sovereignty. The existence of sovereignty is as necessary in the freest republic as in the most absolute monarchy. Blackstone says : " How the several forms of government, as we now see them in the world, began, is a matter of great uncertainty, and has occasioned infinite disputes. It is not my business or intention to enter into any of them. However they began, or by what right soever they subsist, there is, and must be, in all of them, a supreme, irresistible, absolute, uncontrolled authority, in which the *jura summi imperii*, or the rights of sovereignty, reside." [1]

The necessity of sovereignty may be readily recognized, but its residence cannot be so easily found. In a democracy the sovereignty is said to reside in the people, but the suffrage, the instrument by which the sovereignty is supposed to be exercised, nowhere belongs to all the people.[2] In our own land it is withheld from women ; from all male residents who

[1] *Com.*, Introduction, Sec. 2.

[2] Judge Cooley says in his *Constitutional Limitations:* "Sovereignty as applied to States, imports the supreme, absolute,

were born in a foreign country until they comply with
certain terms and forms of naturalization ; from all
native-born males, who are under twenty-one years
of age ; who have not resided in the state, county, and
precinct a prescribed time before the election ; from the
inmates of insane asylums and almhouses ; and from
all who have been convicted of an infamous crime.
But by whom withheld? By the sovereign. But who
and where is the sovereign ? If the ballot is given or
withheld by the sovereign it cannot be itself a mark of
sovereignty, or a guide to its residence. When women
set up a claim to the ballot on the ground that it belongs
to them by natural right, it is answered that the elective
franchise is not the natural right of any body, but a
privilege conferred upon those who possess it. When
they argue that being taxed, they ought to have representation in the government, it is answered that taxation
gives no right to representation ; that also is a privilege,
given or denied, as the sovereign may think best. Great
numbers of men, citizens as well as aliens, own property
and are taxed where they have no right to vote. It is
answered, also, that it has been ordained by the sovereign that the officers, elected by the few upon whom

uncontrollable power by which any State is governed." 1,
(Fourth Edition).

" The theory of our political system is that the ultimate sovereignty is in the people, from whom springs all legitimate
authority. . . What are we to understand by the *People* in
this connection ? . . . As a practical fact the sovereignty is
vested in those persons who are permitted by the Constitution
of the State to exercise the elective franchise." 36, 37.

"The authority of the people is exercised through *elections*
by means of which they choose legislative, executive, and judicial officers, to whom are to be entrusted the exercise of powers
of government." 752.

the privilege of the suffrage has been conferred, shall be the representatives of all, men and women, adults and minors, the taxed and the untaxed. It appears from the arguments of those who are contending for the real existence of this something, that all of the so-called political rights are not rights at all, but privileges, granted by the sovereign ; and it becomes therefore all the more important that we should know who, or what, this supreme authority is. As a matter of course, it cannot be those male citizens who have the suffrage, for they are recipients of the grant, and the same persons cannot be both grantors and recipients. It must be then something or somebody, above and antecedent to, the exercise of the elective franchise, above and before any action of any or all of the citizens ; and we still have to ask what, or who is it. The difficulty of answering this question has led to the hypothesis of an individual existence antecedent to all governmental organization, and from which the government derives all its authority.

Resort is had to this hypothesis to justify certain measures of the government ; for example, it is argued that the State has an absolute dominion over the property of the citizen because its antecedent existence has made property possible,—a superfluous and impertinent argument, since if the sovereign has conferred all rights, he must be the possessor of all rights ; if he is the source and author of all law, he must himself be above all law, and it follows that " where no law is, there is no transgression." The sovereign can do no wrong. His own nature is his only law, and the supposition that he would violate his own nature is inadmissible. It is argued also that this hypothetical existence—the State —may have interests of its own different from, and even

13

antagonistic to, the interests of the people, or, at least, to their opinion of what their interests are ; in which case, its own self-preservation must be the first and supreme law ; and the maxim, *salus populi suprema est lex* is converted into *salus civitatis suprema est lex.*

But how does this sovereignty come into being? It is said that it springs up necessarily from the living of men in proximity to one another. It cannot get its being from any act of organization performed by them, for then it would be their creature, and not their sovereign. It has therefore a necessary, independent, and antecedent existence ; and the question still remains, What is it?

It is conceived of so vaguely by those who contend for it that they apply to it the terms, people, state, nation, society, and brotherhood, interchangeably, as though these terms were equivalent, or as though they stood for different stages in the development of the same thing. The last generalization,—the universal brotherhood of man,—is supposed to be the ideal State, the ultimate abode of sovereignty. This theory, captivating as it is to the benevolent heart and the scientific imagination, is, like Plato's Republic, a dream of mysticism, not the product of an induction. Better be a thorough-going Platonist and hold that the idea of the State, as of all other things, is an eternal individual existence ; and that the government, like all other things, derives its being from the eternal idea, of which it is but an imperfect realization.

A scientific induction will show that the sovereignty in government is nothing but preponderating force, which enables those who possess it to do as they will. They will be governed in the exercise of it, more or less, by benevolent, moral and prudential considerations, for they have a sympathetic, moral, and rational nature, but the ultimate basis of sovereignty in government is force, no less so in a democracy than in a monarchy. Prof. William G. Sumner, in one of his essays, ridicules the popular phrase "the peaceable arbitrament of the ballot"; maintaining that the ballot is a weapon of war, and not an implement of peace, and is serviceable for preserving peace only by indicating on which side the preponderance of force lies. A minority of the strong will never be controlled by a majority of the weak; a minority of wolves will never be controlled by a majority of sheep; nor will a minority of men ever be controlled by a majority of women, unless by some revulsion in nature the women become amazons and the men pygmies. Carlyle's assertion that "the ultimate question between every two human beings is 'Can I kill thee, or, Canst thou kill me,'" is only a harsh and extravagant way of stating a truth. Mr. Bagehot, in his *Physics and Politics*, states it much more appropriately when just before referring to the assertion of the rugged Scotchman, he says, "The savage virtues, which tend to war, are the daily bread of human nature."

The preponderance of force in every form of government is ultimately with the people. It is potential energy, and is kept from becoming kinetic, only by the restraint of circumstances, as it is in the physical world by the restraint of position, which, in both cases, is adventitious. Every government, even the most despotic, rests ultimately upon the consent of the governed. A very complex aggregation of influences may move them to give their consent, but without it no government could stand.[1]

[1] Mr. Herbert Spencer, in his essay, entitled "The Social Organism," says: "We all know that the enactments of representative governments ultimately depend on the national will.

That the sovereignty does not reside in a mystical, antecedent, unchangeable something, but in the possessors of the predominating force, seems to follow from the conceded right of revolution. When the preponderance of force is with those who are opposed to the existing government, and they are minded to overthrow the old and establish a new, they put forth an act of sovereignty. They may act unwisely, may mistake what is for the good of the people, as they have often done in the republics of Central and South America, but the possessor of the preponderating force, the sovereign, is under no law, and is accountable for his acts only to himself. All nations recognize a *de facto* government, which gives promise of maintaining itself, without troubling themselves with the question *de jure.* The sovereignty of the East Indies resides in Great Britain, not in a mystical something, aboriginal, and sprung from the soil of India. Before the year 1776 the sovereignty over the British colonies in America resided in England ; or if in both England and America, that mystical something was nevertheless a unit. There are two sovereigns now where there was

They may, for a time, be out of harmony with it, but eventually they must conform to it. . . . In the case of a government, representing a dominant class, the same thing holds, though not so manifest. For the very existence of a class, monopolizing all power, is due to certain sentiments in the commonalty. But for the feeling of loyalty, on the part of retainers, a feudal system could not exist. . . . Even where the government is despotic the doctrine still holds. The character of the people is, as before, the original source of this form. . . . Moreover, such regulations as a despot makes, if really operative, are so because of their fitness to the social state . . . . and when they are out of harmony with the national character they are soon practically abrogated.''

only one before. Did that one multiply itself in 1776 by fission ?

The genesis of the State may be easily traced. Blackstone says that "the only true and natural foundations of society are the wants and fears of individuals " [1] ; a statement which needs a slight modification and the addition of two or three items :

The duties of man may be classified under four heads : Self-development, Reproduction, Service to his Fellowmen, and the Worship of God.

The first, to realize the archetypal idea of man, the image of God, the likeness to Christ.

The second, to make up to the world the losses caused by death, to keep the world in perpetual possession of the beauty and joy of youth, and to secure, through heredity, the gains made by individual effort and by divine assistance as a cumulative inheritance.

The third, to mitigate the woes and promote the development of mankind.

The fourth, to elevate the nature and supply the proper motive and inspiration for the performance of all duty.

These duties are enforced by divine inculcation and command. Man is instructed to regard God as his father, and therefore, himself as a child, whose great object in life must be to grow unto the likeness of the father, and these commands are given him : " Be ye perfect even as your Father in heaven is perfect " ; " Be fruitful and multiply, and replenish the earth " ; " Love thy neighbor as thyself " ; " Whosoever will be chief among you, let him be your servant ; even as the Son of man came, not to be ministered unto, but to minister, and to give his life a ransom for many " ; " Thou shalt love the Lord thy God with all thy heart,

---

[1] *Com.*, Introd., section 2.

and with all thy soul, and with all thy mind, and with all thy strength " ; " Thou shalt worship the Lord thy God, and Him only shalt thou serve." In order to secure the fulfilment of these duties, appropriate impulses, desires, sympathies, and aspirations have been implanted in man, and these are the forces by which all social organization has been produced. The first desire, in the order of nature, is the desire for food, whereby the welfare and development of the body are promoted ; and even in the lowest stages this desire begets the idea of property, especially when the same object will serve for more than one gratification. The suckling will soon claim property in the mother's breast. If the animal taken in the chase cannot all be eaten at once, the same desire that prompted to the taking of it will prompt to the preservation of it, to satisfy the hunger when it shall return, and will give the idea of the right of possession, soon to be followed by the general idea of property, founded on the labor of obtaining that which satisfies desire. Now, since man is moved primarily by his desires, with little restraint from a sense of right, one will take by force from another whatever he may want, and a combination of the weak will be made for protection against the strong ; while natural sympathies will act as co-operating forces to draw men into association. We have then, as the result of this one desire, the embryo of social organization and government. The desire which prompts to reproduction will tend more directly to this end, for the co-operation of two are necessary to the gratification of that desire. If there are as many women as men, and numbers of them are not at once available, the man will be prompted to retain the first woman to whom he has been united, as his own. The woman being physically the weaker will be governed by the man, and division of labor, the first step toward civilization, will begin. While reason would suggest, to the lowest intellect, that there would be greater gain to all if the different parts of labor were assigned to the persons best fitted to perform it, yet the division is determined at first by mere brute force. The man compels the woman to relieve him of all toil but that which is easiest and most agreeable to himself. She becomes, therefore, his burden-bearer and his slave. Here we have government, with sovereignty, and the sovereignty has its basis in mere force. Children, when they come, will form a new element in the social organization, but the sovereignty of superior force remains the same, softened and restrained, in some degree, by the tenderness of the parental instinct.

The man, observing that the satisfaction of his desires is affected by powers not of himself, and over which he has no control, such as accidents and diseases, heat and cold, drought and deluge, projects the attributes of his own nature into the outer world, and imagines it to be governed by beings of like passions with himself, only greater ; and he fixes upon the use of certain things, and the performance of certain rites, which he fancies will propitiate or defeat these powers. He now has the rudiments of a religion, but it contemplates nothing more than averting bad luck and bringing good luck. It will be regarded as a matter of the greatest importance, for to do anything which would bring bad luck to the family, clan, or tribe would be a crime worse than treason. It will therefore be governed by the strictest regulations, and those regulations will be prescribed by the sovereign, the possessor of the predominant force.

Deeds of valor, done by the man himself, or by others, he delights to recount to his fellowmen, and his imagination, stimulated by the pleasure derived from the recollection, adds embellishment to the account. The story is handed down to his posterity, from whom it receives further embellishment, till finally the hero is deified and associated with the beneficent or the destructive powers of nature ; and the religion advances from fetichism to mythology. The rites of religion will be assigned to particular persons, who will constitute a priesthood, but still the religion will be a matter of State, and the power of regulating it will be in the hands of the sovereign.

The rapacity of other men will cause families to unite in tribes for mutual protection, while all the social impulses will be tending to the same end. The organization will become more complex, and there will be greater specialization of work. The possessor of the sovereignty will see that the more elaborate and comprehensive regulations, now necessary, need a specialized administration, and the final arbiter, force, will be in some degree veiled from sight behind a council of chiefs, and a series of customs which have become institutions.

When the hunter stage gives place to the pastoral, the idea of property will become more definite ; the family will become the patriarchate, a more complex social and governmental organization, and the institutional limitations to the exercise of sovereignty or brute force will be multiplied.

When the wandering herdsman ceases to subsist entirely upon the produce of his herds and the spontaneous products of the earth, and begins to make cereals a part of his subsistence, he will take up his abode on the fields he cultivates ; there will be a larger need of implements, which will cause a more extended division of labor and a more extensive barter ; society and government will go on in its development to a still higher stage. From this stage specialization of function and organ will go on more and more rapidly ; the divisions of labor will be multiplied ; money, and after that the machinery of credit, will be invented to facilitate exchanges ; institutions will become more fixed ; the government, sharing in the progress and carried along by the same laws of progress, will become more complex ; its various functions will be distributed among a larger number of agencies, and force, the final arbiter, will be so far withdrawn from view that many will find difficulty in telling what the final arbiter they now call sovereignty is, or where it resides.

It is very plain now, we think, that the resumption by the government of any of the distributed functions would be a reversal of progress ; or, if there were conditions which rendered such resumption necessary, it would be evidence that the people had turned about and were making their way towards barbarism. It is just as plain, we think, that to set up a hypostatized something—State, or whatever else it may be called— as the original possessor of all governmental power, in order to justify any particular act of the so-called sovereignty, is to look backwards. If we should admit that the whole subject of education and religion belonged originally to the State, the admission would furnish no ground for the resumption of the control of either, or both, in whole, or in part, by the government at the present time. It would be just as absurd as to plead, what embryologists tell us of the development of the individual man, that he passes through all the gradations of animal life, from that of the amœba upwards, to justify his swimming to shore when his boat is sunk,

or his going on all fours through a narrow tunnel to
escape from a military prison in which he is held cap-
tive by an enemy. The possessor of the force necessary
to do a needed thing will neither ask nor offer any other
justification than the necessity.

Sovereignty is nothing but preponderating force,
which, among civilized peoples, is veiled from sight and
powerfully restrained by a wondrously complex and
firmly fixed system of institutions. There is no antecedent existence in which that ghost of kingship, sovereignty, resides. The State is not an eternal idea ; nor
is it an autocthonous something, sprung from the earth,
as Aphrodite sprang from the foam of the sea ; existing before all government, and imparting to government all its powers.

The ever-present political problem is, not the discovery and the exposition of the powers of a supposed
primordial something in which sovereignty resides ;
but the bringing of enlightenment, a sense of justice,
the love of man and the fear of God, to act upon the
possessors of the preponderating force.[1]

---

[1] It may be objected that the genesis of the State, as above
given, is purely imaginary, entirely unlike the actual genesis ;
that it is not only unhistorical, but is in contradiction to a history which is of the greatest antiquity and of the highest authority. According to that history, man was created either at
the highest stage of civilization ; in which case the savages, like
the vicious and criminal classes of our cities, are witnesses to
a degeneration, not to an elevation ; or, man was created at a
middle stage, and the savages are witnesses to degeneration,
while the civilized peoples are witnesses to an elevation. It
may be said, also, that there is no example now on earth of the
extremely low condition which the scheme requires as its start-
ing point.

It may be answered that the science of anthropology has

CHAPTER V.

RELIGIOUS AMENDMENT OF THE CONSTITUTION OF THE UNITED STATES.

THE omission of all recognition of the existence of God and of the Christian religion in the Constitution of the United States has been regarded by many worthy citizens as a very serious defect, if not a grievous sin. An organization has been formed for the purpose of securing an amendment to the Preamble of the Constitution which, it is supposed, will remedy the defect and avert the evil consequences of the sin.

It appears that the placing of a recognition of the Divine Being in the Constitution, which is now deemed to be a matter of so great importance, was not spoken

found, in the geological and archæological fields of its investigation, almost conclusive proof that the low stage in question did exist, and was prevalent in pre-historic times. This fact, at the one extreme, and our high civilization, at the other, with every gradation between, warrants the belief that the scheme, as presented, does set forth the actual course of human progress.

In a scientific investigation, whether it be of the divine works, or of the divine word, our only concern is the ascertainment of facts, not the bearing of facts, in the one domain, upon facts in the other. If, upon independent grounds, we believe the Bible to be the word of God, that question is settled ; it is no longer an open one. If it be not settled, very much more than a few instances of seeming conflict between Science and Revelation will have to be taken into consideration ; and a range of learning and scientific investigation, much wider than the field of natural science, will have to be traversed, in order to settle it. A seeming conflict will only show that there has been a fault in the ascertainment of facts ; and the thing to be done in such a case, is the discovery of the fault ; not the denunciation of Science on the one hand, nor the rejection of the Bible on the other.

of in the convention, nor even thought of outside of the convention, until after the Constitution had been completed and submitted for adoption. It is said that the Rev. Dr. John Rogers, an eminent divine of the Presbyterian Church, in New York City, inquired of Alexander Hamilton on his return from the convention why some suitable recognition of the Almighty had not been placed in the Constitution, and that the reply was, " Indeed, Doctor, we forgot it."

A statement made by Luther Martin, a member of the convention from Maryland, after its adjournment, has been cited to show that the matter had not been entirely forgotten, viz. : " However, there were some members so unfashionable as to think that a belief of the existence of a Deity and a state of future rewards and punishments would be some security for the good conduct of our rulers, and that in a Christian country it would be at least decent to hold out some distinction between the professors of Christianity and downright infidelity or paganism." This statement, however, taken in its connection cannot serve the purpose for which it is cited. Mr. Martin upon his return addressed the House of Delegates of Maryland, giving a long and elaborate discussion of the work of the convention. Among other things he said : " The part of the system which provides that no *religious* test shall be required as a qualification to any office or public trust under the United States was adopted by a great majority of the convention and without much debate. However, there were some members so unfashionable," etc.[1]

Mr. Martin was on other grounds strenuously opposed to the adoption of the Constitution ; he did not sign it, and the probability is that this objection to it

[1] Elliot's *Debates*, vol. i., pp. 385, 386.

was an after-thought. At any rate it is evident that his objection was not to the omission of a bare recognition of the existence and authority of the Divine Being, but the omission of something which would have been far different in its practical effect. The security for the good conduct of our rulers which he thought necessary was a religious test. It was by this means the distinction between the professors of Christianity and downright infidelity or paganism, which he thought necessary to decency, was to be made.

If it be true as Hamilton is reported to have said it was, that a recognition of the Almighty was omitted from the Constitution through mere oversight, nevertheless the oversight cannot but be regarded as remarkable, and every Christian citizen will be ready to ask how it happened to occur. An examination of the circumstances in which the Constitution was formed will furnish ample explanation of the fact, and will also afford entire relief from even a suspicion that the omission was made with any anti-Christian purpose.

I. It is to be remarked in the first place that the public mind, of which the Constitutional convention was a reflection, was especially intent upon guarding against the evils of a union between Church and State, and for that reason gave too little attention, perhaps, to the opposite evils. The lessons of history, especially as connected with the founding of some of the colonies, aroused a fear of the complication of religion with the civil government ; and to this fear the omission must be, in large measure, attributed.

It cannot be denied that the infidelity prevailing in France at that time had become fashionable with a particular party in this country, the party whose political predilections were with the French. It was not fashionable, however, with that large and very respectable party which cherished an admiration for the British Constitution, and desired to establish a modification of that Constitution in this country. The Christian sentiment of the country was still so prevalent and powerful as to render it impolitic for the unbeliever to show any wanton disrespect to it. This will appear from the following letter of Benjamin Franklin, who was reputed to be a deist and a friend of Thomas Paine, the person to whom the letter is supposed to have been addressed :[1]

" I have read your manuscript with some attention. By the argument it contains against a particular Providence, though you allow a general Providence, you strike at the foundations of all religion. For without the belief of a Providence that takes cognizance of, guards and guides, and may favor particular persons, there is no motive to worship a deity, to fear his displeasure, or to pray for his protection. I will not enter into any discussion of your principles, though you seem to desire it. At present I shall only give you my opinion, that, though your reasonings are subtle and may prevail with some readers, you will not succeed so as to change the general sentiments of mankind on that subject, and the consequence of printing this piece will be a great deal of odium drawn upon yourself, mischief to you and no benefit to others. He that spits against the wind spits in his own face.

" But were you to succeed, do you imagine any good would be done by it ? You yourself may find it easy

---

[1] Sparks, in a note, says, " This letter was first published by William Temple Franklin, but without the name of the person to whom it was directed. . . . It is supposed to have been written to Thomas Paine, and the circumstances are such as to render this supposition in the highest degree probable."

to live a virtuous life without the assistance afforded by religion ; you having a clear perception of the advantages of virtue and the disadvantages of vice, and possessing strength of resolution sufficient to enable you to resist common temptations. But think how great a portion of mankind consists of weak and ignorant men and women, and of inexperienced, inconsiderate youth of both sexes, who have need of the motives of religion to restrain them from vice, to support their virtue, and retain them in the practice of it till it becomes habitual, which is the great point for its security. And perhaps you are indebted to her originally, that is, to your religious education, for the habits of virtue upon which you now justly value yourself. You might easily display your excellent talents of reasoning upon a less hazardous subject, and thereby obtain a rank with our most distinguished authors. For among us it is not necessary, as among the Hottentots, that a youth to be raised into the company of men should prove his manhood by beating his mother.

"I would advise you, therefore, not to attempt unchaining the tiger, but to burn this piece before it can be seen by any other person ; whereby you will save yourself a great deal of mortification by the enemies it may raise against you, and perhaps a good deal of regret and repentance. If men are so wicked *with religion*, what would they be *if without it*. I intend this letter as a proof of my friendship and therefore add no professions to it, but subscribe simply

"Yours,   B. FRANKLIN."[1]

Judge Story says, in his *Commentary on the Constitution :* "Probably at the time of the adoption of the

[1] *Franklin's Writings.* Sparks, vol. x., pp. 281-282.

Constitution and of the amendment to it, now under
consideration (Congress shall make no law respecting
an establishment of religion, or prohibiting the free
exercise thereof), the general, if not the universal sentiment in America was that Christianity ought to receive
encouragement from the State, so far as it is not incompatible with the private rights of conscience and the
freedom of religious worship.   An attempt to level all
religions and to make it a matter of State policy to hold
all in utter indifference would have created universal
disapprobation, if not universal indignation." [1]

Judge Story lived so near to the time of the adoption
of the Constitution that these words may be taken as
not merely an opinion formed upon a careful study of
the materials of history, but as at least hearsay testi-
mony to the fact.

It cannot be maintained that there was in the general
public any demand either open or tacit, that an atheistic or anti-Christian character should be given to the
Constitution ; nor can it be maintained that in the convention there was a covert purpose to impart to it such
a character.   The refusal of the convention to adopt
the resolution offered by Dr. Franklin, proposing that
the daily sessions be opened with prayer, cannot in view
of the whole record of the case, which we here give,
be taken as revealing an irreligious bias in the convention.

"DR. FRANKLIN :—' Mr. President, the small progress we have made after four or five weeks' close attendance and continual reasonings with each other ;
our different sentiments on almost every question,
several of the last producing as many noes as ayes, is,
methinks, a melancholy proof of the weakness of the

[1] P. 700.

human understanding. We indeed seem to feel our want of political wisdom, since we have been running about in search of it. We have gone back to ancient history for models of government, and examined the different forms of those republics which having been formed with the seeds of their own dissolution, now no longer exist. And we have viewed modern States all round Europe, but find none of their Constitutions suitable to our circumstances.

" ' In this situation of this Assembly, groping, as it were, in the dark to find political truth, and scarce able to distinguish it when presented to us, how has it happened, Sir, that we have not hitherto once thought of humbly applying to the Father of lights to illuminate our understandings. In the beginning of the contest with Great Britain, when we were sensible of danger, we had daily prayer in this room for the divine protection. Our prayers, Sir, were heard and they were graciously answered. All of us who were engaged in the struggle must have observed frequent instances of a superintending Providence in our favor. To that kind Providence we owe this opportunity of consulting in peace on the means of establishing our future national felicity. And have we now forgotten that powerful friend ? I have lived, Sir, a long time, and the longer I live the more convincing proofs I see of this truth, that *God governs in the affairs of men.* And if a sparrow cannot fall to the ground without His notice, is it probable that an Empire can rise without His aid ? We have been assured, Sir, in the sacred writings, that ' except the Lord build the house they labor in vain that build it.' I firmly believe this, and I also believe that without His concurring aid we shall succeed in this political building no better than the builders of

14

Babel. We shall be divided by our little partial local
interests ; our projects will be confounded, and we ourselves shall become a reproach and by-word down to
future ages. And what is worse, mankind may hereafter from this unfortunate instance despair of establishing governments by human wisdom and leave it to
chance, war, and conquest.

"'I therefore beg leave to move that hereafter prayers,
imploring the assistance of Heaven and its blessings
on our deliberations, be held in this assembly every
morning before we proceed to business, and that one or
more of the clergy of this city be requested to officiate
in that service."

" Mr. Sherman seconded the motion. Mr. Hamilton
and several others expressed their apprehension that,
however proper such a resolution might have been at
the beginning of the convention, it might at this late
day, in the first place, bring on it some disagreeable
animadversions ; and in the second place, lead the
public to believe that the embarrassments and dissen-
tions within the convention had suggested the measure.
It was answered by Dr. Franklin, Mr. Sherman, and
others, that the past omission of a duty could not
justify a further omission ; that the rejection of such
a proposition would expose the convention to more unpleasant animadversions than the adoption of it ; and
that the alarm out of doors that might be excited for
the state of things within would at least be as likely
to do good as ill.

" Mr. Williamson observed that the true cause of the
omission could not be mistaken. The convention had
no funds.

" Mr. Randolph proposed, in order to give a favorable
aspect to the measure, that a sermon be preached at

the request of the convention on the fourth of July, the Anniversary of Independence, and thenceforth prayers, etc., be read in the convention every morning.

" Dr. Franklin seconded this motion. And after several unsuccessful attempts for silently postponing this matter by adjourning, the adjournment was at length carried without any vote on the motion, Thursday, June 28th." [1]

Unless the three reasons against the adoption of Dr. Franklin's motion can be proved to have been without ground, and to have been disingenuously given, the defeat of that motion cannot be regarded as, in itself, a sufficient proof that an anti-Christian bias prevailed in the convention, and that the members, controlled by such a bias, purposely made the Constitution what it is now charged with being, an atheistic document.

In at least two of the State conventions objection was made to the last clause of Article VI. of the Constitution, prohibiting all religious tests and qualifications to any office or public trust under the United States. It will be seen from the arguments urged in favor of the prohibition, and from the character of the persons contending for it, three of them being clergymen, that the motive which prompted the proposing and adopting of that prohibition was a fear of the evils that might result from a religious establishment, and a desire to give all citizens equal rights, with eligibility to all offices and public trusts without discrimination on account of their religious belief or unbelief. There is no evidence whatever of an intention to disparage Christianity or to make an atheistic Constitution ; and it is

[1] *Journal of the Federal Convention.* Kept by James Madison. Edited by E. H. Scott. Chicago, Albert Scott & Co. 1893, pp. 259–261.

fair to assume that if there was no such intention in
this matter that there was none in the omission of a
recognition of the existence of God and of the authority
of the Lord Jesus Christ.

Convention of Massachusetts.—Mr. Parsons, of
Newburyport, said : " It has been objected that the
Constitution provides no religious test by oath, and we
may have in power unprincipled men, atheists and
pagans. No man can wish more ardently than I do
that all our public offices may be filled by men who
fear God and hate wickedness, but it must remain with
the electors to give the government this security. An
oath will not do it. Will an unprincipled man be en-
tangled by an oath ? Will an atheist or a pagan dread
the vengeance of the Christian's God, a Being in his
opinion a creature of fancy and credulity ? It is a
solecism in expression. No man is so illiberal as to
wish the confining places of honor or profit to any one
sect of Christians, but what security is it to the government that any public officer shall swear that he is a
Christian ? . . . Sir, the only evidence we can
have of the sincerity of a man's religion is a good life,
and I trust that such evidence will be required of every
candidate by every elector." [1]

" In the conversation of Thursday on the Sixth
Article . . . several gentlemen urged that it was
a departure from the principles of our forefathers
who came here for the preservation of their religion ;
and that it would admit deists, atheists, etc., into the
general government ; and people being apt to imitate
the examples of the court a corruption of morals ensue.
Gentlemen on the other side applauded the liberality of
the clause and represented in striking colors the impro-

[1] Elliot's *Debates*, vol. ii., p. 90.

priety of, and almost impiety of the requisition of a test as practised in Great Brittain and elsewhere. In this conversation the following is the substance of the observation of Rev. Mr. Shute :

" ' Mr. President, to object to the latter part of the paragraph under consideration which excludes a religious test is I am sensible very popular, for the most of men somehow are rigidly tenacious of their own sentiments in religion, and disposed to impose them upon others as the *standard* of truth. If in my sentiments on the point in view, I should differ from some in this honorable body I only wish from them the exercise of that candor with which true religion is apt to inspire the honest and well-disposed mind.

" ' To establish a religious test as a qualification for office in the proposed Federal Constitution it appears to me, Sir, would be attended with injurious consequences to some individuals and with no advantage to the *whole*. By injurious consequences to some, I mean that some who in every other respect are qualified to fill some important post in government will be excluded, by their not being able to stand the religious test, which I take to be a privation of a part of their civil rights.

" ' Nor is there to me any conceivable advantage, Sir, that would result to the whole from such a test. Unprincipled and dishonest men will not hesitate to subscribe to *anything* that may open the way for their advancement, and put them in a situation the better to execute their base and iniquitous designs. Honest men alone, therefore, however well qualified to serve the public would be excluded by it and their country be deprived of the benefit of their abilities.

" ' In this great and extensive empire there is and will

be a great variety of sentiments in religion among its inhabitants. Upon the plan of religious test the question I think must be, Who shall be excluded from National trusts. Whatever our bigotry may suggest, the dictates of candor and equity, I conceive, will be *None*.

" ' Far from limiting my charity and confidence to men of my own denomination in religion, I suppose and I believe, Sir, that there are worthy characters among men of every denomination ;—among Quakers, the Baptists, Church of England, the Papists, and even among those that have no other guide in the way of virtue and heaven than the dictates of natural religion.

" ' I must therefore think, Sir, that the proposed plan of government in this particular is wisely constructed ; that as all have an equal claim to the blessings of the government under which they live and which they support, so none should be excluded from them for being of any particular denomination in religion.

" ' The presumption is that the eyes of the people will be upon the faithful in the land, and from a regard to their own safety they will choose for their rulers men of known abilities, of known probity, of good moral characters. The apostle Peter tells us that God is no respecter of persons, but in every nation he that feareth Him and worketh righteousness is *acceptable* to Him. And I know of no reason why men of such a character in a community of whatever denomination in religion, *cæteris paribus*, with other suitable qualifications should not be *acceptable* to the people, and why they may not be employed by them with safety and advantage in the important offices of the government. The exclusion of any religious test, therefore, clearly appears to me, Sir, to be in favor of its adoption.' '

¹ *Ibid.*, pp. 117-119.

" REV. MR. PAYSON : ' Mr. President, after what has been observed relating to a religious test by gentlemen of acknowledged abilities, I did not expect that it would again be mentioned as an objection to the proposed Constitution, that such a test was not required as a qualification for office. Such were the abilities and integrity of the gentlemen who constructed the Constitution as not to admit of the presumption that they would have betrayed so much vanity as to attempt to erect bulwarks and barriers to the throne of God. Relying on the candor of this convention, I will take the liberty to express my sentiments on the nature of a religious test and will endeavor to do it with such propositions as will meet with the approbation of every mind.

" ' The great object of religion being God supreme, and the seat of religion in man being the heart or conscience, *i. e.*, the reason God has given us employed on our moral actions in their most important consequences, as related to the tribunal of God, hence I infer that God alone is the God of the conscience, and consequently attempts to erect human tribunals for the consciences of men are impious encroachments upon the prerogatives of God. Upon these principles, had there been a religious test as a qualification for office, it would in my opinion have been a great blemish upon the instrument.''

" REV. MR. BACKUS : ' Mr. President, I have said very little in this honorable convention, but I must beg leave to offer a few thoughts upon some points in the Constitution proposed to us, and I shall begin with the excluding of any religious test. Many appear to be much concerned about it, but nothing is more evident, both in

¹ *Ibid.*, p. 120.

reason and the Holy Scriptures, than that religion is ever a matter between God and individuals, and therefore no man or men can impose any religious test without invading the essential prerogatives of the Lord Jesus Christ. Ministers first assumed that power under the Christian name, and then Constantine approved of the practice when he adopted the profession of Christianity as an engine of State policy. And let the history of all nations be searched from that day to this, and it will appear that the imposing of religious tests hath been the greatest engine of tyranny in the world. And I rejoice to see so many gentlemen who are now giving in their rights of conscience in this great and important matter. Some serious minds discover a concern lest if all religious tests be excluded the Congress would hereafter establish Popery or some other tyrannical way of worship. But it is most certain that no such way of worship can be established without any religious test.' " [1]

The Convention of North Carolina.—" Mr. Henry Abbot : 'Some are afraid, Mr. Chairman, that should the Constitution be received they would be deprived of the privilege of worshipping God according to their consciences ; which would be taking from them a benefit they enjoy under the present Constitution. They wish to know if their religious and civil liberties would be secure under this system, or whether the general government may not make laws infringing their religious liberties. The worthy member from Edenton mentioned sundry political reasons why treaties should be the supreme law of the land. It is feared that by the power of making treaties they might make a treaty engaging with foreign powers to adopt the Roman

[1] *Ibid.*, pp. 148, 149.

Catholic religion in the United States, which would prevent the people from worshipping God according to their own consciences. The worthy member from Halifax has in some measure satisfied my mind on this subject, but others may be dissatisfied. Many wish to know what religion shall be established. I believe a majority of the community are Presbyterians. I am for my part against any exclusive establishment, but if there were any I would prefer the Episcopal. The exclusion of religious tests is by many thought dangerous and impolitic. They suppose that if there be no religious test required pagans, deists, and Mahometans might obtain office among us, and that the senators and representatives might all be pagans. Every person employed by the general and State governments is to take an oath to support the former. Some are desirous to know how and by whom they are to swear, since no religious tests are required ; whether they are to swear by Jupiter, Juno, Minerva, Proserpina, or Pluto. We ought to be suspicious of our liberties. We have felt the effects of oppressive measures, and know the happy consequences of being jealous of our rights. I would be glad if some gentleman would endeavor to obviate these objections in order to satisfy the religious part of the society. Could I be convinced that the objections were well founded, I would then declare my opinion against the Constitution.'

"Mr. Iredell : 'Mr. Chairman, nothing is more desirable than to remove the scruples of any gentleman on this interesting subject. Those concerning religion are entitled to particular respect. I did not expect any objection to this particular regulation, which in my opinion is calculated to prevent evils of the most pernicious consequences to society. Every person in the

least conversant with the history of mankind knows
what dreadful mischiefs have been committed by religious persecutions. Under the color of religious tests,
the utmost cruelties have been exercised. Those in
power have generally considered all wisdom centred in
themselves ; and that they alone had a right to dictate
to the rest of mankind ; and that all opposition to their
tenets was profane and impious. The consequences of
this intolerant spirit has been that each Church has in
turn set itself up against every other, and persecutions
and wars of the most implacable and bloody nature
have taken place in every part of the world. . . .

" ' The power to make treaties can never be supposed
to include the right to establish a foreign religion among
ourselves, though it might authorize a toleration of
others. But it is objected that the people of America
may perhaps choose representatives who have no religion at all, and that pagans and Mahometans may be
admitted into offices. But how is it possible to exclude
any set of men without taking away that principle of
religious freedom which we ourselves so warmly contend for ? This is the foundation on which persecution
has been raised in every part of the world. The people in power were always right and everybody else
wrong. If you admit the least difference, the door to
persecution is opened. Nor would it answer the purpose, for the worst part of the excluded sects would
comply with the test, and the best men only kept out
of our counsels. But it is never to be supposed that the
people of America will trust their dearest rights to persons who have no religion at all or a religion materially
different from their own.

" ' It would be happy for mankind if religion was permitted to take its own course and maintain itself by

the excellence of its own doctrines. The divine author of our religion never wished for its support by worldly authority. Has he not said that the gates of hell shall not prevail against it ? It made much greater progress for itself than when supported by the greatest authority on earth.' '' [1]

These expressions, coming as they do from the opposite ends of the Republic, indicate the purpose that was uppermost in the public mind in forming and adopting the Constitution, and its prevalence. One party desired a religious test that would exclude not only atheists, pagans, and Mahometans, but Roman Catholics also, from all offices and public trusts under the United States. The other party, advocating the largest religious freedom, and regarding it as fraught with no perils to the public welfare, desired a Constitution so formed that every citizen qualified to serve the people in a political capacity might be eligible to office ; a Constitution so formed that an Aristides, a Cato, a Marcus Aurelius, or a Frederick II. would not be barred if the people should desire their service in office. There was no one seeking to place in the Constitution a bare and impotent recognition of the existence of God. Nobody seems to have thought of it. Had the latter party offered to the former such a recognition as a concession or compromise, the offer would have been spurned. The latter party prevailed, and as a natural result of the contest, neither a religious test nor a recognition of the existence of God was to be found in the Constitution. Neither the prohibition of a religious test nor the omission of the name of God can be justly taken as evidence of an intention to make a Constitution which should be atheistic or anti-Christian in its character and effect.

[1] *Ibid.*, vol. iv., pp. 191–194.

II. A Constitution is that part of legislation which is enacted directly by the people for the purpose of giving instructions to the legislature and prescribing limits to its action ; courts being established to declare when the legislature has failed to comply with the instructions given or to confine itself to the limits prescribed. The Constitution is framed for this practical purpose, and not for the proclamation of the sentiments of the people upon subjects which may be deemed to be of importance. Such proclamation, if made at all in connection with a Constitution, is made in a preface, styled a Bill of Rights. That the members of the convention which framed the Constitution of the United States intended to confine themselves strictly to the practical purpose of such an instrument, appears in the fact that they framed no Bill of Rights, and gave to the Constitution throughout a restrictive rather than a declarative character. They did not see fit to affirm in the Constitution even those few and fundamental principles which were set forth in the Declaration of Independence, that all men are created free and equal, that they are endowed by their Creator with certain inalienable rights, that among these are life, liberty, and the pursuit of happiness, that to secure these rights governments are instituted among men deriving their just powers from the consent of the governed. In the State conventions fault was found with the Constitution because it did not contain any such declarations. The convention of North Carolina adopted a long Declaration of Rights, including the principles set forth in the Declaration of Independence ; and resolved that it be submitted and acted upon by a National convention, to be called for the purpose before the ratification of the Constitution on the part of the State of North Carolina.[1]

[1] Elliot's *Debates*, vol. iv., 242–244.

Judge Story, in his *Commentary on the Constitution*, speaking of the Amendments, says that they "principally regard subjects properly belonging to a Bill of Rights" (p. 698). And of the amendment denying to Congress the power to make a law respecting an establishment of religion or prohibiting the free exercise thereof, he says : " The real object of the amendment was not to countenance, much less to advance Mahometanism, or Judaism, or infidelity, by prostrating Christianity ; but to exclude all rivalry among Christian sects, and to prevent any National ecclesiastical establishment which should give to a hierarchy the exclusive patronage of the National government. It thus sought to cut off the means of religious persecution (the vice and pest of former ages) and the power of subverting the rights of conscience, in matters of religion, which have been trampled upon almost from the days of the apostles to the present age " (p. 701).

III. The omission in the Constitution is to be attributed, in some measure, to a like omission in the Articles of Confederation, as one of its producing causes.

The delegates of the States, in promulgating the Articles of Confederation, do for themselves make the following acknowledgment, viz.:

" *And whereas*, it has pleased the Great Governor of the world to incline the hearts of the legislatures we respectively represent in Congress, to approve of and to authorize us to ratify the said Articles of Confederation and perpetual union : Know ye . . ." Yet in the articles themselves there is no mention of the name of God or declaration of a belief in the Christian religion. The members of the Constitutional convention regarded themselves as bound by their instructions to adhere as closely as possible to the Articles of Confederation. At the very outset, Mr. Randolph offered a series of resolutions, of which the first was,

" *Resolved*, That the Articles of Confederation ought to be so corrected and amended as to accomplish the object of their institution, namely, ' common defence, security of liberty, and general welfare.' " [1]

It would be puerile, however, to allege the mere copying of the Articles of Confederation as a sufficient explanation of the omission in the Constitution. The features of both the Articles of Confederation and the Constitution which have been noticed as remarkable—their restrictive character, and the omission of all declarative statements—are to be traced to a common cause.

The delegates of the States, in framing the Articles of Confederation, never supposed for a moment that they were doing anything so solemn and important as the framing of a new system of government. They had not been commissioned to do any such thing. The people were familiar with the thirteen State governments and regarded them with that reverence and affection which men bestow upon old institutions with which are associated all the interests and experiences of their lives ; and they were jealous lest the general welfare should be made a pretext for encroachment upon the prerogatives of those governments. They would not allow the Continental Congress to assume the powers of a government. It could recommend but had no power to execute. The Congress under the Articles of Confederation could not do much more, and it was this rigid reservation of all the powers of government to the States that caused the failure of the Confederation. The Articles of Confederation were intended to be nothing but a league or

[1] *Ibid.*, p. 61.

compact between the States for certain specified purposes,— not a new government superadded to that of the States, and the object of the Constitutional convention was nothing more than correcting and enlarging those articles, so that they might the better serve the purpose for which they were intended. The convention spent a long time in a fruitless effort to accomplish this purpose, till at last the members felt constrained to transcend the limits of their instructions and frame a Constitution, the adoption of which would be a new government. So great, however, was the jealousy of the people for the prerogatives of their State governments, that large numbers of them, after the adoption of the Constitution, contended that it was only a compact between sovereign States, and not a government to which the States were to be subject against their interest or will. Various incidents in our history, such as the alien and sedition laws of 1798, the tariffs of 1824 and 1828, and the extension of the system of African slavery to the new Territories, have served to keep the question open.

The legislature of Kentucky, in 1798, passed certain resolutions, of which the first was :

" *Resolved*, That the several States composing the United States of America are not united on the principle of unlimited submission to their general government, but that by compact under the style and title of a Constitution for the United States, and of amendments thereto, they constituted a general government for special purposes, delegated to that government certain definite powers, reserving each State to itself the residuary mass of right to their own self-government ; and that whensoever the general government assumes undelegated powers, its acts are unauthoritative, void, and

of no force ; that to this compact each State acceded as
a State, and is an integral party ; that this government
created by this compact was not the exclusive or final
judge of the extent of the powers delegated to itself,
since that would have made its discretion, and not the
Constitution, the measure of its powers, but that, as in
all other cases of compact among parties, having no
common judge, each party has an equal right to judge
for itself, as well as of infractions, as of the mode and
manner of redress.''

These resolutions were sent to the several States, and
all the replies received being unfavorable, excepting
that of Virginia which had passed a resolution the
same year declaring the same principles, the legislature of Kentucky in 1799 re-affirmed the resolution of
the previous year, adding the declaration, ''that the
several States who formed that instrument being sovereign and independent have the unquestionable right
to judge of its infractions, and that a nullification by
those sovereignties of all unauthorized acts done under
color of that instrument is the rightful remedy.''

These resolutions of Kentucky and Virginia were intended to be only solemn protests, nothing more being
contemplated than a conference of the States, or other
movement, to secure a repeal of the obnoxious laws.

The labor of slaves being too rude and wasteful to
be profitably applied to manufacturing, the Southern
States became agricultural, while the Northern States
became more distinctively manufacturing. In addition
to this the invention of the cotton gin and the repeal
of the English tariff on cotton, the long staple cotton
of America being necessary to enable the English to
compete with American manufacturers, caused the interest of the Southern States to be more exclusively

agricultural, and the people of those States to become very strongly opposed to a tariff for the protection of manufacturers. The duty on imports was increased in 1824, and in 1825 the legislature of South Carolina declared, " that it is an unconstitutional exercise of power on the part of Congress to lay duties to protect domestic manufactures." The higher tariff of 1828 was regarded as an aggravation of the wrong, and a convention which was called by the legislature October 26, 1832, and which met on the 24th of the following November, adopted an ordinance asserting the principles set forth in the Kentucky and Virginia resolutions of 1798, but going on still further to " nullify certain acts of the Congress of the United States, purporting to be laws, laying duties and imposts on the importation of foreign commodities " ; the ordinance declared it unlawful to attempt to enforce the collection of such duties by an officer of the State or of the United States ; enjoined upon the legislature the passage of acts to enforce this ordinance ; and finally declared that if any attempt should be made by the Federal government to coerce the State, they would hold themselves absolved from all further obligations to maintain or preserve their political connection with the people of the other States, but would organize a separate government. President Jackson was firmly determined to enforce the collection of the duty on imports, and a conflict of arms was averted only by a compromise, Congress enacting that there should be a progressive reduction of duties until 1842.

The question whether the Constitution was a compact between States or whether it established a government, was so far an open one that Mr. Calhoun, senator from South Carolina, offered on the 22d of January,

15

1833, a series of resolutions in the Senate embodying the former doctrine. Mr. Webster of Massachusetts, in his famous speech of February 16, 1833, on those resolutions, gave the question its final settlement as one of logic and interpretation, proving that the Constitution was not a mere league or compact between sovereign States, but that it established a government; that this government derived its authority from the people, the same source from which the State governments derived their authority; that it was as sovereign within its prescribed sphere as the governments of the States were within their spheres, and that its authority was ordained by the people to be paramount, they having declared in Article VI. that "This Constitution and the laws of the United States made in pursuance thereof . . . shall be the supreme law of the land, and the judges in every State shall be bound thereby, anything in the Constitution and laws of any State to the contrary notwithstanding." [1]

The question was settled, however, only as a question of logic, for when the interests of people are involved their opinions and actions are not determined by logic.

Opposition to slavery as a system began to rise in the North, which as it grew begot a determination to prohibit the extension of the system into new territory, while the profits of cotton raising created in the South a determination to perpetuate and extend the system. The controversy was growing in earnestness year by year, till at last the election of Abraham Lincoln to the Presidency and Hannibal Hamlin to the Vice-Presidency in 1860, both Northern men, was taken by the South as a final and irreversible subjection of their special interests to the dictation of the North.

[1] *Works*, vol. iii., pp. 448—505.

The legislature of South Carolina on November 7, 1860, called a State convention, which met at Charleston, December 17th, and passed "an ordinance to dissolve the union between the State of South Carolina and other States united with her under the compact entitled the Constitution of the United States of America," declaring that "the ordinance adopted by us in convention on the 23d day of May in the year of our Lord 1788, whereby the Constitution of the United States was ratified, and also all acts and parts of acts of the general assembly of the State ratifying amendments of the said Constitution, are hereby repealed, and that the union now existing between South Carolina and other States under the name of the United States of America is hereby dissolved." Ten other Southern States took similar action. The forces of South Carolina seized the United States Custom-house, post-office, and arsenal in Charleston and took possession of Forts Moultrie and Pickney in Charleston harbor. On the 12th of April, 1861, they fired upon Fort Sumter, and the great Civil War began, which continued until April 9, 1865, when General Lee, commander of the Confederate army, surrendered to General Grant, and war, the last arbiter in the affairs of nations, decided that the Constitution of the United States established a government, and not a mere league of States.

It is not to be wondered at that the Constitutional convention, knowing that it had gone beyond the instructions given it, and aware of the deep-rooted and strong prejudice in favor of the State governments, should deem it expedient to omit those formal declarations which in other circumstances would have been included in an instrument intended to found a new government. The impression was prevalent at the time that the Declaration of Independence had brought a new Nation into existence, and that the Articles of Confederation and the Constitution were simply adjustments of the internal affairs of the nation. The Declaration of Independence began the work, but came very far short of completing it. Had there been nothing more it would have brought into being thirteen Nations instead of one. But under the prevailing impression that the work had been fully done by the Declaration of Independence, it was perfectly natural that there should be a recognition of the Divine Being in the one instrument, and not in the other. The omission was not made in the latter with impious intent, nor by an oversight which would imply any lack of piety in the members of the convention. The Nation had not been converted from Christianity to atheism in the brief period between 1776 and 1787.

We have a case perfectly analogous in the Constitution of the German Empire, dated April 14, 1871, which, if the words "of God's grace," be excepted, says nothing about religion and requires no religious tests as qualification for civil and political offices under the National government. No one ever thinks of denouncing it as an atheistic document or charging its framers with impiety. It was simply a new adjustment of the internal affairs of a nation already existing; it provided for no official connection with the Church, but left the subject of religion to the several States, each of which has its own State church.[1]

The Christian people of this country, knowing all the circumstances and sharing in the general impression referred to, accepted the Constitution as it was, content with the indisputable fact that the civil government of

[1] *Church and State*, Schaff, pp. 91, 92.

a Christian people is necessarily Christian. They were perhaps the more reconciled to the acceptance of it by the fact that nearly all the State Constitutions contained the recognition desired, the State governments being then regarded as of paramount importance.

Of late years, however, the omission has been seized upon as a means of enforcing a particular theory of civil government ; the theory that civil government in its proper form must be destitute of all religious character. This theory has been held principally and has been urged most strenuously by those who deny the truth of Christianity and of all religion. During a comparatively brief period, after the middle of the present century, atheism gained in respectability by the philosophical speculations of certain men who had attained to great eminence in natural science. These men, having passed over into the domain of philosophy, gave forth their pronouncements with the authority of discoverers and first occupants. They soon found, however, that the new territory had been long occupied, much longer than that from which they came, and that there were giants in that land. Their authority was, therefore, of brief duration, but while it was at its height the unbeliever was emboldened to demand that the administration of the whole government be conformed to his dogmas on the subject of religion. A national organization, called the Liberal League, was formed for the purpose of accomplishing this end. It was demanded that the employment of chaplains by the government should cease ; that the administration of oaths should be abandoned ; that the crime of blasphemy should be blotted from the statute book ; that the Sabbath laws should be repealed ; that the holding of religious exercises and the reading of the Bible in the

public schools should be prohibited. The demand was
so far yielded to, that in some States provision for the
salaries of chaplains was either neglected or prohibited ;
the law relating to blasphemy was repealed ; the Sabbath laws were either repealed or greatly modified, and
with the co-operation of a certain religious denomination, the reading of the Bible in the public schools was
prohibited.   It is not strange that a goodly number of
Christian people began to feel the need of some organized effort to secure their rights and to defeat the attempt to substitute an atheistic for the Christian basis
of their government.

The Civil War, happening to be nearly coincident with
the new movement, was looked upon by a number of
Christian citizens as a judgment of God upon the nation for its failure to honor him in its fundamental law.
It was during the darkest days of the Civil War that the
organized effort to secure a religious amendment to the
Constitution of the United States took its rise.

On Feb. 3, 1863, a convention met at Xenia, Ohio,
which had been called for prayer and Christian conference, with special reference to the state of the country.
On the second day of the convention John Alexander,
then of Xenia, presented a paper in which the sins of
the nation were confessed and the importance of repentance and reformation insisted upon.   After speaking of President Lincoln's Emancipation Proclamation,
then recently issued, and the hopeful prospect of an
anti-slavery amendment to the Constitution, the paper
proceeds as follows :

"We regard the neglect of God and his law, by
omitting all acknowledgment of them in our Constitution, as the crowning original sin of the nation, and
slavery as one of its natural outgrowths.   Therefore,

the most important step remains yet to be taken, to amend the Constitution so as to acknowledge God and the authority of His law ; and the object of this paper is to suggest to this convention the propriety of considering the subject and of preparing such an amendment to the Constitution as they may think proper to propose, in accordance with its provisions."

Mr. Alexander gave an outline of the amendments to the preamble to the Constitution which seemed to him to be needed, and the whole paper was approved by the convention.

On February 6th, just three days after the meeting at Xenia, and without any knowledge of that meeting, a convention of Christians of various denominations met in Sparta, Illinois, and adopted resolutions pledging the members of the convention to "labor to bring the nation to repentance toward God and to a faithful administration of the government according to the principles of the word of God."

After several adjourned meetings of these conventions it was thought best to call a national convention of all citizens favorable to the measure, without any distinction of party or creed. This convention met in Allegheny City, January 27, 1864, and formed a permanent organization under the title, *The National Association for the Amendment of the Constitution*, which has since been changed to the National Reform Association.

The amendment proposed is to the preamble, and in the body of the Constitution only such changes as may be necessary to give effect to that amendment. The preamble as amended would be as follows, the amendments being in brackets :

" We,-the people of the United States, [humbly acknowledging Almighty God as the source of all author-

ity and power in civil government, the Lord Jesus
Christ as the Ruler among the nations, his revealed
will as the supreme law of the land, in order to constitute a Christian government,] and in order to form a
more perfect union, establish justice, insure domestic
tranquillity, provide for the common defence, promote
the general welfare, and secure [the inalienable rights
and] blessings [of life], liberty [and the pursuit of hap-
piness] to ourselves, our posterity, [and all the inhabitants of the land], do ordain and establish this
Constitution for the United States of America.[1]

Men of high position in all the walks of life have

[1] The amendment proposed has undergone several modifications, but its final form may be regarded as embodied in a joint
resolution which was presented to both houses of Congress
January 26, 1894, and by them referred to the appropriate
committees :

"*Resolved by the Senate and House of Representatives of
the United States of America in Congress assembled, two thirds
of each House concurring therein,* That the following amended
form of the Preamble of the Constitution of the United States
be proposed for ratification by conventions in the several
States, which when ratified by conventions in three fourths of
the States shall be valid as a part of said Constitution, namely :

PREAMBLE.

" We, the people of the United States [devoutly acknowledging the supreme authority and just government of Almighty
God in all the affairs of men and nations ; grateful to Him for
our civil and religious liberty ; and encouraged by the assurances
of His Word to invoke His guidance, as a Christian nation,
according to His appointed way, through Jesus Christ,], in order
to form a more perfect union, establish justice, ensure domestic
tranquillity, provide for the common defence, promote the general welfare, and secure the blessings of liberty to ourselves
and our posterity, do ordain and establish this Constitution for
the United States of America."

joined in the movement, but it has never been regarded with favor by a large majority of the Christian people of the land, and of late years has been losing rather than gaining in strength. It would be uncharitable to attribute the failure of Christian people to enter into the movement to lack of the true Christian spirit, and it would be unreasonable to attribute it to mere immobility. They have reasons for their refusal of co-operation, some of which are obvious :

1. The prevailing conviction that our civil government is, now without any such amendment, Christian, necessarily so while the people are Christian, and that for all practical purposes the amendment would not make it any more so than it is.

2. The universal opposition to the imposition of a religious test as a qualification for office or public trust, and the fear that the amendment might be made to operate as such a test. The advocates of the amendment disavow any intention of establishing a religious test; what they desire, they say, is simply something declaratory, nothing that would coerce the conscience of any man, nothing that would debar any one from any right or privilege on account of his religious belief. The amendment, they say, is intended only to preserve the nation from the sin of dishonoring God in its fundamental law, and to exert a wholesome educational influence upon the people ; yet they argue in its favor that it will furnish a basis for coercive legislation on Christian subjects, which does not now exist ; it will furnish a legal basis for the enactment of Sabbath laws, for the requirement that legislation on all moral subjects shall conform to the law of God, and for resistance to the prohibition of the Bible in the common schools. So far as these objects are proper, we have already ade-

quate basis for legislation in the fact that the civil institutions of a Christian people are necessarily Christian. Besides it is doubtful whether a mere declaration in the preamble of the Constitution would serve as a basis for the legislation desired. Judge Story in discussing the preamble in his *Commentary on the Constitution* says : " The preamble never can be resorted to, to enlarge the powers confided to the general government or any of its departments. It cannot confer any power *per se.* It can never amount, by implication, to an enlargment of any power expressly given. It can never be the source of any implied power when otherwise withdrawn from the Constitution" (p. 164).

The preamble, if it could furnish any basis for the legislation desired, has already furnished a sufficient basis in the declaration that the object of the Constitution is to "establish justice." More than justice no Christian should desire, and ample provision for securing that end has been made in the establishment of courts.

The decisions of the courts may vary, but as the needle of the compass after oscillating from one side to the other is brought to rest at last on the magnetic meridian by the power of the ever-present and unseen world currents, so will the action of the courts be brought by a like power to rest upon the line of exact justice. It is not necessary in order to establish justice that every right should be secured by a special written law. It has not been necessary in order to secure the rights of the people that the common law should all be converted into statute law. Submission by general consent to those principles of right which are embodied in the system of rules, entitled international law, and submission by special agreement to

the decisions of international arbitration have secured
justice between nations without any international constitution or a word of enacted law. We are told that
the " law was added because of transgressions, till the
seed should come to whom the promise was made " ;
and we are sure that when the promise of God that
" They shall not hurt nor destroy in all my holy mountain " shall be fulfilled, it will not be by the restraints
of written Constitutions and laws, but by the power of
the law of righteousness and love written in the hearts
of men, for " The earth shall be full of the knowledge
of the Lord, as the waters cover the sea." [1]

[1] So long as man dwells in the body, his manifold inward life
will need to be embodied in outward form ; but both principles
and facts warrant the belief that undue attention to the outward
form will be followed by a decline in the vigor of the inward
life. The ancient Phariseeism has shown this to be true of the
spiritual life, as the modern prize ring and excess in athletics
have shown it to be true of the physical life.

In California nearly every mountain, valley, river, bay and
city is made, by its name, a memorial of a Christian saint, and
if there were any virtue in a formal public recognition of Christianity the atmosphere of that State ought to be as redolent of
sanctity as it is of the eucalyptus and the orange blossom ; but
California is the only State in the Union which has repealed its
Sabbath laws.

In no other State, of equal age and wealth, does so large a
proportion of the churches receive aid from the Home Missionary contributions of the churches outside of its boundaries. (59.6
per cent. of the Presbyterian churches in 1894 ; while in Iowa,
which is only four years older, it was 43.5 per cent., and there is
no reason to regard the Presbyterian churches as exceptional.)

In no other State has the baser element in politics succeeded
in so befouling the nation with an unjust prejudice against a
peaceable and industrious class of foreigners. And in no other
Northern State does so large a proportion of the white inhabitants set so low a value upon human life.

If it be said that the proposed amendment will serve
a practical purpose in proclaiming to the world the true
character of our government and in exerting an educational effect upon our own people, the reply may be
made that it is seriously defective.   It will make a false
proclamation and give an erroneous education.   There
is no mention in it of the third person of the Trinity,
nor any recognition of his existence.   It will proclaim
and teach a duo-unity, not a tri-unity, in the God-head.
If to omit the name of God in the Constitution is to
dishonor God, surely then to mention the name of any
other person of the Trinity and to omit that of the
Holy Spirit, is to dishonor him.   And it is a dishonor
which cannot be regarded as a light matter since our
Lord has declared a penalty against it above that for
dishonoring any other member of the Trinity : ''Therefore I say unto you, all manner of sin and blasphemy
shall be forgiven unto men, but the blasphemy against
the Holy Ghost shall not be forgiven unto men.   And
whosoever speaketh a word against the Son of man it
shall be forgiven him, but whosoever speaketh against
the Holy Ghost it shall not be forgiven him, neither in
this world, neither in the world to come.'' [1]

3. If the amendment be simply declaratory, it cannot be expected to affect the dealings of God with the
nation, unless the nation, as such, is under obligation
to make the declaration.   It is not reasonable to suppose that if the nation be Christian in fact God would
withhold his blessings on account of the absence of any
verbal declaration of the fact ; nor that if the nation be
not Christian in fact God would be induced by the mere
verbal declaration to mitigate the severity of his judgments against it.   On the contrary, it is rather to be

[1] Matthew, xii. 31, 32.

supposed that in this latter case he would add to his judgments, for the sin of hypocrisy and falsehood would call for punishment in addition to that of withholding the honor which is his due. It may be remarked in passing that the force of the argument in favor of the amendment which was drawn from the Civil War, regarded as a punishment inflicted upon the nation for the dishonoring of God in its organic law, has been greatly weakened by the fact that blessings of incalculable value have resulted from the war ;—the extinction of slavery, and the industrial regeneration of the Southern States. The war may have been a divine infliction upon the nation for its sins, but surely it could not have been for this sin of omission, for the blessings resulting from the war have been accumulating, while the alleged sin has been persisted in.

The advocates of the amendment, in order to hold that the nation, as such, is under obligation to make the declaration, are constrained to adopt the mystical theory of the State. The argument is that the State is a moral person, and that it is therefore under all the obligations to God that bind any other moral person ; one of which is to profess His name and to acknowledge His authority. "*Resolved*, That the State, as a power claiming and exercising supreme jurisdiction over vast numbers of human beings as the sovereign arbiter of life and death, and as an educating power, has necessarily a moral character and accountability of its own." [1]

"If the State has a character, then it must also have some sort of personality. . . . Moral character be-

---

[1] *Proceedings of the National Convention to secure the Religious Amendment of the Constitution of the United States*, 1872, p. 50.

longs only to rational beings. . . . But whatever
that personality may be, and I cannot discuss that question here, in it the moral character of the State inheres. ·
. . . Whatever then may be the opinion of any one
as to what constitutes the character of the State, it is
certain that it is not the character of any one of its subjects ; neither is it the sum, or sum and differences of
all their characters. . . . The State is an official
person, ordained by God, and holds a delegated authority from him. . . . Men associated under a
Constitution and laws in keeping with it form a com-
posite person or an associated personality." [1]

"The State is not only an organism, so to speak ;
even Hobbes arguing against its organic being, yet
represented it as a colossal living man; but it is a
sovereign, conscious, moral personality. . . . Its
life does not consist of a body of enactments, but in the
limitation of its being in a moral personality. . . .
It needs, therefore, to regulate the relations of its members as moral personalities, and to assert justice, which
is only the recognition of the relations among the moral
personalities of its members, and between them and its
own moral personality. And in doing this it derives
all its sanctions of administration from morality and
religion." [2]

It is very plain that the advocates of the amendment
do not wish to be understood as speaking of the State
as a person by a mere play of the imagination, in the
use of the common figure of speech, personification, as
when we apply the feminine pronoun to the ship, or
speak of the breeze as whispering, the wind howling, or

---

[1] Prof. O. N. Stoddard, LL.D. *Ibid.*, pp. 50, 52, 53.
[2] Hon. M. B. Hagans, Judge of the Superior Court of Cincinnati. *Ibid.*, p. 10.

the brook babbling. But if the State be, as they hold that it is, an actual person, it must be held to possess, not one or two, but all the attributes of personality. If it may have a belief of its own, either coincident with or differing from that of the persons who are its subjects; if it may profess its belief; if it may have a responsibility of its own to God, it must also be capable of hearing God's commands and threatenings, of repenting and praying for the forgiveness of its sins, and of rejoicing in forgiveness in *propria persona*, apart from the hearing, repenting, praying, and rejoicing of any other person whatever. These acts performed by one person cannot be the acts of another and a distinct person.

The legal maxim " *Qui facit per alium facit per se*," making the principal responsible for the act of his agent, has made us familiar with the transfer of the *responsibility* for an act from one person to another; and the theological doctrine of imputation has made us familiar with the transfer of the *consequences* of an act from one person to another; but no legal maxim and no theological doctrine teaches anything so absurd as the transfer of the act itself from one person to another.[1]

The advocates of the amendment, driven on by their

---

[1] The theological doctrine of Realism seems to imply such a transfer, and yet those who hold it would probably deny the implication. Realism denies the doctrine of imputation as an explanation of the state of sin and misery into which mankind are fallen; that is, the transfer of the consequences of Adam's sin to his posterity, upon the ground of a covenant or representative relationship; and explains the present state of mankind by the hypothesis that all mankind were in Adam, and that they acted when he acted. They may have been constrained to act by him in whom they were contained, but their present condition is the consequence of their own act.

zeal, do not stop to define personality or to follow the definition to its necessary consequences. A person in the proper sense of the term is a *suppositum intelligens*, a distinct individual existence, having a power of knowing, feeling, and willing of its own, and a consciousness of its own ; that is, the power of knowing that it knows, feels, and wills. In speaking of itself it must use the personal pronoun of the first person. If this nation, therefore, be a person and in the Constitution speaks as a person, it should have said "I, the Nation, do ordain and establish this Constitution " ; or, if common sense revolt at such a consistent carrying out of the theory, then at least, "We (*pluralis majestatis*), the Nation, and not We, the People."

A personality may be constituted of a part of one vast substance, and yet that substance be in no respect a person. The iceberg is of the same substance as the ocean, but it does not follow that the ocean possesses all the specific properties of the iceberg. The latter is an individual concrete thing, entirely different from the water of the ocean in gravity, solidity, and in the property of refracting and reflecting light.

Three persons in the Godhead are represented in the Scriptures as having all the attributes of personality, not of a figurative or modal, but an actual personality ; but the one substance or essence of which these three divine persons are composed is not a person. Pantheists do not hold that "the All " is a person, but that it comes into the self-consciousness of personality only in man. If, therefore, the State were a substance or thing distinct from the personality of its subjects, it does not necessarily follow that it is a person.

The hypothesis of the personality of the State leads

to absurd consequences if fully and consistently carried
out, and it is unnecessary. God is competent in knowledge and power to deal with individual men in accomplishing all his purposes on earth ; for he is omniscient
and omnipotent, and is a discerner of the thoughts and
intents of the heart. He is represented in the Scriptures
as dealing directly with individuals and with masses
of men in accordance with the character of the individuals composing the masses. The calls to repentance
addressed to Israel in old times were calls for changes
in the spirit and conduct of individual kings and people,
and not for changes in the utterances of a body supposed to have a personality different and apart from
that of the individual Israelite. It can hardly be supposed that God would send judgments upon the nation
as a person for a constructive dereliction when the individuals composing the nation were pure in their
intentions and faithful in their conduct. Did he
do so, the judgments sent upon the national person
would fall upon the innocent individual persons.
Neither can it be supposed that if the individual
persons had become corrupt, he would withhold his
judgments from the national person because of the
piety expressed in its fundamental law. In that case
the guilty would find immunity under the shelter of the
innocent national person.

It must be admitted that the political parties within
a State possess all the attributes of personality that are
said to belong to the State itself. They are great organized bodies, characterized by unity in the apprehension
of truth, in feeling and will, and also in action. They
are spoken of as having an individuality of their own,
distinct from that of the persons of whom they are com-

16

posed. They are regarded with contempt and hatred, while persons belonging to them are honored and beloved. The variation in the constituent elements may be greater, in the political party, than it is in the State, but no one holds that invariability and permanence of the constituent elements are essential to the personality of the State, and if not essential in the one case they cannot be in the other. Like the State, the great political parties are included in the providential government of Him who notices the fall of the sparrow and numbers the hairs of our head. He uses them, in the determination of the history and destiny of the nation, as He does the nations, in the determination of the history and destiny of the world. He deals with them as individuals, holding them responsible for their principles and acts. He visits them with defeat or overthrow for their follies, errors, and iniquities, just as He does the nations. But if the political parties are persons and the State is a person, then we have two or more persons within a person, a dichotomy and, it may be, a trichotomy or more, in that which is atomic.[1]

The people composing the State are actual persons, amendable to the laws of God. The State is a metaphorical person, amenable only to the laws of Rhetoric.

---

[1] We do not overlook the fact that we, who are persons, are in God, and that God, in whom there are three persons, is in us ; but we hardly think that the mystery of the omnipresence and the trinity can properly be made available to relieve this case of its absurdity. Mystery is to be believed only in the extreme of logical necessity. It is not to be made a convenient resort for the support of every theory, that is unable to stand without it. A theory needing such support may be, justly, set aside as belonging to the realm of the clouds.

CHAPTER VI.

EXCEPTIONS TO LIMITATIONS.

WE have seen that the law of progress, differentiation in form and specialization in function, applies to civil government as well as to everything else : and that as a general rule this law will limit the functions of government to purely secular affairs. From this rule certain special cases are to be excepted.

When the State takes to itself for any length of time the charge of the whole life of the subject, as it does in the army and navy, in the prisons, reformatories, homes for soldiers and outcast children, almshouses, hospitals, asylums, academies, colleges and universities, it is under obligation of the strongest character to teach religion, and the religion which it is under obligation to teach is the Christian religion. If it be granted that man has a religious element in his nature,—and a vast majority of the people in a Christian land do grant it,—then, not to develop that part of his nature equally with the rest is to distort and dwarf the man ; it would be the same as to develop his sense of hearing to the highest degree while keeping him in total darkness until his eyes had become atrophied ; the same as to give all attention to the development of his body and none at all to the development of his mind. Not to supply him with the consolations of religion in his trials and troubles would be the same as not to supply him with medicines in his sickness. To eliminate the truths of religion from the teaching given him would be the same as to eliminate an essential element, such as starch, albumen, lime or phosphorus from the food given him. Not to teach him the Ten Commandments, the Lord's Prayer and the Sermon on the Mount would be the same as not to teach him the multiplication table and the rules of syntax. For the State, while it has charge of the whole man, to be indifferent or neutral while he is becoming a Mormon, a Buddhist, or an atheist would be the same as to be indifferent or neutral while he is becoming a whiskey drinker, an opium eater, or a clay eater. To allow him to depend for his Christian teaching and nurture upon extraneous and voluntary agencies would be the same as to allow him to depend upon such agencies for his food and medicine and secular knowledge.

In the case of Warner *v.* Smith, 8 Conn. 17., an apprentice had escaped from his master and suit was brought by the master against the guardian for the return of the apprentice. It was pleaded in defence that the master had denied him the ordinary opportunities for religious nurture, and the Supreme Court of Connecticut said: "As the master stands *in loco parentis*, he is under higher obligation to instruct him in the principles of morality and religion; but instead of performing this parental duty this master compelled this apprentice, unnecessarily, to work on the Lord's day. From such an apprenticeship, it was the right, it was the *duty* of the ward to escape, and of the guardian to receive him."

Surely the State is itself to be governed by the principles which it prescribes for the government of the citizen. When it takes the whole man in its charge, it is under obligation to provide for the whole man. The practical difficulty arising from the diversity of creeds and sects in the Christian Church is not to be pleaded as insuperable, and therefore rendering the performance of the duty impossible. It is to be met with judgment and prudence, just as the like difficulty is met in other similar cases. There are almost as many schools of medicine and dietetics as there are sects in religion ; yet the government has not been deterred by any difficulty arising from this fact from providing medical attendance and a course of diet for those who are in its charge. The United States government has already recognized the obligation resting upon it to provide for the teaching of Christianity in such cases.

When the general government adopted the policy of civilizing the Indians by the establishment of schools among them for the instruction of their children, it was felt that it would be incongruous with all enlightened ideas of civilization to provide schools for these wards of the nation and exclude all religious instruction from those schools ; yet under the impression that the government could not legitimately teach Christianity it was thought necessary to adopt a plan for the accomplishment of the good work which would at least seem to transfer the responsibility to other parties. What was called the "contract system" was therefore adopted by which those Christian denominations which had competent missionary organizations were given severally the charge of particular Indian schools. In these schools religious and secular instruction was to be given, and the denominations in charge were to receive from the government a stipulated amount for each pupil.

In carrying out the plan of contract schools for the Indian children it was found necessary in order to allay the opposition that might arise from the assumption that the government could not in any case legitimately engage in the work of teaching Christianity, to resort to such empty and pitiable pleas as—that the money appropriated for this purpose belonged to the Indians by right and was not taken out of the national treasury, and indeed that none of it was used to pay for religious instruction, since the religious bodies in charge of the schools contributed from their benevolent resources more than enough to pay for the time and labor employed in giving such instruction. This plan, so far as it was intended to transfer the responsibility of the religious teaching of the Indian children to other parties, was utterly futile, for the government as principal is responsible for everything that its agent does with its knowledge and consent, even when the agent works under contract. By this plan the government becomes a teacher, not only of Christianity, but of sectarianism, for it cannot be pretended that the religious teaching given by Roman Catholics, Episcopalians, Presbyterians, Methodists, and Friends will not be more or less in accordance with the peculiar doctrines of those denominations. The teaching of religion by this plan is therefore far more incongruous with the principles of our government than such teaching by persons appointed for the purpose by the government would be. If in such a case it would be a barbarous method of civilizing, to establish schools and exclude all religious teaching from them, the government ought to teach religion openly, avowedly, and not by a subterfuge.

Had not the government, while placing the Indian on reservations of land, recognized his independence by making treaties with him and purchases of him, it would have been under obligation to teach the adult Indian the Christian religion, and not to leave him as it has done to depend on voluntary agencies for such teaching: it would have been under obligation to enforce with prudence and consideration a prohibition of his paganism.

In the lease of the fur seal fisheries on the islands of St. George and St. Paul in the territory of Alaska made by the government to the North American Commercial Company, one of the stipulations requires the company to provide school-houses and competent teachers eight months in the year, and a house of religious worship ; and by the latter clause is meant a house of Christian religious worship, not a house of pagan, or Jewish, or Mohammedan religious worship.

In all the cases mentioned, it is the duty of the State not only to provide for the teaching of the Christian religion, but to prohibit the teaching of any other religion, or of irreligion. It should require that Christian religious exercises be maintained in its schools, academies, colleges, and universities : and should also require that all the teaching therein should be professedly in accord with the truths of the Christian religion.

CHAPTER VII.

RELIGION IN THE PUBLIC SCHOOLS.

THE fact that our civil government is Christian does not in itself furnish sufficient ground for the requirement of religious teaching in our public schools ; nor is the relation between the mental, moral, and spiritual in man so intimate as to render the separate development of any one department of his nature either impracticable or necessarily pernicious. There may be such an order of dependence that it will be possible to develop in some degree the mental nature without at the same time developing the moral and spiritual ; in a less degree, the moral without the mental ; and in still less degree, the spiritual without the moral and mental. There can be no education, in the proper sense of the term, unless the development of the three parts of our nature be carried forward abreast and with equal pace ; but it is not necessary that this should all be done at the same hour or by the same agency. In this case the State is not *in loco parentis ;* it does not take charge of the whole life of the pupil. It is charged with providing for only one of the wants of his nature. Were it in charge of the whole life of the pupil, it would be under obligation to provide for the nourishment of his body. It knows however that another and better agency, the family, is making provision for that want ; and while it may be true that all families are not competent to provide the most wholesome food, yet the State is not chargeable with inhumanity in refusing to make this provision. It does not thereby leave the pupil to starve. So in refusing to make provision for the religious development of the pupil in the public schools it cannot be justly accused with being irreligious or anti-Christian. It does not thereby deprive him of all spiritual nurture. It knows that other and better agencies, the family and the church divinely appointed for the purpose, are making provision for that want ; and it simply leaves that very important provision to be made by those agencies. Those Roman Catholics, Lutherans, and Reformed, who withdraw their children from the public schools and send them to parochial schools, and who seem to have a just ground of opposition to the public-school system in that they are taxed for a public provision which they cannot conscientiously use, do not over-estimate the importance of religious instruction for the young ; but they mistake in thinking that the State is under obligation to give such instruction or none at all. The public-school system has not been fitted for that work, and in this country it would be impracticable to fit it for that work. It requires of its teachers, besides a good moral character, only qualifications for teaching certain branches of secular learning ; it does not require the qualifications necessary for the conducting of religious services or the imparting of religious knowledge. It cannot be true that a particular work belongs to the public school system and is obligatory, when the regulations of the system do not and cannot require of the teachers the qualifications necessary for the performance of that work. An atheist might possess all the qualifications required for teaching in our public schools, and it would certainly be an incongruous thing to have an established order which would require such a one to lead in the reading of the Scriptures and in the repeating of the Lord's Prayer as an act of worship.[1]

[1] Unless it shall be decided that the teacher in the public school is, like the janitor, an employé, and not the incumbent of an office or the fiduciary of a public trust, the requirement of a religious qualification as a condition of his appointment would be a violation of that clause in the State and Federal Constitutions which prohibits a religious test as a qualification to any office or public trust. The requirement of a religious qualification is undoubtedly made in the case of chaplains, and the qualification required is more than merely religious,—it is Christian, no minister of any other religion being eligible ; but the requirement is only tacitly, not formally, made. This qualification being essential to the performance of the functions of the office, the requirement of it is necessarily involved in the institution of the office. Since none but ministers of the gospel are ever appointed to the office, it is not necessary that the requirement of a religious qualification should be formally made ; their ordination being a formal guaranty of their possessing it. Teachers in the public schools, however, occupy no position which furnishes any such guaranty. The requirement, if made in their case, would have to be formally made, and it is

It may not be impertinent to notice the fact that the persons making the demand for religious instruction in the public schools are not consistent in carrying out the principle on which they say the demand is based, in that they do not insist upon the application of the principle in those cases in which they might do so with justice and with a reasonable prospect of success. The master, teaching the apprentice his trade, the private tutor, and the music teacher are not required to begin their lessons with prayer, or to combine the communication of religious with secular knowledge. Such a requirement is not made of the commercial college, the medical college, or the law school, and yet all these are patronized by all Christian people without objection. Why is not all the teaching in these cases denounced as "godless" and therefore pernicious, as well as the teachings in the public schools. Indeed it is practically conceded in these cases that secular instruction, unaccompanied with religious instruction, is not necessarily pernicious.

There are, however, two other ostensible grounds upon which the demand for religious instruction in our public schools may be based. One of these we shall now consider; the other we shall notice incidentally farther on.

The first attaches itself very closely to the ground upon which the system itself is supposed to be based.

not probable that such a requirement, so made, would be tolerated by the public or sustained by the courts. If the requirement were deemed to be as essential to the office of teacher as it is to the office of chaplain, that office ought to be expressly excepted from the Constitutional prohibition. Indeed it would have been better had the office of chaplain been so excepted.

The theory may be stated thus : Intelligence is necessary to good citizenship ; therefore the State is bound to furnish all the youth of the land with such instruction as will enable them to avail themselves of the ordinary means of intelligence, and also to compel attendance upon the instruction provided. In syllogistic form, the theory would be thus stated, viz.:

Major premise. Self-preservation is a law that binds the State as well as the individual, and under this law the State is bound to provide whatever is essential to good citizenship.

Minor premise. Education is essential to good citizenship.

Conclusion. Therefore the State ought to provide common schools and compel attendance upon them.

It is very plain that if any other subject than education may be properly put before the predicate in the *Minor premise,* the syllogism will be as conclusive for that subject as it is for education. If it be true that "the fear of the Lord is the beginning of wisdom,"— if it be true that an illiterate disciple of Christ whose "delight is in the law of the Lord" will be a better citizen than the educated unbeliever who walks "in the counsel of the ungodly," then, according to this theory, it is just as conclusive that the State should provide for religious instruction in the common school as that it should provide the school itself. But the theory is too comprehensive by far to be tenable. Suppose that the *Minor premise* of the syllogism affirm that the influence of religion not only in *childhood,* but *throughout life,* is essential to good citizenship (and who will deny the truth of the affirmation ?), then it is just as conclusive that the State should provide for the religious instruction of the adult as for that of the child. There is no open link in this logic ; it cannot be parted in the middle ; it reaches all the way from the compulsory attendance of children upon the public school to the compulsory attendance of adults upon public worship. The logic of this theory of the public-school system is the same as that of Article III. of the Bill of Rights, adopted by Massachusetts in 1780 :

"As the happiness of a people and the good order and preservation of civil government essentially depend upon piety, religion, and morality ; and as these cannot be generally diffused through a community but by the institution of the public worship of God, and of public instructions in piety, religion, and morality. Therefore, to promote their happiness and to secure the good order and preservation of their civil government, the people of this commonwealth have a right to invest their legislature with power to authorize and require the several towns, parishes, precincts, and other bodies politic, or other religious societies, to make suitable provision at their own expense for the institution of the worship of God and for the support and maintenance of public Protestant teachers of piety, religion, and morality in all cases where such provision is not made voluntarily.

" And the people of this commonwealth have a right, and do invest their legislature with authority to enjoin upon all the subjects an attendance upon the instructions of the public teachers aforesaid at stated times and seasons, if there be any on whose instructions they can conscientiously and conveniently attend."

The logic, granting the assumption on which it is based, is as unanswerable in the one case as it is in the other.

This theory of the public-school system, notwithstanding that it is affirmed in all the school journals, in all teachers' associations, County, State, and National, by all County and State superintendents of public schools, and acted upon by all the State legislatures, has been practically abandoned by all its advocates. It has been abandoned in the establishment of high-schools and State universities. Nobody pretends that a knowledge of algebra, geometry, conic sections, calculus, physics, chemistry, geology, astronomy, of the French, German, Greek, and Latin languages, is essential to good citizenship, or that the provision for the teaching of these things in our public schools and State universities rests on any such basis. These things are taught to the few at the expense of the many, in direct violation of the fundamental postulate of the theory. Yet nobody seems disposed either to object to the violation or to confess an abandonment of the theory. The reason of the inconsistency is to be found in the fact that a different theory is half-consciously held, but is so simple and obvious that it is hardly thought of, much less propounded as a theory. It is the theory of general consent. This theory, on account of its simplicity, has held its place in practice while the other has continued to hold its place in discourse.

While the primary function of civil government is the protection of the citizen from the unjust interference of his fellow-citizen with his person and property, and while as a general rule the public welfare will be highest when the government confines itself to its primary function, leaving all else to individual freedom; yet, because what Terence said of himself is also true of all men,—"I am a man, and I count nothing human as foreign to me,"—consent is readily given that the government shall do many things which do not belong to its primary function, the provision understood being that it does not renounce the principles of freedom and assume the principles of paternalism.

Without considering whether there is a natural right of property in the form in which thought is expressed or conception realized, as well as in the paper, marble-canvas, or machine upon which the hand has wrought, we readily concede that the government may very properly promote literature and art by giving a copyright to the author and artist; it may encourage invention by giving a patent to the inventor; it may also promote science by fitting out expeditions for exploration and discovery, by providing for astronomical observations and meteorological investigations, and by maintaining museums; it may establish a weather service, and make daily announcements of the coming of storms and changes in temperature; it may maintain parks for the pleasure of the people; it may diminish the perils of the sea by making surveys and charts of all the coasts, establishing light-houses and maintaining life-saving stations, along all our shores; it may maintain a postal system, carrying the letters, the newspapers, and periodicals of the people,—all this upon the ground of general consent, and not upon the ground of inherent prerogative or indispensable obligation.

The postal system is one that contributes very greatly to the promotion of intelligence among the people, and supplies a facility of immense importance to the business of the country, but that system has not its basis in the duty of the government, in its paternal character to promote the intelligence and prosperity of the people. Why when it added the carrying of parcels to that system did it not also add the whole business of transportation ? Why when it added the transmission of small sums of money to that system did it not also add the whole banking business of the country ? Why is the telegraph system, which promotes intelligence by the transmission of the daily news and affords a facility of immense importance to the business of the country, left in private hands? May it not be safely predicted that if the telegraph system shall ever be incorporated with the postal system, it will be to protect the citizen from the unjust exactions of a monopoly, and not because the government is bound in its paternal character to make the intelligence and prosperity of the people one of its chief concerns. Would any one think of arguing that because the postal system promotes the intelligence of the people and was provided for that purpose, every citizen should be compelled to receive through the mails certain periodical publications graded according to his intelligence, and to exercise himself in composition by writing a certain number of letters every week.

The postal system and the public-school system, alike, have their basis in general consent, which is given on account of economy, efficiency, uniformity, equal and perpetual availibility for all the people. If the alleged basis of the public-school system in the paternal prerogative of the State and its right of self-preservation should be abandoned in theory, as it has been in practice (of which, it must be admitted, there is not the least reasonable prospect), it would be far more just if, as in the postal system, the public provision were made, only the cost charged for the use of it, only those who use it required to pay for the maintenance of it, and they to pay only in proportion to the use they make of it. Under such a plan arrangements might be made which would remove some present difficulties, without developing others not now existing. The postal laws allow railroad, express, and navigation companies to carry their own correspondence, and make no exactions of them for the support of the postal system. So under a public-school system similarly organized, those Christian people who feel bound in conscience to maintain parochial schools might be allowed to do so, without being subject to the injustice of paying taxes for the teaching of the children of other people, while bearing all the expense of teaching their own ; and without being liable to the charge of hostility to a system which has been established to secure the welfare and safety of the State. The State might prohibit the teaching of any other children in the parochial schools, as it prohibits the corporations referred to carrying any other than their own correspondence ; it might also prohibit the establishment of parochial schools where, on account of the sparseness of the population, they would cripple or destroy the public schools ; and it might require that the teaching in the parochial schools be in the English language.

Objection might be made that, while the plan of requiring those who use the public schools to pay the cost of maintaining them might be more just, it would fail to reach the very persons who were in most need of its advantages, and would deprive the State of the very benefit the system was intended to secure. It may be a question, however, whether gratuitousness is the only or the best means of securing the prevalence of a common education. There can be no doubt that with all its advantages it is attended with counteracting evils. People do not appreciate that which costs them nothing as they do that which they have to pay for.

To pauperize the people is to shrivel the nerves of energy and to destroy the spirit of self-reliance,—evils
which an enlightened public policy regards as of no
small moment. It is probable that the requirement of
an educational qualification for the exercise of the elective franchise, with other co-operating influences, would
be quite as effective to the end desired as mere freedom
from charge. This opinion is not without the support
of facts. The State derives a very important benefit
from the prevalence of religion among the people, but
that benefit is left by the State to be provided entirely
at the expense of those who desire it, and there can be
no doubt that the public benefit from that source is as
large in this country under this system as it is elsewhere under a Church and State system. De Tocque-
ville in his *Democracy in America* says : " There is no
country in the whole world in which the Christian
religion retains a greater influence over the souls of
men than in America. . . . Upon my arrival in
the United States the religious aspect of the country
was the first thing that struck my attention, and the
longer I stayed there the more did I perceive the great
political consequences resulting from this state of
things. . . . I questioned the members of all the
different sects, and I more especially sought the society
of the clergy. . . . I found that they differed upon
matters of detail alone, and that they mainly attributed
the peaceful domain of religion in their country to the
separation of Church and State." [1]

Mr. James Bryce says : "To estimate the influence
and authority of religion is not easy. Suppose, however, we take either the habit of attending church or
the sale of religious books as evidences of its influence

[1] 1848, vol. i., pp. 332, 337.

17

among the multitude ; suppose that as regards the more cultivated classes we look at the amount of respect paid to Christian precepts and ministers, the interest taken in theological questions, the connection of philanthropic reforms with religion. Adding these various data together, we may get some sort of notion of the influence of religion on the American people as a whole. . . . In all these respects the influence of Christianity seems to be, if we look not merely to the numbers but also to the intelligence of the persons influenced, greater and more wide spread in the United States than in any part of western Continental Europe, and I think greater than in England." [1]

This fact thus attested by discerning and impartial foreigners is pertinent by way of analogy, but we have a fact more directly pertinent in the condition of education in Iceland. That island is outside of the world's great currents of intelligence and literature, and yet it is said to be the best educated country on the face of the earth. Mr. John Thorgeirson, in a communication to one of our religious journals, says : " The general education in Iceland is wholly domestic, and there are no public schools in the country ; neither any direct compulsory educational law. But the laws and customs of the country demand that every parent or guardian of children shall under the direction of the parish minister teach those in their care to read, write, and cipher, and instruct them in domestic science, general history, and especially in the literature of their own country. . . . Persons that can neither read nor write in Iceland are by law and custom regarded as mental imbeciles. They are not regarded competent to manage any inheritance left to him or her, but must

[1] *The American Commonwealth*, vol., ii., p. 583.

remain wards. They are not allowed to marry, as they would be incapable of educating children ; neither are they regarded as bright enough to understand the meaning of an oath, and hence are not competent witnesses in court." [1]

These statements are confirmed, in general, by one of the authors of the article in the *Encyclopedia Britannica* on " Iceland," J. A. Hjaltalin, who says : " The Icelanders have long been famous for their education and learning, and it is no exaggeration to say that in no other country is such an amount of information found among the classes which occupy a similar position. A child of ten unable to read is not to be found from one end of the island to the other. A peasant understanding several languages is no rarity, and the amount of general information which they possess might be envied by many who have had greater facilities for acquiring knowledge. Till within the last few years there were no elementary schools on the island ; all the children were taught by their parents or near neighbors. Now a few elementary schools have been started, but their number is still too small to make any general difference in the education." [2]

[1] *The Independent*, 1893, p. 1336.

[2] We are aware that any state of things which has become institutional in any country is the product of all antecedent conditions and is fixed by its adaptation to present circumstances. To suppose, therefore, that the educational methods of Iceland could be transplanted and flourish in this country would be almost as unreasonable as to suppose that the Iceland moss could be transplanted and made to flourish on all our mountains ; yet, such examples if kept in mind will encourage and reinforce the sense of justice until a way shall be found to remove all unnecessary hardship and remedy all injustice.

The public school must be accepted as an established institu-

The exercise of paternal prerogatives on the part of the government is not necessary to the attainment of the end aimed at in the establishment of a public-school

tion of this land. Whatever may be the defects of the theories invented to serve as the basis of it, the benefits to be derived from it are so obvious and so great that it is not likely ever to be abandoned. There is no more probability that it will ever be transferred to private hands than there is that the postal system will be transferred to the express companies. The latter system was not by any means perfect when first adopted. It has undergone many modifications, improving it and adapting it to new conditions, and all without a word of opposition, simply because the defects were pointed out and the changes suggested by those who were known to desire its improvement and not its destruction. It is not unreasonable to believe that the public-school system will undergo modification when the defects are pointed out and the alterations are proposed by persons who cannot be suspected of secret unfriendliness or of a covert purpose to destroy it.

The Roman Catholic Church, which is by far the most conspicuous complainant of the injustice of our public-school system, has itself put a check upon any tendency there might be to remove the injustice complained of. Holding an un-catholic theory of the Church, a remnant of the *hortus siccus* of mediæval logic, it is unwilling to admit that it is only a part of the kingdom of Christ on earth, a branch of the true vine, and —to use its own phraseology—a sect among sects, and, like the Apostle John, who said, "Master, we saw one casting out devils in thy name and he followeth not us, and we forbade him because he followeth not us," it has laid the ban on all Protestantism, affirming that all religious teaching by Protestants, or by others than regularly authorized Roman Catholic ecclesiastics, is so pernicious as to be worse than none. It denounces as "godless" schools in which there is no religious teaching, and proclaims by its actions that it regards all schools in which there is unsectarian religious teaching by Protestants as worse than "godless." Its protest against our public-school system is twofold : a protest against a purely secular education ; and a

system. Neither is the paternal theory of government
necessary as a basis for a public-school system. That
theory may be rejected, with all its logical conse-

protest against any non-sectarian or Protestant religious instruction therein. The latter, though kept in the background in
all public discussions of the subject, is held to be of equal importance with the former. Where it could not have its own
sectarian teaching established in the public schools it has attempted to exclude all religious instruction therefrom (see the
cases, presently to be cited, of Donahue *v.* Richards in Maine,
and John D. Minor *et al. v.* the Board of Education of the City
of Cincinnati *et al.* in Ohio), and in some cases, by the co-operation of those who hold the anti-Christian theory of the State, it
has succeeded in the attempt, thus causing the rights of a great
majority of Christian people to be trampled upon, and a serious
injury to be inflicted upon the public. (See the case of Weiss
et al. v. District Board of School District No. 8, of the City of
Edgerton, in Wisconsin, presently to be cited.)

Is it at all strange that Protestants are slow to accede to a demand which involves such unfavorable implications against
themselves, and which no Protestant sect is narrow and bigoted
enough ever to think of making for itself? Protestants are willing to fulfil the Lord's injunction, "All things, whatsoever ye
would that men should do to you, do ye even so to them," but
they do not feel under obligation to go beyond it. It is probable
therefore that the great mass of the people will be content with
the public-school system as it is, whatever may be its basis, so
long as it may be made Christian without being sectarian. They
count it no injustice that their own sectarian teachings are excluded, and it is therefore difficult for them to regard the exclusion of Roman Catholic sectarian teaching as an injustice.
Could a new system be proposed which would afford the relief
desired, and at the same time secure all the beneficent results
of the old, without producing any new evils, they would no
doubt readily make the change. The presentation of such a
system, and not complaint of the injustice of the old, is the
thing to be done. When the conditions of the public welfare
are such that hardship must fall upon persons whose consciences

quences, and yet may the State properly maintain such a system.

Mr. Macaulay, in his review of Gladstone's *The State in its Relations with the Church*, states very clearly and illustrates very aptly the principle for which we are contending. He says : " We consider the primary end of government as a purely temporal end, the protection of the persons and property of men. . . . We think that government should be organized solely with a view to its main end, and that no part of its efficiency for that end should be sacrificed in order to promote any other end, however excellent. But does it follow from thence, that governments ought never to pursue any end other than the main end ? In no wise. Though it is desirable that every institution should have a main end, and should be so formed as to be in the highest degree efficient for that end ; yet if, without any sacrifice of its efficiency for that end, it can pursue any other good end, it ought to do so. Thus the end for which a hospital is built is the relief of the sick, not the beautifying of the street. To sacrifice the health of the sick to splendor of architectural effect ; to place the building in a bad air, only that it may present a more commanding front to a great public place ; to make the wards hotter or cooler than they ought to be in order that the columns and windows of the exterior may please the passers-by, would be monstrous. But if, without any sacrifice of the chief object, the hospital can be made an ornament to the metropolis, it would

will not permit them to conform to those conditions, those persons have no just ground of complaint so long as they are not compelled to do what their conscience forbids. In that case the individual must endure hardship for conscience' sake ; the public welfare should not be sacrificed for his relief.

be absurd not to make it so. In the same manner, if a government can without any sacrifice to its main end promote any other good work, it ought to do so. The encouragement of the fine arts, for example, is by no means the main end of government, and it would be absurd in constituting a government to bestow a thought upon the question, whether it would be a government likely to train Raphaels and Domenichinos. But it by no means follows that it is improper for a government to form a national gallery of pictures. The same may be said of patronage bestowed on learned men, of the publication of archives, of the collecting of libraries, menageries, plants, fossils, antiques, of journeys and voyages for purposes of geographical discovery or astronomical observation. It is not for these ends that government is constituted. But it may well happen that a government may have at its command resources which will enable it, without any injury to its main object, to pursue these collateral ends far more effectually than any individual or voluntary association could do. If so, government ought to pursue these collateral ends.'"[1]

Upon the theory we have been setting forth, religion may very well have a place in the public schools, just as music, pictures, flowers, and calisthenics have, by general consent. And let it be remembered that the consent which gives legal validity to a usage is *general*, not *necessarily unanimous* consent. The tenure would be a valid and strong one, but religious exercises ought not to be made an indispensable requirement. On the one hand, pupils whose parents are conscientiously opposed to such exercises ought not to be compelled to attend upon them. On the other hand, such exercises

[1] *Edinburgh Review*, April, 1839, and *Essays.*

ought not to be prohibited upon the demand of unbelievers, any more than pictures and music and flowers
ought to be prohibited upon the demand of boors. On
the one hand, nobody has a right to demand that the
State should provide sustenance for the pupils in the
common schools. On the other hand, nobody has a
right to demand that every provision looking to the
bodily welfare of the pupils, hygiene and calisthenics,
for example, should be excluded. So on the one hand,
nobody has a right to demand that full courses of religious instruction be given in our common schools ; and
on the other hand, nobody has any right to demand that
everything of a religious character be excluded.[1]

It is a happy circumstance that so large a proportion
of the teachers in our common schools have the es-
thetic and religious feelings which make it a pleasure to
them to bring into the school-room, not only the refining and elevating influence of music and pictures and
flowers, but also of a simple unsectarian Christian worship. Those who do so ought not to be interfered with
either upon the plea that our civil institutions are destitute of religious character,—an untenable plea, as we
have already shown,—nor upon the plea of injustice to
the unbelieving taxpayer,—also an untenable plea, as we
shall presently show. All these means of refining and
elevating the character, however, should be kept in a
subordinate position, as accessories to the main purpose
of the school. The State is not qualified to give full
courses of religious instruction, that not being among
the main objects of its organization. It may therefore
very well leave the great bulk of such instruction to be
given by the family and the church, the two divine in-

[1] See case of Foster North *v.* Board of Trustees, University of
Illinois, presently to be cited.

stitutions appointed especially for that work. The work will be better done by an organ specialized for that purpose than by one that had been specialized for another purpose.

Decisions of the Courts on Religion in the Public Schools.—The Board of Education of the city of Cincinnati, Ohio, on the 1st day of November, 1869, adopted the following resolutions, viz. :

"*Resolved*, That religious instruction and the reading of religious books, including the Holy Bible, are prohibited in the Common Schools of Cincinnati, it being the true object and intent of this rule to allow the children of the parents of all sects and opinions in matters of faith and worship, to enjoy alike the benefit of the Common-School fund.

"*Resolved*, That so much of the regulations on the course of study and text-books in the Intermediate and District Schools (p. 213, Annual Report) as reads as follows : 'The opening exercises in every department shall commence by reading a portion of the Bible by or under the direction of the teacher, and appropriate singing by the pupils,' be repealed."

John D. Minor and others brought action before the Superior Court of Cincinnati, by petition for an order to restrain the Board of Education from carrying out the above resolutions.[1] The parties were heard by the Court in general term, November 30, 1869; W. M. Ramsey, George R. Sage, and Rufus King appearing for the plaintiffs, and Judges F. B. Stallo, George Hoadly, and Stanley Matthews for the defendants;

[1] The statement and history of the case, the arguments of counsel on both sides, and the opinions of the justices have been published in full in *The Bible in the Public Schools*, Cincinnati, Robert Clarke & Co.

Judges Storer, Taft, and Hagans on the bench. The cause was argued with great ability and almost exhaustively on both sides.

The Court decided that " The injunction must be perpetual," Taft dissenting.

Judge Hagans in his opinion, referring to the incorporation of *Article III Ordinance of 1787*, with the Constitution of Ohio, says : " It is admitted that the common schools of Ohio are in operation under the present Constitution, adopted in 1851. The last sentence of the seventh section of the Bill of Rights declares : ' Religion, morality, and knowledge, however, being essential to good government, it shall be the duty of the General Assembly to pass suitable laws to protect every religious denomination in the peaceable enjoyment of its own form of public worship, and to encourage schools and the means of instruction.' There is a vast difference, however, between *omitting* or *not requiring*, and the *prohibition* of a thing. It could not be claimed that if the Legislature had omitted to pass suitable laws to protect religious worship that it would be competent for the City Council to enact an ordinance to prohibit the police from doing it. This last clause provides two modes of reaching the declared end :

" 1st. To protect every religious denomination in the peaceable enjoyment of its own mode of public worship. . . . There shall be no respect to the consciences or opinions of nullifidians or other sects of belief, by law, nor shall any rights of conscience they have be allowed as against the ' peaceable enjoyment of their own mode of public worship' by ' every re-religious denomination,' and the reason is because ' religion, morality, and knowledge ' are essential to good government.

" As another, and the last mode, which the Constitution enjoins on the Legislature to provide for reaching the desired end, it enacts, ' And '—mark the copulative conjunction—' to encourage schools and the means of instruction.'

" Both the State and religion grow out of the same element of the human soul, and they cannot therefore be separated or treated as one independent of the other. Hence, we shall find that religion of some sort was always a necessary adjunct of the State, furnishing both bonds and sanctions as pledges of its safety and perpetuity. And just in proportion as these bonds and sanctions were weak, growing out of the relative purity of the religion of the people, more or less force was necessary for government. But there never was a State that existed long without the bonds and sanction of some religion. The mistake of most governments has been that the State has allied itself with religion, has erected establishments with a view of producing uniformity of faith ;—an alliance which has been hurtful to both parties to it. But while the State and religion are thus inseparably connected with each other in their origin, and necessary to each other's existence and perpetuity, their objects, spheres, means, and ends are widely different.

" *Tenth.* If we should in any sense worship science, or art, or the collective wisdom of all ages, or the souls of our ancestors and of posterity, like Comte, or intellect like Buckle, or virtue like Bentham, or any other divinity, and make that worship the manifestation of our religious convictions, these resolutions would prohibit instruction therein, and emasculate the schools ; besides doing violence to some consciences.

" It appears from a careful survey of the character

and spirit of the Constitutional provisions we have been examining, and of the legislation in pursuance thereof, that it must be true for the purposes of the State that Christianity, not in the sense of ecclesiasticism, is the prevailing religion in the State. . . . The framers of the Constitution felt that the moral sense must necessarily be regulated and controlled by the religious belief; and that whatever was opposed to religious belief, estimated by a Christian standard, and taking into consideration the welfare of the State, would be in the highest degree opposed to the general public sense, and have a direct tendency to undermine the moral support of the laws and corrupt the community. . . . It is not claimed anywhere that the Holy Bible does not impress on the children of the common schools the principles and duties of morality and justice and a sacred regard for truth, love of country, humanity, universal benevolence, sobriety, industry, chastity, moderation, temperance, and all other virtues, which are the ornaments of human society. . . . Nor is it claimed seriously that the Bible is adverse in any translation to any of these virtues as proper to be inculcated. On the contrary, its sublime morality furnishes those teachings best fitted to develop the morals and promote the virtues that strengthen and adorn both social and public life. In any view we can take of these resolutions, in this case, they are unconstitutional and void."

Upon the plea made by the counsel for the defence that the Bible containing the New Testament was to the Jew, and King James's version read without note or comment was to the Roman Catholic, a sectarian book, and that its use in the public schools was a violation of the Constitution which provides that " No preference shall be given by law to any religious society," and that "No religious or other sect or sects shall ever have any exclusive right to, or control of, any part of the school funds of this State," Judge Storer in his opinion said : "The whole argument that seems to us reaches the real question before us is predicated upon the supposition that the Bible is a volume whose teachings lead to sectarianism, and which ought not therefore to remain in the schools. We do not admit the assertion, either in whole or in part. What we understand by sectarianism is the work of man, not of the Almighty. . . . We marvel not that the admixtures and devices of men have obscured revelation when scarcely a week passes by without the annunciation of some new annotation or analysis or the defence of some peculiar dogma. All these we admit tend to the same result, which is necessarily a devotion to a sect. But we cannot admit that the Bible necessarily induces any such consequences. If it is candidly examined, studied without preconceived prejudice, its truths admitted to the test of enlightened conscience, we doubt not the answer always will be, as it ever has been, the acknowledgment of its sacred character and a veneration for its truthfulness. . . . The Catholic does not deny the inspiration of the Scriptures, but does not admit the accuracy of what is called King James's version. Yet, with comparatively few exceptions, the omission of the Apocryphal Books and the rendering of some peculiar passages, we do not suppose there is any essential difference between the versions. . . . It is urged, however, that the conscience of the Catholic parent cannot permit the ordinary version to be read as an exercise, as no religious teaching is permitted by his Church unless it is

directed by the clergy or authorized by the Church itself, and it is therefore offensive to the moral sense of
those who are compelled to listen when any portion of
the Bible is read ; but the rule has long since been
abolished requiring children to be present, or to read
from the version now in use, if it should be the expressed wish of the parents first communicated to
the teachers. . . . But is it consistent with this
claim of counsel that, even if the Bible should be prohibited, Catholic children would not attend the common
schools unless subject to the teachings of their spiritual
guides. The schools have been denominated godless,
while the Scriptures are yet read as a daily exercise.
What must they become, and what will they be termed,
when the Scriptures are forbidden ? What appears to us
to underlie this view of the case is the alleged injustice
that Catholic parents, in common with other property-
holders, should be taxed for the support of schools that
are independent of the control of the church, and consequently opposed to its whole economy. This has
been pressed in argument, though no one of the counsel for the plaintiffs or defendants have intimated there
should be a division of the school fund. With the justice or injustice, therefore, of the mode of taxation we
have nothing to do in deciding the questions submitted
to us. If the point should ever arise, we trust we shall
attentively consider all the objections that may be raised
to the present organization of the schools ; but it furnishes no ground of argument against the reading of
the Bible that the taxes for the support of the schools
are not equally assessed or properly distributed. . . .
If then, ' no religious test,' to use the language of
the Bill of Rights, is required of teacher or scholar, if
no act of worship in a sectarian sense is performed, if

no sectarian or denominational teaching is introduced, and even the possibility of either is prevented by the resolution long since promulgated, that those who desire may be exempted from the general rule, we cannot see how the defendants can justify the exclusion from the schools of what has been permitted there for nearly half a century without rebuke. . . . We are satisfied, . . . that the resolutions prohibiting the Bible and all religious instruction are *ultra vires*, and therefore void. . . . While we hold that every form of religious worship is to be alike protected by law, and the conscience of every man cannot be questioned, while the broad shield of the Constitution is over all citizens without distinction of race or sect, we cannot ignore the right of the petitioners for the relief they have sought ; nor can we with our views of legal duty sustain the action of the defendants.

" A majority of the court are of this opinion, and a perpetual injunction will therefore be decreed, as prayed for in the petition." [1]

[1] This decision was reversed by the Supreme Court of Ohio upon the ground that the mandate of the Constitution (quoted above by Judge Hagans) applied to the Legislature alone, and that the Legislature had taken no action in the matter further than to establish a common-school system and to commit the management and control of it exclusively to Directors, Trustees, or Boards of Education.

The Court said, *inter al. :* " It is claimed in behalf of the defendants in error (1) that these provisions of the Constitution require and enjoin religious instructions, or the teaching of religious doctrines, in the public schools, irrespective of the wishes of the people concerned therein ; and (2) that this requirement and injunction rests, not upon the legislature alone, but, in the absence of legislation for that purpose, is a law of the State *proprio rigore,* binding upon courts and people.

" If it is not conceded, it must be conceded that the legislature

In the case of Weiss *et al. v.* District Board of School District No. 8, of the City of Edgerton, the Superior Court of Wisconsin, March 18, 1890, gave a decision, which was unanimous, and of which the following is the authorized summary, viz.:

"1. In a petition for a writ of mandamus to compel the discontinuance of Bible reading in the common

have never passed any law enjoining or requiring religious instructions in the public schools, or giving the courts power in any manner, or to any extent, to direct or determine the particular branches of learning to be taught therein, or to enforce instructions in any particular branch or branches. . . .

" There is a total absence, therefore, of any legislation looking to the enforcement of religious instruction in the reading of religious books in the public schools ; and we are brought back to the question, What is the true meaning and effect of these Constitutional provisions on this subject ? Do they enjoin religious instructions in the schools, and does this injunction bind the courts, in the absence of legislation ? We are unanimously of the opinion that both of these questions must be answered in the negative. . . .

" Equally plain is it that if the supposed injunction to provide for religious instructions is to be found in the clause of the Constitution in question, it is one that rests exclusively upon the legislature. In both sections the duty is expressly imposed on ' the general assembly.' The injunction is to ' pass suitable laws.' Until these ' laws ' are passed it is quite clear to us that the courts have no power to interpose. The courts can only execute the laws when passed. They cannot compel the general assembly to pass them." 23 Ohio, N. S., 211. Dec., 1872.

The question still remains whether, if the Legislature had passed laws enjoining or authorizing any form of religious instruction or exercise in the public schools, this Court would hold those laws to be constitutional. From the tenor of a disquisition at the conclusion of the decision we infer that it would not do so.

schools, averments that petitioners are taxed for the support of the schools and are equally entitled to the benefit thereof, and that the reading of the Bible therein is contrary to the rights of conscience, and is sectarian instruction, such as is prohibited by Constitution, Wisconsin, Art. 10, S. 3, are sufficiently broad to cover every valid objection that may be made to such readings.

"2. Averments, in answer to such petition, that the reading of the Bible in the schools is not sectarian instruction, and that there is no material difference between the King James version used in the schools and the Douay version, are not admitted by demurrer; the former being a conclusion of law, and the latter not well pleaded because against common knowledge.

"3. The 'sectarian instruction,' prohibited in the common schools by Constitution, Wisconsin, Art. 10, S. 3, is instruction in the doctrines held by one or other of the various religious sects and not by the rest; and hence the reading of the Bible in such schools comes within the prohibition, since each sect, with few exceptions, bases its peculiar doctrines upon some portion of the Bible, the reading of which tends to inculcate those doctrines.

"4. The practice of reading the Bible in such schools can receive no sanction from the fact that pupils are not compelled to remain in the school while it is being read, for the withdrawal of a portion of them at such time would tend to destroy the equality and uniformity of treatment of the pupils, sought to be established and protected by the Constitution.

"5. The reading of the Bible is an act of worship, as that term is used in the Constitution, and hence the tax-payers in any district who are compelled to

18

contribute to the erection and support of common schools, have the right to object to the reading of the Bible therein, under Constitution, Wisconsin, Art. 1., S. 18, cl. 2, declaring that "No man shall be compelled . . . to erect or support any place of worship."

"6. As the reading the Bible at stated times in a common school is religious instruction, the money drawn from the State treasury for the support of such school is "for the benefit of a religious seminary" within the meaning of Constitution, Wisconsin, Art. 1., S. 18, cl. 4, prohibiting such an appropriation of the funds of the State."

Lyon, J., in giving his opinion said :

"II. In considering whether such reading of the Bible is sectarian instruction the book will be regarded as a whole, because the whole Bible without exception has been designated as a text-book for use in the Edgerton schools. . . .

"III. The courts will take judicial notice of the contents of the Bible, that the religious world is divided into numerous sects, and the general doctrines maintained by each sect. . . . Thus they will take cognizance without averment of the facts that there are numerous religious sects called 'Christians,' respectively maintaining different and conflicting doctrines ; that some of these believe the doctrine of predestination, while others do not ; some, the doctrine of eternal punishment of the wicked, while others repudiate it ; some, the doctrines of the apostolic succession and the authority of the priesthood, while others reject both ; some, that the holy Scriptures are the only sufficient rule of faith and practice, while others believe that the only safe guide to human thought, opinion, and action is the illuminating power of the Divine Spirit upon the

humble and devout heart ; some, in the necessity and
efficacy of the sacraments of the church, while others
reject them entirely ; and some, in the literal truth of
the Scriptures, while others believe them to be allegori-
cal, teaching spiritual truth alone, or chiefly.   .   .   .

" V. . . . The question therefore seems narrowed
down to this : Is the reading of the Bible in the
schools—not merely selected passages therefrom, but
the whole of it--sectarian instruction of the pupils?
In view of the fact already mentioned, that the Bible
contains numerous doctrinal passages upon some of
which the peculiar creed of almost every religious sect
is based, and that such passages may reasonably be
understood to inculcate the doctrines predicated upon
them, an affirmative answer to the question seems unavoidable.   Any pupil of ordinary intelligence who
listens to the reading of the doctrinal portions of the
Bible will be, more or less, instructed thereby in the
doctrines of the divinity of Jesus Christ, the eternal
punishment of the wicked, the authority of the priesthood, the binding force and efficacy of the sacraments,
and many other conflicting sectarian doctrines.   .   .   .

" It should be observed, in this connection, that the
above views do not, as counsel seemed to think they
may, banish from the district schools such text-books
as are founded upon the fundamental teachings of the
Bible, or which contain extracts therefrom.   Such
teachings and extracts pervade and ornament our secular literature, and are important elements in its value
and usefulness.   Such text-books are in the schools
for secular instruction, and rightly so ; and the Constitutional prohibition of sectarian instruction does not
include them, even though they may contain passages
from which some inference of sectarian doctrine might

possibly be drawn. Furthermore, there is much in the Bible which cannot justly be characterized as sectarian. There can be no valid objection to the use of such matter in the secular instruction of the pupils. Much of it has great historical and literary value, which may be thus utilized without violating the Constitutional prohibition. It may also be used to inculcate good morals; that is, our duty to each other, which may and ought to be inculcated by the district schools. No more complete code of morals exists than is contained in the New Testament, which re-affirms and emphasizes the obligations laid down in the ten commandments. Concerning the fundamental principles of moral ethics the religious sects do not disagree. . . .

"XI. The drift of some remarks in the argument of counsel for the respondent, and perhaps also in the opinion of Judge Bennett, is that the exclusion of Bible reading from the district schools is derogatory to the value of the holy Scriptures, a blow to their influence upon the conduct and consciences of men, and disastrous to the cause of religion. We most emphatically reject these views. The priceless truths of the Bible are best taught to our youth in the church, the Sabbath and parochial schools, the social religious meetings, and above all by parents in the home circle. There, these truths may be explained and enforced, the spiritual welfare of the child guarded and protected, and his spiritual nature directed and cultivated in accordance with the dictates of the parental conscience. The Constitution does not interfere with such teaching and culture. It only banishes theological polemics from the schools. It does this, not because of any hostility to religion, but because the people who adopted it believed that the public good would thereby be promoted, and they so declared in the preamble. Religion teaches obedience to law, and flourishes best where good government prevails. The Constitutional prohibition was adopted in the interests of good government, and it argues but little faith in the vitality and power of religion to predict disaster to its progress because a Constitutional provision, enacted for such a purpose, is faithfully executed.''

Orton, J., said : ''As the State can have nothing to do with religion except to protect every one in the enjoyment of his own, so the common schools can have nothing to do with religion in any respect whatever. They are as completely secular as any other institutions of the State, in which all the people alike have equal rights and privileges. The people cannot be taxed for religion in schools more than anywhere else. . . . The clause ' No sectarian instruction shall be allowed therein,' was inserted *ex industria* to exclude everything pertaining to religion. They are called by those who wish to have not only religion, but their own religion taught therein, ' Godless schools.' They are Godless and the educational department of the government is Godless, in the same sense that executive, legislative, and administrative departments are Godless. So long as our Constitution remains as it is, no one religion can be taught in our common schools. . . . There is no such source and cause of strife, quarrels, fights, malignant oppositions, persecutions, and war, and all evils in the State, as religion. Let it once enter into our civil affairs, our government would soon be destroyed. Let it once enter into our common schools, they would be destroyed. Those who made our Constitution saw this, and used the most apt and comprehensive language in it to prevent such a catastrophy." [1]

The Constitution of Wisconsin might very well have prohibited *partisan* instruction also in the public schools, for partisanship is as prominent a feature of our social life as sectarianism. The partisan publications, daily and weekly, read by the people of that State, it is safe to say, outnumber the sectarian publications in the proportion of a hundred to one ; and while the religious discourses outnumber the political addresses delivered, yet it cannot be denied that an immensely large proportion of the former dwell upon themes on which all Christians are agreed, and are not sectarian, while every one of the latter is intensely partisan. Such a prohibition no doubt would have been placed in the Constitution had the convention that framed it been perfectly free from a very prevalent bias. The words of Justice Orton in this decision, "There is no such source and cause of strife, quarrels, fights, malignant oppositions, persecution and war, and all evils in the State, as religion," reveal an excessive fear of the Christian religion which can hardly be attributed to anything else than a bias in favor of an ill-digested and tacitly assumed anti-Christian theory of our civil institutions,—a bias which seems to avail itself of every opportunity to establish that theory. Supposing that the Constitution of Wisconsin had prohibited *partisan* as well as sectarian instruction ; would this court have adjudged the Constitution of the United States to be a partisan document? Would it have given as the ground of this opinion the fact that there are now over one hundred volumes of decisions upon conflicting claims, based upon different views of the meaning of that

[1] *The N. W. Reporter*, vol. 44, pp., 967–982.

document ; that almost from the beginning two great political parties have been in contention as to the construction to be put upon it ; that every Congress has debated its meaning ; and that a great war grew out of conflicting interpretations of it ?

And, further, had the Constitution of the United States been written in a dead language ; were there now in common use two versions of it ; both derived from a received text, the one a translation into the vernacular, the other a translation into another dead language and re-translated into the vernacular ; the two differing only as such translations might be expected to differ ; and did the political leaders of a small minority, say one tenth of the population, lay it down as one of the doctrines of their party that the common people were incompetent to form any correct opinions of the meaning of the Constitution, and therefore were not to read it or hear it read, but were to accept implicitly the interpretations of it promulgated by the Supreme Court of the United States, and to receive those interpretations only from persons who had been regularly admitted to the Bar ; would this court hold that both of these versions were partisan documents ; that the reading of either of them in the public schools even without note or comment would be partisan instruction, and that such reading was therefore prohibited by the Constitution of the State ?

Any one will be able to see that, by the subtle potency of the definition of partisan instruction here given, the partisan tenet of a small minority is put in operation as the law of the State. The tenet of the majority is rejected, and that majority is compelled to pay taxes for the purpose of establishing the tenet of the minority in the administration of the public schools. A decision

having such an effect ought to be based upon a definition of partisan instruction less obviously defective than
the one here given. It is little wonder that the Supreme Court of a neighboring State declined to recognize the validity of the principles laid down in this
decision.

James H. Nichols *v.* The School Directors. Appeal
from the Circuit Court of Livingston County, Illinois.
Bill for an injunction by complainant as a citizen, tax-
payer, and freeholder of the school district, to restrain
the directors from allowing the school-house of that district to be used by any society or organization for the
purpose of a religious meeting-house.

The Supreme Court of Illinois, September, 1879, said,
Mr. Justice Sheldon delivering the opinion of the court,
Hon. N. J. Pillsbury (Judge) presiding :

"The grievance as set forth in the bill is that the
defendants have as such directors given permission to
different church organizations to hold religious services
in the school-house against the protest of complainant
and other tax-payers of the district ; that under this
permission some of the church organizations purpose
holding stated meetings in the school-house ; that by
this means complainant is compelled to aid in furnishing
a house of worship for religious meetings contrary to
the law of the land ; that he is opposed to such use of
the house by the societies, and that such meetings are
about to be held in the same contrary to his wishes.

"*Statute.* '. . . and who may grant the temporary
use of school-houses, when not occupied for schools, for
religious meetings and Sunday-schools, for evening
schools and for literary societies, and for such other
meetings as the directors may deem proper.' [1]

[1] *Revised Statutes,* 1874, p. 958, S. 39.

" There is clearly sufficient warrant in the statute, if that be valid, for the action of the school directors. But the statute is assailed as being unconstitutional. The clauses which are pointed out as being supposed to be violated by this statute are the following only :

' Art. II., S. 3. No person shall be required to attend or support any ministry or place of worship against his consent ; nor shall any preference be given by law to any religious denomination or mode of worship.'

" 'Art. VIII., S. 3. Forbidding among other public bodies, the General Assembly, or any school district, from ever making any appropriation or paying from any public fund whatever, anything in aid of any church or sectarian purpose, etc. ; and forbidding the State or any public corporation from making any grant or donation of land, money, or other personal property to any church, or for any sectarian purpose.'

" ' Art. VIII., S. 2. All land, moneys, or other property, donated, granted, or received for school, college, seminary or university purposes, and the proceeds thereof, shall be faithfully applied to the objects for which such gifts or grants were made.'

" The thing contemplated by the Constitutional provision first above named, was a prohibition upon the legislature to pass any law by which a person should be compelled without his consent to contribute to the support of any ministry or place of worship. Such a matter as the subject of complaint here, we do not regard as within its purview.

" Religion and religious worship are not so placed under the ban of the Constitution that they may not be allowed to become the recipient of any incidental benefit whatever from the public bodies or authorities of the State. That instrument itself contains a provision authorizing the legislature to exempt property used for religious purposes from taxation ; and, thereby, the same as is complained of here, there might be indirectly imposed upon the tax-payer the burden of increased taxation, and in that manner the indirect supporting of places of worship. In the respect of the possibility. of enhanced taxation therefrom, this provision of the Constitution itself is even more obnoxious to objection than this permission given by the school directors to hold religious meetings in the school-house. There is no pretence that it is in any way in interference with the occupation of the building for school purposes.

" We think the court rightly sustained the demurrer and dismissed the bill as making no case for an injunction. The decree is affirmed.[1] "

In the case of Donahue *v.* Richards *et al.*, 38 Maine, p. 376, suit had been brought by the father of Bridget Donahue against the superintending school committee of the town of Ellsworth, Me., for expelling her from school for a refusal to comply with the orders of her instructor to read in the common version of the Bible, designated in the report as the Protestant version ; such reading being a part of the general course of instruction, and this version being directed to be read in this course.

The nonsuit was confirmed on the ground that " In no case can a parent sustain an action for any wrong done to the child, unless he has incurred some direct pecuniary injury therefrom, in consequence of some loss of service, or expenses necessarily consequent thereupon." It was decided that for injury to the person, the reputation, or the property of the child, the suit must be brought in her own name. Whereupon action was brought by plaintiff who was fifteen years of age,

[1] 93 Illinois, 61.

through her father, as her *prochein ami*, against the superintending school committee, to recover damages for maliciously, wrongfully, and unjustifiably expelling her from one of the town schools in Ellsworth.

In this case, Donahue, *prochein ami, v.* Richards *et al.* 38 Maine, 379, Appleton, J., giving the decision, the Court said :

" The present suit is by the minor for the alleged wrongful exclusion from school in consequence of her refusal to read one of the books directed by the defendants, who are the superintending school committee of the town of Ellsworth, to be used in the school of which she was a member.

" The questions involved in the decision of this case are their liability, when acting in good faith in the discharge of their duty, to an action at the suit of the individual expelled, even if the exclusion was erroneous ; their powers as to the selection of the books to be used ; their legal right to expel a scholar in case of a refusal to read in a book by them prescribed ; the Constitutionality of a regulation by which the Bible, or any version of it, is designated as one of the books to be read.

" The defendants are public officers, discharging an important public trust, and in the exercise of this authority, necessarily clothed to a certain extent with judicial powers. In doing the act of which complaint is made, they were acting under the obligations of official duty and the sanctions of an oath. The plaintiff claims that when thus acting, and without malice or intentional wrong on their part, they can be held responsible in damages for an erroneous decision, an error in judgment, either as to the facts or as to the consequences rightly deducible from them. In fine, that they should be held liable if they erred in judgment in a matter submitted to their determination, and upon which they were bound to act. . . .

" Her claim to be exempt from a general regulation of the school rests entirely on her religious belief, and is to the extent that the choice of reading books shall be in *entire subordination to her faith, and because it is her faith.* . . . The preference [of a religious sect] is manifestly given, if in the selection to be made the defendants were bound to defer to the doctrines and authority and teachings of the sect of which she is a member. The right of negation is, in its operation, equivalent to that of proposing and establishing. The right of one sect to interdict or expurgate would place all schools in subordination to the sect interdicting or expurgating. If the claim is that the sect of which the child is a member has a right to interdict, and that any book is to be banished because under the ban of her church, then the preference is practically given to said church, and the very mischief complained of is inflicted on others. . . . If Locke and Bacon and Milton and Swift are to be stricken from the list of authors which may be read in the schools, because the authorities of one sect may have placed them among the list of heretical writers, whose work it neither permits to be printed, nor sold, nor read, then the right of sectarian interference in the selection of books is at once yielded, and no books are to be read to which it may not assent. . . . If one sect may object, the same right must be granted to others. This would give the authorities of every sect the right to annul any regulation of the constituted authorities of the State as to the course of study and the books to be read. It is placing the legislation of the State, at once and forever, in subordination to the decrees and the teachings of any and all sects when their members conscientiously believe such teachings. It at once surrenders the power of the State to a government not emanating from the people, nor recognized by the Constitution, . . . and the use of books would be made to depend not upon the judgment of those to whom the law entrusts their selection, but upon that of the authority of a Church ; so that each sect would have precedence, as a sect, and for that cause. . . . The claim so far as it may rest on conscience is a claim to annul any regulation of the State made by its constituted authorities. As a right existing on the part of one child it is equally a right belonging to all, . . . and thus, the power of selection of books is withdrawn from those to whom the law entrusts it, and by the right of negation is transferred to the scholars. The right, as claimed, undermines the power of the State. It is that the will of the majority shall bow to the conscience of the minority, or of one. . . ."

Mr. Foster North, a student of the University of Illinois, after nearly six years of acquiescence in the regulation requiring attendance upon chapel exercises, absented himself from those exercises.

On April 17, 1885, the Faculty, after having had conference with Mr. North and having entered upon its minutes that "He would be expected to comply with the regulations of the University as long as he remains a student therein," voted the following order, viz. :

" Case of F. North referred to Regent. If he claims conscientious scruples against attendance at chapel, he may be excused ; if not, he will be suspended."

On the 24th of April, Mr. North replied in writing, refusing the offer to be excused on account of the repugnance of the chapel exercises to his religious convictions, saying that he had "no religious convictions for the chapel exercises to be repugnant to"; and secondly, he took the ground that the Faculty had no right to make any regulation requiring students to attend chapel ; and that the act of formally expressing his wish not to attend would be a recognition of a right which he strenuously denied. Whereupon the following communication was addressed to him, viz.:

"ILLINOIS INDUSTRIAL UNIVERSITY,
"REGENT'S OFFICE,
"Urbana, Ill., April 30, 1885.
"MR. FOSTER NORTH,

"Dear Sir :—It is in evidence before the Faculty of this University that during most of the current term you have purposely absented yourself from the general assembly of the students, required daily of them by the regulations of this institution. You aver that you have not done this on account of any conscientious objections to any of the exercises there held, religious or other, but because you deny the authority of the Faculty to require your attendance there, so long as any part of the exercises are religious in form. You therefore deny the authority of the Faculty as now administered.

·"The Faculty cannot accept your view of the case or admit your propositions thereupon ; nor can they allow you to nullify their regulations. I am therefore directed to say to you that you are from this date suspended indefinitely from the University.

"S. H. PEABODY,
"*Regent.*

"By order of the Faculty."

Mr. North appealed to the Board of Trustees, a majority of whom sustained the action of the Faculty. The Board asked the advice of the Attorney-General of the State, Hon. George Hunt, their legal adviser, who gave an elaborate opinion sustaining the action of the Board.[1]

In 1890 Mr. North petitioned the Supreme Court of Illinois for a writ of mandamus against the Trustees of the University requiring them to reinstate him in the University.

Upon the hearing of this petition the Court said, Mr. Justice Wilkin delivering the opinion of the court :

". . . It certainly will not be insisted that the rule requiring students to attend chapel exercises is unreasonable or unlawful, as applied to those who are willing to obey it. The legality of the rule is questioned on the sole ground that it violates that clause of Section 3, Article II. of the Constitution of this State, which says, ' No person shall be required to attend or support any ministry or place of worship against his consent.' It is not pretended by the petitioner that the exercises at chapel meetings were sectarian, and therefore objectionable ; but the only objection to those exercises was, and is, that they were in part religious worship, within the meaning of the above-quoted language of the Constitution. In the view we take of the case that fact may be conceded. The real question on this branch of the case is, Was it a violation of that constitutional provision for respondents to adopt the rule, and require obedience thereto by those attending the University, unless excused therefrom ?

" There is certainly nothing in this section of our Con-

[1] *Report of the Board of Trustees of the University of Illinois to the Governor of Illinois*, 1886, pp. 39, 43, 62, 63, 66, 72.

stitution prohibiting this and like institutions of learning from adopting reasonable rules requiring their
students to attend chapel exercises of a religious nature,
and to use at least moral suasion and all argumentative
influences to induce obedience thereto. . . . Shall
a court say such a requirement is, in and of itself, a violation of said Constitutional provision, merely because
some one or more students attending the University *may*
object to obeying it? More especially should this be
done when, as is here shown by the answer, the rules
expressly provide that for good cause students may be
excused from obedience to the regulations. We have
said, in construing this section of the Constitution,
'Religion and religious worship are not so far placed
under the ban of the Constitution that they may not be
allowed to become the recipient of any incidental benefit whatever from the public bodies or authorities of the
state' (Nichols *v.* The School Directors, 93 Illinois, 61).
It may be said with greater reason that there is nothing
in that instrument so far discountenancing religious
worship that colleges and other institutions of learning
may not lawfully adopt all reasonable regulations for
the inculcation of moral and religious principles in
those attending them.

"We are clearly of the opinion that the rule is not
unlawful. At most it could only be fairly contended
that under said clause of the Constitution one so desiring it should for reasonable cause be excused from its
observance. The whole of said Section 3 being considered, it is clear that it is designed to protect the
citizen in the free exercise of his religious opinions,
and it should be liberally construed to that end.

"As we have seen, he was requested to base his application to be excused from attending chapel exercises

on the only reasonable ground that it could be based. He not only refused to do that, but according to the allegations of the answer, which he admits, refused to ask to be excused on any ground. His expulsion was the result of his own wrong. Neither the respondents or the Faculty have been guilty of a violation of law, or of doing any wrong.

" The authorities cited by counsel for the petitioner do not militate against this conclusion. The case of the State *ex rel.* Weiss *et al. v.* District No. 8, etc., decided by the Supreme Court of Wisconsin, in 1890, (*N. W. Reporter*, vol. xliv, p. 967) is much relied on as sustaining the petitioner's right to the writ. The case is wholly unlike this. The relators in that case were members of the Roman Catholic Church and tax-payers in the school district. Their children attending the school were also members of that church. The complaint was that, Bible reading in the school was exclusively from ' King James's Version,' and therefore sectarian instruction in violation of Section 3, Article X, of the Constitution of that State, which ordains that ' No sectarian instruction shall be allowed in the district schools of this State.' Lyon, J., who wrote the principal opinion in the case, confines his discussion and decision to that question only, and as we read the petition that was the only Constitutional question raised by it. In the concurring opinions filed by Casody and Orton, J. J., there is a discussion of the questions as to whether or not such Bible reading, as alleged in the petition, was a violation of the rights of conscience, and amounted to compelling the relators to aid in the support of a place of worship against their consent, within the prohibition of other sections of that Constitution.

19

"It is manifest all that is said in that case could not be approved by this court consistently with our former decisions, as is there expressly recognized ; but, if it could, still it would by no means follow that a peremptory writ should be issued in this case. None of the questions there decided are necessarily involved here.

"We are clearly of the opinion that there is no sufficient ground here shown to authorize the ordering of the peremptory writ of mandamus, and it is therefore denied." [1]

CHAPTER VIII.

FULL LIBERTY.

THE government should allow full liberty of belief and unbelief, and the largest liberty of action to the believer and unbeliever alike, which is consistent with justice and the good order of society.

It will happen that Christian considerations will enter into some of the legislation of the State, and that certain Christian observances will be established by law,—an inevitable result where the people are almost wholly Christian, as we have shown, but in all these cases the State should show its Christian character, first of all, in not usurping the place of God, and assuming the right to coerce the consciences of men. It should show its confidence in the truth by not desiring to employ against those who deny the truth any other force than the force of truth itself. The State, Christian though it be, should not compel any man to

[1] North *v.* Board of Trustees of the University of Illinois, 27 *N. E. Rep.*, 54, March 1891.

act contrary to his convictions ; nor should it impose
any coercive disabilities upon any man for refusing so
to act.   It should not require the Quaker or the atheist
to take an oath ; nor should it exclude either from the
witness stand, or from office, on account of his refusal
to take an oath.   It has appointed the Lord's day as a
day of rest.   It should not require of the unbeliever,
the Jew, or the Christian Sabbatarian, any observance of that day which would imply on his part that
he was observing it as a Christian duty, or for the
Christian reason of the appointment.   It should require
of these citizens only that they abstain from all acts on
that day which would offend the sensibilities of Christian people, disturb them in their worship, or disturb
the good order of society.   Any prohibitions or penalties
laid upon them for the non-observance of the day ought
to be based on these reasons, and on these alone.
Were a man alone in the depths of a forest, the State
ought not to punish him for felling trees, or hunting,
or fishing, on the first day of the week.   Were there
a company of persons away by themselves in such a
solitude, and did they choose to divert themselves on
that day with the game of base-ball, or with the music
of a brass band, or with a dramatic performance, it ought
not to punish them for so doing ; but it might prohibit
all such diversions where they would offend the sensibilities of Christian people or disturb them in what
they regard as the proper use of the day.   This difference in action on the part of the State would imply
and would be based upon a just discrimination in principle.   While establishing a Christian ordinance, and
establishing it as such, it would not be requiring the
unbeliever to observe it as Christian, or for the Christian reasons, upon which the observance is based.

The old laws upon the observance of Sunday, which
are still in force in most of the older States, go further
than this ; but the later jurists, and a few of the States
in their legislation, and in the decisions of their courts,
have adopted the principle of discrimination we have
been setting forth.[1] To this extent the regulations of
the State ought to be governed by a respect for the
personal liberty and the feelings of the unbeliever.

CHAPTER IX.

UNTENABLE THEORIES.

THE abstaining of the government from the propagation of Christianity, and from the enforcement upon
the unbeliever of the observance of a legally established Christian ordinance, as a religious duty, or for
the Christian reasons upon which the ordinance is based

---

[1] The older States, in framing their Sunday laws, have followed the old English statute, which prohibited the doing or exercising of any worldly labor, business, or work, on the Lord's
day, works of necessity and charity excepted. Under these
laws a great number and variety of questions have been brought
to the courts for decision, such as the validity of contracts and
promissory notes, made on Sunday ; damages for injuries received upon public highways, and from public carriers, by accident in travelling on Sunday, or for failure of a public carrier to
transport perishable freight on Sunday. One or two cases may
serve as examples of the decisions rendered under this form of
the statute.

Michael Connelly, in passing over Dover Street, Boston, at
nine o'clock Sunday night, Oct. 6, 1872, walked off an open
drawbridge, which was not protected by any guard or barrier.
Upon suit for damages, the court decided that " One who works
by night, instead of by day, and who travels on Sunday, for the

does not work a divestiture of all Christian character, and does not remove all Christian basis from its regulations. That such a divestiture has somehow been made is coming to be a general impression. Even Christian jurists, and also courts, which cannot be charged with any prejudice against Christianity, have made affirmations which seem to imply it. The natural history of this impression can easily be made out.

In the first place, almost any one, upon finding that these two propositions must be accepted : *(a)* That it is not the proper function of the government to inculcate, propagate, or foster Christianity : *(b)* That full liberty of conscience is to be guaranteed to the believer and unbeliever alike, and finding that the regulations prescribed for the observance of a Christian ordinance, established by law, are such as not to imply on the part of the unbeliever observance as a Christian duty

purpose of seeing his master and inducing him to change his hours of labor from night to the day, in order that he may sleep better is not travelling from necessity or charity, and cannot maintain an action, against the town, for an injury sustained by him, while so travelling, by reason of a defect in the highway which the town is by the law obliged to keep in repair." Connelly *v.* City of Boston, 117 Mass., 64. Jan., 1875.

"One who travels on Sunday, to ascertain whether a house he has hired, and into which he intends to move the next day, has been cleaned, is not travelling from necessity or charity, and cannot maintain an action, for injury sustained at a railroad crossing, through the negligence of the servants of the railroad corporation." Smith *v.* Boston & Maine R. R., 120 Mass., 490. Sept., 1876.

Mr. Geo. E. Harris, of the Washington, D. C., Bar, has made a classification and a brief digest of the decisions upon the Sunday laws in the United States, filling an octavo volume of over three hundred pages. Published by The Lawyers Co-operative Pub. Co., Rochester, N. Y., 1892.

or for Christian reason thereof; would be led to suppose that the government, if Christian at all, is so only in name. Hence we think it is that we find in the latest writings of some jurists and in the recent decisions of some of the courts, affirmations that our civil government is Christian, but connected with these affirmations, others which imply that it is so in nothing but the name. Hence also the growing tendency to give up the name. If it be Christain only in name, that were better given up, for an empty name is a pretence that there is something where there is nothing.

In the second place, co-operating with this cause of the impression, there may be a visionary theory of the ideal government,—the theory that in such a government there would be no trace of a religious character, as in an ideal church there would be no trace of a secular character. A person of an ingenuous mind can hardly help believing that the ideal ought to be realized, and he would very naturally take the progress which has been made in the enlargement of the boundaries of personal liberty as having for its end the realization of that ideal. But if the correctness of the ideal should be conceded, as a matter of theory, yet it would be true in this case, as in all others, that the realization of the ideal is impossible in this world. That ideal would be like the point, the line, and the surface in mathematics; available for abstract processes but impossible of realization in material things. It would be in politics, analogous to Sir William Thomson's theory of matter in physics, that it is " the rotating portions of a perfect fluid, which continuously fills space," a beautiful theory as an abstraction, but liable to this practical objection that a perfect fluid, one that is absolutely without viscosity, and free from internal friction, cannot be conceived of as existing. So in this case, the ideal State cannot exist or even be conceived of as existing. It would be, in the nature of things, impossible, as we have shown, to keep the religion of a people from entering into their civil institutions. This ideal, as such, may be a harmless fancy, but to attempt to carry it out in the practical affairs of the world would be injurious, as it is always injurious to attempt to conduct the affairs of life upon an impossible hypothesis.

Whatever may be the natural history of the impression in question, there can be no doubt that it is becoming prevalent among writers of eminence ; and that some of our courts, or rather, perhaps, some of our legislatures, for the courts have been governed generally in their decisions by the letter and intent of the statutes, have shown a disposition to establish it in the law of the land.

The Rev. M. B. Anderson, D. D., in a paper read before the Social Science Association, at Saratoga Springs, September, 1879, on the *Relations of Christianity to the Common Law*, and published in the Albany *Law Journal* of October 4th and 11th of that year, says : "The common law has taken account of Christianity as a positive system for the purpose of punishing blasphemy and malicious ridicule of Christian doctrines and rites. The common law has recognized these as *crimes* against the *State*, and not as *sins* against *God*. It has regarded them in the light of moral nuisances, against which the believers in Christianity have a right to be protected. . . . That portion of the common law which makes blasphemy, Sunday desecration, the disturbance of religious assemblies, indictable offences, seems naturally to fall into the class of laws which provides for the community protection against nuisances whether physical or moral in their nature."

Judge Cooley, in his *Constitutional Limitations* (pp. 588, 589), says : "It is frequently said that Christianity is part of the law of the land. In a certain sense and for certain purposes this is true. The best features of the common law, and especially those which regard the family and social relations, which compel the parent to support the child, the husband to support the wife ; which makes the marriage tie permanent and forbids polygamy ; if not derived from, have at least been improved and strengthened by the prevailing religion and the teachings of its sacred book. But the law does not attempt to enforce the precepts of Christianity on the ground of their sacred character or divine origin. . . . Christianity is not a part of the law of the land in any sense which entitles the courts to take notice of and base their judgments upon it, except so far as they can find that its precepts and principles have been incorporated in and made a component part of the positive law of the State."

He questions the correctness of Justice Story's statement in the Girard will case, that Christianity is a part of the common law in the sense that "its divine origin and truth are admitted, and therefore that it is not to be maliciously and openly reviled and blasphemed against to the annoyance of believers or to the injury of the public," saying, "it may be doubted, however, if the punishment of blasphemy is based necessarily upon an admission of the divine origin or truth of the Christian religion, or incapable of being otherwise justified." He shows that the punishment of blasphemy is capable of being otherwise justified. He says : "Blasphemy has been defined as consisting in speak-

ing evil of the Deity, with an impious purpose to
derogate from the Divine majesty and to alienate the
minds of others from the love and reverence of God.
It is purposely using words concerning the Supreme
Being calculated and designed to impair and destroy
the reverence, respect, and confidence due him, as the
intelligent Creator, Governor, and Judge of the world.
It embraces the idea of detraction as regards the character and attributes of God, as calumny usually carries the same idea when applied to an individual. It
is a wilful and malicious attempt to lessen men's reverence of God by denying his existence or his attributes as an intelligent Creator, Governor, and Judge
of men, and to prevent their having confidence in him
as such. Contumelious reproaches and profane ridicule of Christ or of the Holy Scriptures have the same
evil effect in sapping the foundations of society and
of public order, and are classed under the same head "
(pp. 589,590).

His objection to Justice Story's statement seems to be
that the common law cannot properly admit the divine
origin and truth of the Christian religion, nor base any
action on the admission. It is clear enough that blasphemy may be punished as sapping the foundations of
public order, so long as the people believe in the divine
origin and truth of Christianity. It is not so clear how
it can be punished as sapping the foundations of *society*,
unless the divine origin and truth of Christianity be
admitted. In the one case, only the fact that such is
the belief of the people is admitted. In the other, that
belief is admitted to be true. Upon the question, what
the decision of a court, under the statute and common
law, ought to be, we should be very far from setting up
an opinion of our own, against that of one who is prob-

ably the most eminent living jurist in the land; but our question is, what ought the statute to be; would a statute, having a positive Christian character, be fundamentally wrong; and would the courts be bound to declare it so to be. Upon this question, we flatter ourselves that we shall be in agreement with Judge Cooley. He says: "But while thus careful to protect and defend religious freedom and equality, the American Constitutions contain no provisions which prohibit the authorities from such solemn recognition of a superintending Providence, in public transactions and exercises, as the general religious sentiment of mankind inspires, and as seems meet and proper in finite and dependent beings. Whatever may be the shades of religious belief, all must acknowledge the fitness of recognizing, in important human affairs, the superintending care and control of the great Governor of the Universe; and of acknowledging, with thanksgiving, his boundless favors or bowing in contrition when visited with the penalties of his broken laws. No principal of Constitutional law is violated, when thanksgiving or fast days are appointed; when chaplains are designated for the army and navy; when legislative sessions are opened with prayer or the reading of the Scriptures; or when religious teaching is encouraged, by a general exemption of houses of religious worship from taxation for the support of the State government."

He goes on, however, to say that "This public recognition of religious worship, however, is not based entirely, perhaps not even mainly, upon a sense of what is due to the Supreme Being himself, as the author of all good, and of all law; but the same reason of State policy, which induces the government to aid institutions of charity and seminaries of instruction, will incline it

also to foster religious worship and religious institutions, as conservators of public morals, and valuable,
if not indispensable, assistants in the preservation of
the public order." [1]

It is very plain that he regards the public recognition
of religious worship, in the particular acts he has mentioned, as based in part upon a sense of what is due the
Supreme Being ; that is, upon a purely religious consideration, his only question being, whether it is entirely,
or even mainly, so based. This being conceded, it is
difficult to see how the government can be justified in
basing an action upon "the general religious sentiments of mankind," or upon a recognition of the truth
of bare theism, and not be justified in basing an action
on the general Christian sentiment of the people, or
upon a recognition of the truth of Christianity ; for the
ground of the justification, in the latter case, is pre-
cisely the same that it is in the former ; and, although
not so extensive, yet is so ample, that if accepted as a
sufficient basis of action in the one case, it cannot be
rejected as insufficient in the other. Now if it is not a
violation of any principle of Constitutional law for one
department of the government—the executive—to base
an action upon the assumption of the truth of the
Christian religion, or of the fact that the people believe
it to be true, it cannot be a violation of any such principle for the other departments of the government—the
legislative and judicial—to do so. Whether with or
without statute, therefore, the government is positively
Christian. It may, in all its departments, base an action on purely Christian reasons. Not only may it do
so, but there are cases, as we shall presently show, in
which it cannot help doing so.

[1] *Ibid.*, pp. 587, 588.

CHAPTER X.

SUNDAY LAWS, OPINIONS OF THE COURTS.

THE older statutes and the present statutes of the older States prohibit all sport, worldly labor, work, or business, excepting works of necessity and mercy, on the Lord's Day ; thus being based in part upon the consideration of the sanctity of the day. Some of the newer statutes are so framed as to exclude that consideration entirely, and recognize only the secular basis of the law ; for example, the statute of Illinois on Sunday is as follows, viz.:

"261. Whoever disturbs the peace and good order of society by labor (works of necessity and charity excepted) or by any amusement, or diversion, on Sunday, shall be fined not exceeding $25.

"262. Whoever shall be guilty of any noise, rout, or amusement, on the first day of the week, called Sunday, whereby the peace of any private family may be disturbed, shall be fined not exceeding $25."

Under such a statute any acts, not otherwise prohibited, will be allowable which do not disturb the peace and good order of society, or the peace of a private family. Contracts and notes made on Sunday will be valid.

The Supreme Court of Illinois in the case of Richmond *v.* Moore, 107 Freeman, p. 429, October, 1883, Walker delivering the opinion, affirmed the validity of a contract made on Sunday. Moore having engaged Richmond to sail the vessel *Scotia* during the season of 1880, and having prevented Richmond from fulfilling the contract, the latter brought suit for damages. Moore pleaded in defence that the contract having been made on Sunday was void. The Court said : " . . . The common law does not prohibit contracts on Sunday. This is the doctrine of all decisions of English and American courts, with not more than one or two exceptions. The doctrine that contracts made on Sunday are void depends therefore alone on statutory enactments. And in the various States of the Union the statutes vary in language or substance, and the decisions of different courts have been based on the phraseology of their several statutes. The common law, on the other hand, seems always to have prohibited all judicial decisions on Sunday. The 29 Charles 11, C. 7, p. 257, seems to be the basis of the enactments of the various States of the Union. It is this : ' That no tradesman, artificer, workman, laborer, or other person, whatsoever, shall do or exercise any worldly labor, business, or work on the Lord's day.' It contains exceptions, of which are works of necessity and charity. A mere glance at that and our statute will show that they are materially different. That prohibits labor and *business* ; ours only prohibits labor or amusement that disturbs the peace and good order of society. . . . The British statute makes the mere act of labor or business penal. . . . Our statute by its very terms is for the preservation of the peace and good order of society from disturbance. It is not, nor can it be held to be, the purpose of the statute to compel the performance of a religious duty, however necessary to the future welfare of the individual failing to perform it. The object of the statute is to protect persons, keeping the Christian Sabbath as a day of holiness, from disturbance in that observance, and not to compel the performance of a religious duty, as such. That is no part of governmental duty under our statutes. The spiritual welfare of our people is left entirely to the hierarchy of the various churches. The government protects all alike in their religious beliefs and unbelief. It is no part of the function of our government to prescribe and enforce religious tenets. The great purpose of the formation of our system of government is to protect the people in the enjoyment of their temporal and spiritual rights, and to prohibit crime, vice, and wrong, to any portion of the community ; and to pass and enforce laws for the promotion of the temporal interests of the people, and as far as possible secure their temporal welfare and happiness. Although it is no part of the functions of our government to propagate religion and to enforce its tenets, when the great body of the people are Christians in fact or sentiment, our laws and our institutions must necessarily be based upon and embody the teachings of the Redeemer of mankind. It is impossible that it should be otherwise. And in this sense and to this extent our civilization and our institutions are emphatically Christian ; but not for the purpose of compelling men to embrace particular doctrines or creeds of any church, or to support one or another denomination by public burdens ; but simply to afford protection to all in the enjoyment of their belief or unbelief. It may be that in suppressing crime, vice, and immorality it may incidentally enforce religious doctrines. The Christian religion forbids all crime, vice, and immorality, and good government equally requires their suppression. They are suppressed by the government because required for the general welfare ; not because they are religious doctrines.''

The Supreme Court of Ohio in the case of Bloom *v.* Richards, 2, Ohio State Reports, 38, December, 1853, A. G. Thurman delivering the opinion, after noticing

the fact that Christianity was part of the common law
of England, said : " But the Constitution of Ohio having declared that ' All men have a natural and inde-
feasible right to worship Almighty God according to
the dictates of conscience,' . . . it follows that
neither Christianity, nor any other system of religion,
is a part of the law of this State. We have no union
of Church and State, nor has our government ever been
vested with authority to enforce any religious observance simply because it is religious. . . . We are
to regard the statute under consideration as a mere municipal or police regulation whose validity is neither
strengthened or weakened by the fact that the day it
enjoins is the Sabbath day."

In McGatrick *v.* Wasson, 4 Ohio State Reports, 571,
572, the same court two years later said, by the same
justice : " . . . But was it a work of necessity
[Shipping cargo on Sunday when navigation was about
to close] within the meaning of the act? In answering
this question we must always keep in mind that it is
no part of the object of the act to enforce the observance of a religious duty. The act does not to any
extent rest upon the ground that it is immoral or irreligious to labor on the Sabbath any more than upon any
other day. It simply prescribes a day of rest, from
motives of public policy, and as a civil regulation ; and
as the prohibition itself is founded on principles of policy, upon the same principles certain exceptions are
made, among which are ' works of necessity and charity.' In saying this I do not mean to intimate that
religion prohibits works of necessity or charity on the
Sabbath, but merely to show that the principles upon
which our statute rests are wholly secular, and that
they are none the less so because they may happen to

concur with the dictates of religion. Thus the day of
rest prescribed by the statute is the Christian Sabbath ;
yet so entirely does the act rest upon grounds of public
policy that, as was said in Bloom *v.* Richards, 2 O. S.
R., 391, 392, it would be equally Constitutional and
obligatory did it name any other day ; and it derives
none of its force from the fact that the day of rest is
Sunday. For, as was also said in that case, no power
is possessed by the legislature over things spiritual, but
only over things temporal ; no power whatever to enforce the performance of religious duties simply because
they are religious, but only within the limits of the
Constitution, to maintain justice and promote the public welfare. . . . "

A member of a religious society which kept Saturday
sacred as a day of rest was indicted in Pennsylvania
for laboring on Sunday and convicted. In this case,
Specht *v.* Commonwealth, 8 Penn., 312, the Supreme
Court of that State said :

"Though it may have been a motive of the law-
makers to prohibit the profanation of a day regarded
by them as sacred, and certainly there are expressions
used in the statute that justify this conclusion, it is not
perceived how this fact can vitally affect the question
at issue. All agree that to the well-being of society
periods of rest are absolutely necessary. To be productive of the required advantage these periods must
occur at stated intervals, so that the mass of which the
community is composed may enjoy a respite from labor
at the same time. They may be established by common
consent ; or, as is conceded, the legislative power of
the State may without impropriety interfere to fix the
time of their stated return, and enforce the observance
of the direction. When this happens, some one day

must be selected, and it has been said the round of the week presents none which being preferred might not be regarded as favoring some one of the numerous religious sects into which mankind are divided. In a Christian community, where a very large majority of the people celebrate the first day of the week as their chosen period of rest from labor, it is not surprising that that day received the legislative sanction ; and as it is also devoted to religious observances we are prepared to estimate the reasons why the statute should speak of it as the Lord's day, and denominate the infraction of its legalized rest, a profanation. Yet this does not change the character of the enactment. It is still essentially but a civil regulation, made for the government of man as a member of society, and obedience to it may properly be enforced by penal sanctions.''

Justice Coulter dissented from the grounds assumed for the Constitutionality of the act of the Assembly, holding '' It to be Constitutional because it guarded the Christian Sabbath from profanation, and in the language of the Act, prohibited work or worldly employment on the Lord's day, commonly called Sunday ; and not because of the mere usefulness of the day as a day of rest and cessation from worldly labor.''

CHAPTER XI.

BLASPHEMY.

JUDGE COOLEY says : '' But it does not follow, because blasphemy is punishable as a crime, that therefore one is not at liberty to dispute and argue against the truth of the Christian religion, or of any accepted

20

dogma. Its 'divine origin and truth' are not so far admitted in the law as to preclude their being controverted. To forbid 'discussion on this subject, except by the various sects of believers, would be to abridge the liberty of speech and of the press in a point which with many would be regarded as most important of all. Blasphemy implies something more than a denial of any of the truths of religion, even of the highest and most vital. A bad motive must exist; there must be a wilful and malicious attempt to lessen men's reverence for the Deity or for the accepted religion. But outside of such wilful and malicious attempt, there is a broad field for candid investigation and discussion, which is as much open to the Jew and Mahometan as to the professors of the Christian faith. No author or printer who fairly and conscientiously promulgates the opinions, with whose truths he is impressed, for the benefit of others, is answerable as a criminal. A malicious and mischievous intention is in such a case the broad boundary between right and wrong ; it is to be collected from the offensive levity, scurrilous and opprobrious language, and other circumstances, whether the act of the party was malicious. Updegraph *v.* Commonwealth, 11 S. & R., 394. Legal blasphemy implies that the words were uttered in a wanton manner " with a wicked and malicious disposition, and not in a serious discussion upon any controverted point in religion.'' People *v.* Ruggles, 8 Johns, 293, *per* Kent, Ch. J. The courts have always been careful in administering the law to say that they did not intend to include in blasphemy disputes between learned men upon particular controverted points. The Constitutional provisions for the protection of religious liberty not only include within their protecting power all sentiments and professions concerning or upon the subject of religion, but they guarantee to every one a perfect right to form and promulgate such opinions and doctrines upon religious matters, and in relation to the existence, power, attributes, and providence of a Supreme Being, as to himself shall seem reasonable and correct. In doing this he acts under an awful responsibility, but it is not to any human tribunal." [1]

The Supreme Court of Delaware, in the case of the State *v.* Chandler, 2 Harrington, 553, said : " The common law took no cognizance of offences against God, only when by their inevitable effect they became offences against man and his temporal security. It was never pretended by any common law court that he who did not love his neighbor as himself, or who did not visit the fatherless and widows in their affliction, and keep himself unspotted from the world, was therefore indictable at common law. The same is true of the laws of God, as revealed in the Old Testament. No lawyer ever framed an indictment in a common law court charging that the defendant did not honor his father and mother, or merely coveted his neighbor's property. True, there are many instances in which the divine precepts have been enacted into statutes, and in case of violation of these or of any divine mandate which had been adopted into the common law, because the peace and safety of civil society could not be secured without it, the common law courts become the avengers of the public wrong. . . . It [the common law] became the preserver of the peace and good order of society throughout the land, and noticed what was the religion of the people to the end that it might preserve that peace and good order. It sus-

[1] *Constitutional Limitations*, pp. 591, 592.

tained indictments for wantonly and maliciously blaspheming God, or the founder of the Christian religion, because such blasphemy tended to subvert the peace and good order which it was bound to protect. But it sustained no indictment for a mere sin against God, as a common law offence, where these objects of its care were not affected. It did not look to the condition of man in another world to punish, and thus prepare him for it in this. That was the loathsome duty of some ecclesiastical commissioner, some fiery bigot or Star Chamber judge. While these punished blasphemy as a spiritual offence, *pro salute animæ*, the common law only punished it when it tended to create a riot, or break the peace, or subvert the very foundations on which civil society rested.   .   .   ."

CHAPTER XII.

CHRISTIAN CHARACTER REMAINS.

THE principles set forth in these decisions are in the main unquestionably correct. It is right that the government should carefully abstain from inflicting a penalty for an offence which is against God only, and which does not at the same time threaten the peace and good order of society ; right, also, that it should take pains to make it understood, when the offence is against both God and man, that it punishes only for the offence against man. But the assumption which seems to be made in some of these decisions and in the legislation upon which they are based, that the government in doing this has acted upon some principle which requires the removal of every vestige of Christian basis, motive, and purpose from its laws, is unwarranted. Such removal is not accomplished even when the statute on Sunday observance is so framed that the penalty for its violation can be inflicted only for the disturbance of the peace and good order of society. Besides, the making of laws with penalties attached to them does not cover the whole field of governmental action. There is a large scope in which legislation, not penal, may be rightly determined by Christian considerations. The assumption in question is improbable, unreasonable, and inconsistent with facts.

1st. It might be probable enough that a great body of Christian people, as they become enlightened and imbued with the spirit of their master, would abstain from requiring the unbeliever to observe a religious ordinance for religious reasons ; but when they have the power in their own hands, when their religion is already incorporated with their civil institutions, is it probable that, without any known or possible motive, they would go beyond that, cast their religion entirely out of their civil institutions, and exclude every Christian motive, reason, and consideration from their action as a body politic ?

2d. It is unreasonable. A father might very well make it understood that a waif, happening to be a member of the family, was not required to perform certain acts of respect and obedience as a *filial* duty, but only for the sake of the good order of the family. Should the father take his journey into a far country, leaving the management of his estate to his children until his return, the children likewise might well make it understood that the waif would not be required to do as a *filial* duty anything that the father had required to be done, but only as obligatory for the good order of the family. It would be very strange if any one of the children should argue that, by so doing, they had divested the regulations prescribed for the government of the family of all fatherly authority, and that those regulations were binding, and ought to be recognized as binding upon themselves, not as a filial duty, but only for the good order of the family. For the discrimination in behalf of the waif there is reason and motive enough ; for the extension of it to the children there is neither reason nor motive, and the hypothesis that such extension of it is a necessary consequence of making it in behalf of the waif is absurd.

Again, it is unreasonable because such a divorce of co-existing motives as is supposed in the case is unnatural. When two different motives are known to exist in the same breast at the same time, both of which may prompt to the same action, it is hardly reasonable to affirm that the act has been produced by either motive, to the entire exclusion of the other. A man, looking forward to an action in which a good and a bad motive may be combined, may desire and purpose to suppress the bad and act only from the good motive. But looking back at the action done, it would hardly be proper for him to affirm as a matter of unquestionable fact that the bad motive had been entirely inoperative. Much more difficult and improbable would the divorce of the motives be if both were of such character as to receive the heartiest approval of his conscience. When a man relieves the sufferings and saves the life of a sick horse, his pecuniary interests and his humane feelings will both combine in prompting him to the act, and the assumption must be that both were operative in what he did. If he were a member of a large association which employed many horses in its business, and all the members were possessed of the like humane feelings, then the humane motive must be presumed to have entered, with the economic motive, into every rule of the company regarding the life of the beast. Indeed if the animals were cattle instead of horses, and the association a slaughtering company whose object it was to *take* instead of to *save* the life of the animals, we should still insist that humanity did in some degree enter into the regulations prescribed for the business. It is as unreasonable to suppose that Christian motives have been entirely excluded from the legislation of a Christian people on subjects that have both a religious and secular character, as to suppose that humane motives have been entirely excluded from the legislation of a humane people against cruelty to animals. It is very plain that this supposition springs from an erroneous presupposition as to the nature of our political institutions.

CHAPTER XIII.

SUNDAY LAWS HAVE A CHRISTIAN BASIS.

JUDGE COOLEY in his *Constitutional Limitations* (p. 594) says: "The laws which prohibit the ordinary employments on Sunday are . . . . based upon the demonstrations of experience that one day's rest in seven is needful to recuperate the exhausted energies of body and mind." And the Supreme Courts of Ohio and Illinois in the decisions referred to make the same assumption. When and to whom was the demonstration of experience made? Not to the ancient Greeks, with all their speculative penetration; not to the ancient Romans, with all their practical wisdom; not to the millions of China, nor to the various peoples of India, during all the ages of their civilization. France during the revolution of 1793 substituted one day in ten, for the one in seven, as the day of rest, and the failure of that experiment may have tended to confirm the fitness of the old order to the nature of man. But the fitness of one day in seven rather than one day in ten was no discovery of man. It may be admitted that the demonstration of experience does justify the acceptance of one day in seven, but to say that the fitness of one day's rest in seven was first demonstrated by experience, and that then the Sabbatic legislation was based on the demonstration, is to give an untrue history of that legislation. The actual historical order was: first, the divine institution, or purported divine institution; then legislation based upon that institution, and then the confirmation of experience.

Again. Why was Sunday and not Wednesday, or some other day of the week, made the day of rest? The Supreme Court of Ohio in the case of Bloom *v.* Richards, already referred to, says: "We are to regard the statute under consideration as a mere municipal or police regulation whose authority is neither strengthened nor weakened by the fact that the day of rest it enjoins is the Sabbath day. . . . Regarded merely as an exertion of legislative authority, the act would have had neither more nor less validity had any other day been adopted." [1]

The Supreme Court of Illinois in the case already referred to, says: "Considerations of public policy demanding such periods of rest, and the great body of

[1] 2 Ohio State Reports, 392.

Christians holding the observance of the Sabbath to be a religious duty, it is natural that the law-making power, as a matter of public policy, should specify Sunday as the day of rest ; thereby conforming public policy to religious sentiment. But that Sunday is kept as a holy day by most Christian denominations neither adds to nor detracts from the validity of the enactment. Had any other day of the week been selected the enactment would have had the same binding force." [1]

If these statements were not intended to affirm the identical proposition, that a law, if made by the constituted authority, would be a law, they were intended to affirm that there is a something, called the State, separate from the People, which is governed in all its action by nothing but considerations of public policy, and that this something, though existing in a country in which "The will of the people is the law of the land," is so totally destitute of all religious character that the particular day appointed as the day of rest would have been to it a matter of utter indifference. So far as its own character and the considerations by which it is to be governed are concerned, it might just as well have appointed any other day than Sunday. [2] It has been said that if the people of this country were Mohammedan, the legal day of rest would have been Friday, which, it is alleged, proves that the State is, and must be indifferent to all religious considerations in the appointment of the day. If it did prove

---

[1] 107 Illinois Reports, Freeman, p. 437.

[2] Here we have mysticism employing its phantasm for the support of the anti-Christian theory of the State, as we had it before (p. 237) employing a like creation of its fancy for the support of the Christian theory. There the State was a person. Here it is a nondescript, undefined something.

any such thing, it would be that the State, as an abstraction, is thus indifferent ; but with such a State,—an imaginary State, not composed of people, we have nothing to do. The fact adduced proves, however, the very opposite, viz.: that the religious reasons which induce the people to observe the day, enter of necessity as an effective and determining factor into the legislation prescribing and regulating the observance.

If, upon my returning from the field, after a hard day's work, weary almost to fainting, and very thirsty, I should find on my table a glass of wine and a glass of water, and I should choose the wine, it would be preposterous for me to say that I was determined in my choice solely by the desire to quench my thirst, and not at all by my desire for the invigorating influence of the wine. It is no less preposterous to say, when the State chooses the Lord's Day as the legal day of rest, that it was determined in its choice wholly by temporal and secular considerations, and not at all by religious considerations.

It is beyond all question that part of the law appointing a weekly day of rest—that part which determines that it shall be one day in seven and not one day in six, or eight, or ten, and that part which makes the Lord's Day and not some other day the day of rest—was determined by Christian considerations, and by Christian considerations alone. The choice of the people had been determined by those considerations, and it was the will of the people that gave this feature to the law.

It requires a great leap in logic to assume that the State in exempting the unbeliever from all obligation to observe Sunday as a religious ordinance, and inflicting penalty only when the non-observance is of such a character as to disturb the peace and good order of society, has thereby removed every Christian consideration from the basis of the law and proclaimed itself in all things, non-Christian. The very statute which Mr. Justice Thurman was construing in Bloom *v.* Richards, saying that its prohibition in relation to Sunday was " a mere civil regulation," provides in its first section that " if any person shall be found on the first day of the week, commonly called Sunday, sporting, fishing, shooting, or at common labor," he shall be punished. Surely fishing would be no offence if the law had been intended to be only a civil regulation to preserve the peace and good order of society. Mr. W. M. Ramsey, of counsel for the plaintiff in Minor *et al. v.* The Board of Education of Cincinnati, in alluding to this point in the decision very aptly said : " A quiet seat by the bank of a pleasant stream with a fishing-rod would be an admirable disposition of one's self for a day of rest and reinvigoration after six days of toil."

If we look at the statutes of Ohio and Illinois respectively, as a whole, we shall find in them ample ground for the opinion that the legislatures of those States intended, in the form they gave to their penal Sunday statutes, to restrict the infliction of the penalty to the offence against man, and did not intend to remove every Christian consideration from the laws of the State. The statutes of Ohio which were in force when the decision in Bloom *v.* Richards was rendered provided that the family Bible should be exempt from execution. The Apprentice law bound the master to give to the apprentice at the close of his term a new Bible. The statute regulating county jails required that each prisoner be furnished with a Bible. The Penitentiary act required the warden of the penitentiary to furnish each criminal with a Bible. It required that a Chaplain be employed, that he " shall be a minister of the Gospel, in good standing in some one of the denominations of this State " ; that he " shall devote his whole time and ability to the welfare of the convicts " ; that he shall hold his office for one year, and that he shall receive an annual salary.

The statutes of Illinois, S. 31, C. 108, relating to the penitentiary, which were in force when the decision of the Supreme Court in Richmond *v.* Moore was rendered, provided that " Facilities for attending religious services regularly on Sundays shall be afforded each convict so far as the same can be done judiciously, and upon no pretext shall a convict, on contract, be required to labor on Sunday ; nor shall any convict be required to do any other than necessary labor for the State on that day."

Section 44 provided "That no labor shall be performed by the convicts in the penitentiary of this State in any stone quarry or other place outside the walls of the penitentiary."

If there is any place in the world where labor on Sunday will not disturb the peace and good order of society, is it not inside the walls of a penitentiary? Surely it cannot be maintained that this regulation was intended to be purely civil, merely to preserve the good order of society from disturbance, and is destitute of all Christian character. Can it be truthfully said that it was based upon purely economical reasons derived from the demonstrations of experience, and to no degree and in no respect whatever upon the Christian reason derived from the convictions of the people ? Can it be maintained that purely secular and economical considerations form the basis of the statute which provides for the appointment of a chaplain for the penitentiary, and for the payment of his salary, and which requires him " to perform religious services in the penitentiary, . . . to visit the convicts in their cells for the purpose of giving them moral and religious instruction," and " to furnish at the expense of the State a Bible to each convict " ?

CHAPTER XIV.

SUNDAY IN THE CONSTITUTION OF THE UNITED STATES.

THE 7th Section of Article I. of the Constitution of the United States contains the following provision, viz. :

" If any Bill shall not be returned by the President within ten days (Sundays excepted) after it shall have been presented to him, the same shall be a law, in like manner as if he had signed it, unless the Congress by their adjournment prevent its return, in which case it shall not be a law."

This exemption of the President from the necessity of studying the merits of a bill on Sunday surely could not have been based solely on a regard for the peace and good order of society, and in no degree whatever on a respect for the religious character of the day. How could such study in the privacy of the executive office disturb that peace and good order?

In view of this exemption and the ground upon which it was undoubtedly based, it cannot be maintained that President Lincoln either violated the spirit or strained the letter of the Constitution when he issued the following order, viz. :

" EXECUTIVE MANSION,
" Washington, Nov. 15, 1862.

"The President, Commander-in-Chief of the Army and Navy, desires and enjoins the orderly observance of the Sabbath by the officers and men in the military and naval service. The importance for man and beast of the prescribed weekly rest, the sacred rights of a Christian people, and a due regard for the Divine will, demand that Sunday labor in the Army and Navy be reduced to the measure of strict necessity. The discipline and character of the national forces should not suffer, nor the cause they defend be imperilled by the profanation of the day or name of the Most High. . . ."

It is in no violation of either the spirit or letter of the Constitution that in the military and naval academies, and at all the army posts, Sunday is kept as a day of rest and Christian worship, by the authority of the government.

In 1892 the World's Columbian Exposition, a body incorporated by the legislature of the State of Illinois for the purpose of celebrating the four hundredth anniversary of the discovery of America by an exposition of the world's arts and manufactures, to be held in the city of Chicago in 1893, sought aid of the United States government in carrying forward their enterprise. Congress, by act of August 5, 1892, granted aid to the amount of $2,500,000 which was to be delivered in 5,000,000 half dollar silver souvenir coins. To this grant the following condition was attached, viz. :

" *Section 2.* And it is hereby declared that all appropriations herein made for or pertaining to the World's Columbian Exposition, are made upon the condition

that the said exposition shall not be opened to the
public on the first day of the week, commonly called
Sunday ; and if the said appropriations be accepted by
the corporation of the State of Illinois, known as the
World's Columbian Exposition, upon that condition, it,
is hereby made the duty of the World's Columbian
Exposition Commission, created by act of Congress of
April twenty-fifth, eighteen hundred and ninety, to
make such rules, or modification of the rules of the said
corporation, as shall require the closing of the Exposition on the said first day of the week, commonly called
Sunday.''

The grant was accepted, and on October 25, 1892,
rules were adopted by the corporation and the commission, among which was one providing that the gates
should be open from May 1st to October 30th every day
of the week except Sunday, when the gates should be
closed.   By another rule the Board of Directors of the
corporation reserved "the right to amend or add to
these rules whenever it may be deemed necessary for
the interest of the Exposition."   By act of Congress
March 3, 1893, the Secretary of the Treasury was directed to retain part of the appropriation until the local
corporation had given the government security for a
proposed loan for the payment of awards for foreign
exhibitors, or had paid such awards, since such awards
constituted a debt for which the local corporation was
liable under the act creating the Exposition, and which
the government was in honor bound to see paid.   On
May 12th the board of directors of the World's Columbian Exposition resolved to open the grounds, but not
the buildings, on Sunday, and on May 16th passed certain resolutions which recited that there was a widespread demand that not only the grounds but the main

buildings should be opened, and that the welfare of the
public, and especially the wage-workers, would be promoted by permitting the people to enter the Exposition
on Sunday, and that a large majority of the people of
this country demanded this privilege. Also that the
withdrawal by Congress, by the act of March 3, 1893,
of over one fifth of the entire appropriation made in aid
of the Exposition, had thereby removed all obligation
on the part of the corporation to comply with the conditions of the act of August 5th. It was resolved that
both the buildings and grounds should be opened during
the Sundays of the Exposition period ; that the operation of the machinery should be suspended as far as
practicable, and all exhibitors and employees relieved
from duty except so far as essential to the protection
of life and property ; that there should be religious services and sacred music ; and further, that " In case the
above is carried into effect, this corporation pledges and
obliges itself to return to the government of the United
States that portion of the appropriation received by virtue of act of August 5, 1892, *to wit*, the sum of $1,929-
120, from and out of the net receipts of this corporation,
after the payment of all just and valid obligations,
before any payment shall be made to the stockholders
or the city of Chicago."

The United States brought suit, in the United States
Circuit Court, (N. D., Illinois,) praying that the
World's Columbian Exposition might be enjoined from
opening the Exposition and the grounds and gates
thereof on Sunday, and be commanded to close the
Exposition and grounds and gates on that day.

Objection was made by the defendant to the equity
jurisdiction of the court, but the objection was overruled, on the ground that " The government has suffi-

cient interests at stake, because it has possession of the grounds, has property there, and has pecuniary interest in imported goods subject to duty, and also indirectly in the gate receipts and income from all sources, and, besides, is under the highest obligations of honor and law to protect the property and interests of foreign nations and of the several States of the Union, and of all exhibitors brought there upon its invitation." Also upon the ground that the grant of $2,500,000 to the corporation is a charitable donation.

The court on June 8, 1893, decided that the injunction prayed for should be issued, Woods and Jenkins, circuit judges, concurring, and Grosscup, district judge, dissenting.

The defendant appealed to the United States Circuit Court of Appeals, Seventh District, and the appeal was sustained. The Court on July 26, 1893, said : "We have given to this record patient investigation, and to the able arguments of counsel the attention which their merits deserved and the character of the controversy demanded, and we can discover no tenable ground, excepting the case from the ordinary rule which requires, in order to the exercise of jurisdiction in chancery, some injury to property, whether actual or prospective ; some invasion of property or civil rights ; some injury irreparable in its nature and which cannot be redressed at law. The application of that rule is fatal to the maintenance of the order under review, and whatever temptation to leave the beaten path the record of a particular case may be supposed to afford, it is not for courts of justice in the exercise of an unregulated discretion to remove the settled landmarks of the law.

"The order is reversed, and the cause remanded for further proceedings, not inconsistent with this

21

opinion " ; Fuller, circuit judge, and Brewer and Allen, district judges, all agreeing.

The defendants before the Circuit Court had answered to the prayer of the plaintiff among other things, that, " If the true meaning and intent of Congress as expressed in said act of Congress of August 5, 1892, was to prohibit and restrain the public from their entrance upon and enjoyment of the grounds and appurtenances of Jackson Park and Midway Plaisance, not occupied by buildings erected for the purpose of installation of exhibits at said Exposition, or of the entire Exposition, on the first day of the week commonly called Sunday, then the said defendant avers and charges that said act of Congress is an unlawful restriction of the rights and privileges of the public, is contrary to the laws and Constitution of the State of Illinois, and repugnant to the Constitution of the United States, and is therefore wholly void."

To this Judge Wood in giving his opinion replied : " Whether influenced by the sentiment against such opening or by other considerations, it would be irrelevant to inquire, but Congress in extending further aid saw fit to couple with it the condition and requirement that the Exposition should be closed on Sundays. Without making the gift, the government, as I think, might at any time have enacted or required the adoption of this rule."

Judge Jenkins in his opinion said : " It is said that this legislation by Congress is without the power of Congress ; that it is unconstitutional ; that it seeks to establish religious tests. I cannot concur in the objection. Legislation with respect to the first day of the week has nothing to do with the matter of religious tests, or the compulsion of a particular religious belief or service. It is founded upon the necessities of the human race, as taught by experience, the needed rest which human beings require from the avocations of six days' labor ; and it is justified by that experience outside of and irrespective of any question of creed or any question of religion, and all the laws seek to do—the laws of the several States, which have existed almost from the existence of the States—is to provide for that needed rest, and to provide for noninterruption in that rest and in such religious services in which any citizen may choose to indulge. It is not an imposition upon any one of compulsion in respect to religious belief, or in respect to attendance at church. It provides simply for the protection and for the peace of those who may choose to attend church, that they shall not be interrupted by labor on that day.''

The defendant in his appeal to the Circuit Court of Appeals abandoned his plea that the act of Congress, August 5, 1892, requiring that the Exposition should be closed on Sundays, was '' repugnant to the Constitution of the United States.'' Justice Fuller in his statement of the case said : '' On the 14th of June the corporation, defendant below, appellant here, applied to the Circuit Court for leave to amend its answer, which was granted, and the answer amended by striking out the words, ' *and repugnant to the Constitution of the United States,*' from the paragraph heretofore quoted.'' [1]

---

[1] United States *v.* World's Columbian Exposition *et al.* Circuit Court, N. D., Illinois, June 8, 1893. *Federal Reporter*, vol. 56, pp. 630-653.

World's Columbian Exposition *et al. v.* United States, Circuit Court of Appeals, Seventh District, July 26, 1893. *Ibid.*, pp. 654-675.

The Circuit Court of Appeals took into consideration no facts but those bearing upon the question of the jurisdiction of the Circuit Court in the case as a court of equity, and decided no other question. It decided only that the Circuit Court had no jurisdiction in the case as brought before it by the United States, and that its action thereon was therefore void. It appears, however, that the defendant by his amended appeal conceded that the enforcement of the law of the United States, requiring the gates of the World's Fair to be closed on Sunday, could not be successfully resisted in the courts on the plea that such a law was " repugnant to the Constitution of the United States," and therein conceded the correctness of the opinion of the Circuit Court which pronounced the law in question to be Constitutional.

CHAPTER XV.

SUNDAY IN THE COMMON LAW.

THE supposed principle that all restraint of action on Sunday is based on the purely secular consideration of the peace and good order of society, cannot possibly apply to the common law restriction, which makes Sunday a *dies non juridicus*, so that no valid judicial act can be performed on that day excepting in cases of extreme necessity. In the case of Scammon *v.* The City of Chicago, (40 Illinois Reports, North, p. 146 April, 1866,) legal process had been instituted to condemn certain lots for the failure to pay an assessment for paving a street, notice of which is required by the statute to be given by six days' publication in the corporation paper. In this case, publication on Sunday in the Chicago *Tribune*, was one of the six days. The Supreme Court said : " At common law Sunday is, in legal phrase, *dies non juridicus*. No valid judicial proceeding can be had upon that day. If the service of civil process would be invalid on Sunday, it necessarily follows that a publication of this notice on Sunday, if the law required but one publication, would be equally invalid ; and the same rule must be applied to the present case, in which the Sunday publication must be counted to make out the requisite number. The notice stands in the place of process. To permit it to be given on Sunday is against the spirit and policy of our law."

In the case of Thomas *v.* Hinsdale *et al.*, Myers came to Hinsdale's office, who was an acting Justice of the Peace, early in the morning on Sunday, and made affidavit for attachment against Harriet C. Thomas. The Justice of the Peace issued the writ, and appointed McDonough a constable to execute it. Mrs. Thomas brought action for trespass, which was not sustained by the lower court. The Supreme Court, Breese delivering the opinion, decided that " the magistrate performed an act the law gave him no authority to perform. McDonough executed the writ, having no authority whatever to execute it. No justification is shown, nor can be. The judgment is reversed, and the cause remanded for further proceedings consistent with this opinion." [1]

In this case it may be said that the *execution* of the writ might disturb the peace and good order of society, but it was *issuing* the writ on Sunday which made the execution of it void of authority,—an act done in the

[1] 78. Illinois Reports, Freeman, p. 259.

privacy of the Justice's office and which could not disturb any Christian in his worship, public or private, any more than could the making of a contract in the same office.

In the case of Baxter *v.* The People, Baxter was tried for murder. The jury brought in their verdict on Sunday. The court received the verdict, and pronounced judgment, sentencing Baxter to be hanged. The Supreme Court of Illinois said [3 Gilman, 368, Caton, J., delivering the opinion, December, 1846] : " 'That courts have no right to pronounce a judgment, or do any other act strictly judicial on Sunday, unless expressly authorized by statute, seems too well settled to admit a doubt by the decisions in England and in this country. It appears that anciently, among the Christians, courts did sit on Sunday, but by a canon of the church made in the year 517, this was prohibited, and that rule seems to have been adopted into the common law and may be considered well settled.` . . . The question seems to have been frequently before the English courts, and the courts of most of the States of the Union ; and the decisions are very uniform, that a judgment cannot be entered of record on Sunday. The cases all show that a judgment entered of record on Sunday is not only erroneous but void. But although the law seems to be well settled that a judgment cannot be entered of record on Sunday, yet I think it equally well settled that the verdict of a jury may be entered of record on Sunday. We think the authorities clearly establish that when a cause is submitted to the jury before twelve o'clock on Saturday night, the verdict of the jury may be received on Sunday, but that is not a judicial day for rendering any judgment ; and if it attempt to render a judgment, still in law it would be no judgment

but absolutely void, and will be so declared and may be reversed by this court,—not that such reversal will take from it any force or vitality, for it never had any, not having been rendered by a court having authority to render any judgment whatever at that time. . . .
Suppose, after this verdict had been received, the cause had been continued to the next term for judgment and the court adjourned ; and that sometime during vacation and without appointing a special term, through some misapprehension, the judge had opened court and rendered judgment ; such a judgment would have been a nullity, but no more so than this.'' Koerner, J., dissented, holding that as under the statute of Illinois the jury is made judge of both the law and the facts, the verdict of the jury was a judicial act, and that it, as well as the judgment of the court, was void.

Now taking the history of the common law requirement as it is given in this case, can it be maintained that no religious reason, motive, or consideration is to be found in our legal regulations of the observance of Sunday, that those regulations are based wholly on temporal considerations, nothing being prohibited but what disturbs the peace and good order of society ? Would the rendering of a judgment by a court on Sunday disturb the peace and good order of society, more than the rendering of a verdict by a jury ? Is the latter permitted because it *does not* disturb the public peace, and for no other reason ? Is the former prohibited because it does disturb the public peace, and for no other reason ?

CHAPTER XVI.

THE OATH.

THE administration of the oath is inconsistent with the assumption that the government cannot be determined in anything it does or requires by a religious consideration. Whatever may be its form,—whether putting the Bible to the lips, or laying the hand upon it, or the lifting up of the hand ; whether the words " So help me, God " be omitted or not,—the administration of an oath is a religious act. The whole history of the oath proves that it has a specifically religious character. Why is the crime, in bearing false witness, the violation of the oath, and not the utterance of falsehood ? Is it true that no higher sentiment is appealed to than regard for the truth ? If the oath administered to a witness by a court is entirely destitute of religious character, it is nothing more than a contract made by the witness with the court or with the body-politic as represented by the court, to tell the truth. Why such a contract, and why punish the false witness for violation of the contract, and not for the falsehood? When a man comes into the court-room he is not required to take an oath, or make a contract to respect the court ; yet he will be punished for contempt. Why would it not be enough to punish the false witness for uttering falsehood, making that act the crime, as the act of contempt is the crime in the other case. The oath differs essentially from a contract ; it is not even a contract with the Divine Being, but is an appeal to Him who has said " Thou shalt not bear false witness against thy neighbor," to take cognizance of and punish any departure from the truth in the act of witness-bearing,

Were there among the people no belief in God, were the oath divested of all religious character, no oath ought to be or would be required. The oath is essentially religious.

CHAPTER XVII.

RESTRICTION OF FUNCTION NOT RENUNCIATION.

THAT the government should restrict to the narrowest limits the exercise of its function, as Christian ; that it should decline to engage in the work of propagating, or even to adopt any positive measures for the fostering of Christianity ; that it should carefully avoid any coercion of the conscience of the unbeliever, not requiring of him the performance of a religious duty when it requires of him the observance of a legally established Christian ordinance, allowing him the largest liberty of action compatible with the rights of Christian people and the good order of society, is explicable. Motive enough for so doing can be found in considerations of reasons and justice. But that the government of a people who are, in overwhelming majority, Christian, should go farther than that, and divest itself of all Christian character, would be inexplicable. There would be no practical necessity for so doing ; nor even a theoretical necessity, except upon the part of a few unbelievers who would hardly claim that the theory of the few ought to prevail against that of the many.

There is no doubt that the restriction of the religious function of the government thus far made will be attributed by many to the force of a supposed principle, which as yet lies beneath the public consciousness, but which is struggling upward, and will in the natural

course of evolution finally attain unto full realization
in the entire suppression of that function. But it is to
be remembered that the most rigid restriction does not
always and necessarily imply a latent tendency to suppression. There is no restriction which municipal
governments enforce more rigidly than that which forbids the encroachment of buildings upon the street
line ; even the projection of the capital of a column,
or a cornice beyond that line, is prohibited. But it
would be very absurd to interpret that restriction as
implying a latent opposition, which may be expected
to work out to the final suppression of all building.
Equally absurd is it to infer the existence of a similar
opposition from the limitations the government has put
upon the exercise of its Christian function. The principles of religious liberty are the open highways in the
city of God on earth. Christian laws are the walls of
the buildings that stand on its boundary lines. Neither
can be permitted to encroach upon the other, but to the
detriment of the whole.

CHAPTER XVIII.

THE DEMAND FOR NEUTRALITY.

THE demand which is now being made for the removal of every trace of Christian character from our
civil government is destitute of foundation either in
reason or justice, but the plea made by the unbeliever
for that removal is plausible. He says that what he
asks for is only that the government shall be neutral
on the subject ; neither for nor against Christianity,
or any other religion ; only the omission of all require-

ments based upon Christianity.   In that case, he says, Christian people of course would not be required to pay taxes for the support of what was contrary to their convictions and what they believed to be pernicious. Whereas in the case, as it now stands, that is just what the unbeliever is compelled to do.

Plausible as this plea is, it will be seen at once that a very positive action would have to be taken in order to reach the negative result.   Christianity holds now, as it has held from the beginning, a place in the law of the land, and it would have to be dislodged before the supposed negative position could be reached. Furthermore, the action would of course take its significance from the reasons upon which it was based. Christian people, having abated all injustice arising from the exercise of the Christian function of their government, can have no reason for desiring the dislodgement in question ; and the unbeliever, having received the abatement of all injustice, can have none but a theoretical reason for desiring the dislodgement ; which reason is that Christianity is a superstition, and like all other superstitions false and pernicious.

The term sect is commonly applied to the various schools into which the adherents of a religion are divided.   It is a familiar term as applied to the various denominations of Christians, but in a broad view unbelievers as a class must be regarded as a sect.   Their dogmas on the subject of religion are well defined, and they are divided into sects among themselves ;—Materialists denying the existence of mind or spirit, either finite or infinite ; Pantheists denying the personality of the all-pervading source of all existence ; and Agnostics denying that the primal being, whose existence may be admitted, can be known.   The doctrines of each sect are not only well defined, but like the doctrines of the Christians, are made to rest on an elaborate sub-structure of philosophy and logic. When facing Christianity all of these sects agree in the negation of its truths, and taking all parties to the question into view they are to be reckoned as one sect. They are united in organizations for the purpose of maintaining and propagating their doctrines, to the overthrow of what they regard as the false doctrines of Christianity.

The whole controversy lies in the domain of the religious feelings ; and although they are contending for irreligion, it is very plain that they are not destitute of those feelings of admiration for the true, the beautiful, and the good, which in Christians are expressed in worship. They are worshippers. Truth, or reason, or law, or humanity, or nature is the object of their worship, a worship that leads naturally to some sort of personification. That scene enacted in the Cathedral of Notre-Dame in Paris, November 26, 1793, when Damoiselle Candeille of the opera was borne on a throne upon the shoulders of men to the altar, the worship of the Goddess of Reason supplanting the worship of the blessed Virgin, cannot be easily forgotten. And with that spectacle before our eyes it can hardly be denied that atheists are possessed of those feelings which naturally express themselves in worship.

Seeing then that unbelievers possess all the specific characteristics of a sect ; definite doctrines upon the subject of religion ; organization for the defence and propagation of those doctrines ; and even in some proper sense a worship, they are to be regarded in this controversy as a sect, and the demand they are making of the government is to be regarded as nothing else than the establishment of their sectarian doctrines. Mr. Francis E. Abbot in speaking before the National Reform Association at its meeting in Cincinnati, February 1, 1872, making a protest against the proposed religious amendment of the Constitution of the United States, which that association was organized to secure, said, "I respect this movement very sincerely. It seems to me to have the logic of Christianity, behind it, and if I were a Christian, if I believed in Christianity, I do not see how I could help taking my stand by your side." [1]

It is fair to infer from this declaration that what the members of that association were endeavoring to accomplish for their belief, he was endeavoring to accomplish for his belief, that is, to make it the supreme ruling principle of the government. As they were demanding that the government should be bound to violate no principle of Christianity, so he was demanding that it should be bound to violate no principle of atheism. It is fair to infer that the two parties differed only as to which should be established in the Constitution, Atheism or Christianity. In the *Index*, the organ of the Liberal League, published by Mr. Abbot, for January 4, 1873, the demands of the League were published as follows :

" 1. We demand that churches and other ecclesiastical property shall no longer be exempt from just taxation.

" 2. We demand that the employment of chaplains in Congress, in State legislatures, in the navy and militia, and in prisons, asylums, and all other institutions supported by public money, shall be discontinued.

" 3. We demand that all public appropriations for

[1] *Proceedings*, p. 33.

educational and charitable institutions of a sectarian character shall cease.

"4. We demand that all religious services now sustained by the government shall be abolished, and especially that the use of the Bible in the public schools, whether ostensibly as a text-book, or avowedly as a book of religious worship, shall be prohibited.

"5. We demand that the appointment by the President of the United States or by the Governors of the various States of all religious festivals and fasts shall wholly cease.

"6. We demand that the judicial oath in the courts and in all other departments of the government shall be abolished, and that simple affirmation under the pains and penalties of perjury shall be established in its stead.

"7. We demand that all laws, directly or indirectly enforcing the observance of Sunday as the Sabbath, shall be repealed.

"8. We demand that all laws looking to the enforcement of "Christian" morality shall be abrogated, and that all laws shall be conformed to the requirements of natural morality, equal rights, and impartial liberty.

"9. We demand that, not only in the Constitution of the United States and of the several States, but also in the practical administration of the same, no privilege or advantage shall be conceded to Christianity or any other religion ; that our entire political system shall be founded and administered on a purely secular basis, and that whatever changes shall prove necessary to this end be consistently, unflinchingly, and promptly made."

Upon what ground does the Liberal League make these demands?   Upon the ground that under the government on its present basis, and as it is now administered, they are deprived of the liberty of belief and of acting in accordance with their belief;—on the ground that they are required to do anything which would imply on their part a belief in the doctrines of Christianity;—on the ground that they are subject to any hardships that are not necessarily incident to the rule of the majority? That cannot be, for there is no such ground. It has already been removed; or if a vestige of it remain Christians will join with them in securing its speedy removal.

The demand as now made can be only on the ground that the doctrines of Christianity are false and the doctrines of atheism are true. The demand of the unbeliever is that the government shall adopt and act upon the doctrines which *he* believes to be true. That this is the demand, which is disguised under the plea of neutrality, may be made plain by a simple illustration.

Certain very respectable and eminent philologists desire a reform in the orthography of the English language; among other things the omission of all silent letters, such as the *a* in hear, dear, fear, etc.; the *e* in care, dare, wear, etc. They claim that the adoption of the reform would save in the aggregate an immense amount of labor and money to the public generally, and an immense amount of nervous energy to the pupils in our schools. Those who prefer the old mode of spelling hold that the letters alleged to be superfluous serve as diacritical marks, and serve for that purpose as well as any marks that could be invented to take their place. They maintain that the difference between them and the reformers is only a difference in tenet or doctrine as to diacritical marks. Now should the government, beguiled by the plea of the reformers that all they ask is omission, order the omission of

those letters in all its documents and records and in all
the books used in the public schools, who does not see
that such an order would involve the rejection of the
tenet of the majority and the establishment of the tenet
of the minority. This is a case in which the remark
of Justice Appleton of Maine in the case of Donahue
v. Richards, that " The right of negation is in its
operation equivalent to the right of proposing and establishing," is true. The omissions, negations, and
prohibitions demanded by the unbeliever would be
equivalent to the establishment of his tenets. Such
establishment over a population that is almost wholly
Christian would be a flagrant injustice.

Another simple illustration will serve to show that
acceding to the demand in question, instead of securing
justice, would inflict injustice ; instead of securing the
rights of conscience, would trample on those rights.

Suppose that a vegetarian becomes a member of a
boarding club which has always used meats, and that
he desires the club to change its policy and exclude
meats from the table. He might plead that all he asks
for is omission, negative action ; and that to secure no
more than what is simply just. He pays an equal
share with the rest into the common fund, and part of
his money goes to pay for provisions which he does not
use. Moreover, his conscience is involved in the matter ; he has conscientious scruples against eating the
flesh of animals ; while the other members have no
conscientious scruples against the use of vegetables.
Plausible as this plea of conscientious scruple may
seem, it will appear upon examination to be an adroit
misrepresentation of the other side of the case. They
have no conscientious scruples against the use of vegetables, but they have conscientious scruples against

subsisting on vegetables alone. Why does he use only vegetables? Partly because he believes it to be a duty to keep his body in the fullest vigor possible. They hold the same belief for themselves. He holds that his health would suffer detriment from the use of animal food ; and they hold that their health would suffer detriment from the disuse of it. Conscience is involved as much on the one side as on the other. The only question in the case therefore is who shall rule,—the many over the one, or the one over the many? The rule of the many over the one is democracy ; the rule of the one over the many is despotism. If he is permitted to remain in the club, to enjoy all its privileges and advantages, and is not compelled to partake of animal food ; he has no just ground of complaint if the club refuse to change its old established principles so as to conform with his peculiar views. He has all the rights to which in those circumstances he is entitled.

There will undoubtedly be more or less of hardship incident to the rule of the majority, as evil attends all earthly things ; but hardship is not always injustice. The Quaker is compelled to pay taxes for the support of a government that keeps an army and navy, inflicts capital punishment, carries on war, and administers oaths. Those who believe that the administration of medicines is pernicious are compelled to pay taxes for the support of physicians in government employ who administer medicines. Spelling reformers are compelled to pay taxes for the support of schools in which a system of orthography, to which they are opposed, is taught. A man, who has neither horse nor carriage, but does all his travelling by railroad, is compelled to pay his fare on the railroad and also to pay taxes to keep up the public roads and bridges. The

22

man who furnishes his own water and light is compelled
to pay taxes for building the city waterworks and gas
works. The parent who has no children to go to
school, or who prefers to send his children to a private
school, is compelled to pay tax for the support of the
public schools. The Jew and the member of those
Christian denominations which keep the seventh day
of the week sacred are compelled to pay taxes for the
support of a government which will not allow them to
have a cause heard in court, or to have a legal process
issued, or a petition presented to the legislature, or to
have business done at the bank, or to enforce the payment of a debt on the first day of the week.

These hardships are unavoidable incidents to all social
organization? They furnish no valid reason for taking
the rule from the majority and giving it to the minority.
Nor would such transfer diminish the hardships: it
would only increase them. When these hardships are
reduced to the least possible amount and are made to
fall upon the least possible number of persons; and
when no one is compelled to do what his conscience
forbids, there can be no just ground for complaint.
When the Quaker is not compelled to bear arms, or to
take an oath, he has all the respect shown for his peculiar views that he has a right to demand. When on
the ground that he is conscientiously opposed to war
and that he pays taxes for the support of the government, he goes farther and demands that the government be neutral on the subject of war ; his demand is
not for the securing of his rights, but for the establishment of his doctrines. His grievance is, not that he is
compelled to do anything that his conscience forbids,
but that all other people are not compelled to yield
their conscientious convictions to his ; it is that the

majority conduct the affairs of the government in accordance with their own views of what is right, and are not compelled to conduct those affairs in accordance with his views; or, in other words, that he is not allowed to wield the power of a despot. He has a perfect right to his opinion; a perfect right to advocate it; to endeavor to persuade his fellow-citizens to his way of thinking; and if he should succeed in persuading a majority of them, he has a right to have the government administered in accordance with his views; but, until that be done, he has no right to keep up an outcry of injustice, or to be obstructive in his action. To use an illustration of Lord Brougham. If he should come into a court of justice and say that his conscience not only precluded him from taking an oath, but precluded him also from giving evidence which in the existing state of the laws might bring a fellowman to capital punishment, the answer he would receive would be this: "Sir, the legislature is the only judge of the necessity of taking away a man's life; and neither your conscience nor your notions of jurisprudence must stand in the way of justice."

In the case of Simons Ex. *v.* Gratts, 2 Pennsylvania, 412, Levi Philips, the only plaintiff attending to the preparation of the case, made deposition, stating, "That he had scruples of conscience against appearing in court to-day [Saturday] and attending to any secular business, and that he believes that his presence and aid will be material in the progress of the cause." His honor overruled the objections of the plaintiff and ordered on the cause.

On appeal the Supreme Court said (Gibson, C. J., delivering the opinion); "The religious scruples of persons concerned with the administration of justice will receive all due indulgence that is compatible with the business of the government ; and had circumstances permitted it, this cause would not have been ordered for trial on the Jewish Sabbath. But when a continuance, for conscience' sake, is claimed as a right and at the expense of a Term's delay, the matter assumes a different aspect.

" It never has been held, except in a single instance, that the course of justice may be obstructed by any scruple or obligation whatever. The sacrifice that ensues from conscientious objection to the performance of a civil duty ought, one would think, to be on the part of him whose moral and religious idiosyncrasy makes it necessary ; else the denial of the lawfulness of capital punishment would exempt a witness from testifying to facts that might serve to convict a prisoner of murder ; or to say nothing of other functionaries of the law, excuse the sheriff for refusing to execute one, capitally convicted. That is an exemption which none would pretend to claim ; yet it would inevitably follow from the principle insisted on here. Rightly considered, there are no duties so sacred as those which the citizen owes to the laws. In the judicial investigation of facts, the secrets of no man will be wantonly exposed, nor will his principles be wantonly violated. But a respect for these must not be suffered to interfere with that organ of the government which has more immediately to do with the protection of person and property : the safety of the citizen and the very existence of society require that it should not. That every other obligation shall yield to that of the laws, as to a superior moral force, is a tacit condition of membership in every society, whether lay or secular, temporal or spiritual ; because no citizen can lawfully hold communion with those who have associated on any other terms ; and this ought in all cases of collision to be accounted a sufficient dispensation to the conscience. . . . I am for setting aside this non-suit, certainly not for any supposed interference with the rights of conscience.''

The case of the Quaker given in elucidation of the point we are making, it is hardly necessary to say, is altogether hypothetical. To the honor of the highly respected and truly conscientious society of Friends, be it said, that they keep up no agitation, make no outcry of injustice, and are not persistently obstructive to those measures of the government which they regard as unrighteous. Of the unbeliever, however, more rest-less and less tolerant than the quiet and amiable Friend, it is doubtful whether so much can be truthfully said.

Christian believers can have no motive for divesting their civil government of its Christian character.

Unbelievers can offer no ground in reason or justice for such divestiture.

CHAPTER XIX.

DUTIES OF THE STATE AS CHRISTIAN.

1st. Not to Adopt Positive Measures for the Fostering of Christianity.—At the close of the sec-ond part of our investigation, we arrived at the con-clusion that the government of these United States was necessarily, rightfully, and lawfully Christian. In Part III. we entered upon the question : What may the government do, and what ought it to do in its Chris-tian character ? Our first answer to that question was a negative one, viz. : That it was no part of the proper function of the government to inculcate, propagate, or even foster, Christianity; certain special cases being excepted.

We have been considering throughout the previous discussion the question of inculcating and propagating, but have given no special consideration to the question of *fostering* Christianity. Our negative answer to the latter question may seem to be a step too far in the way of restriction or concession. It can hardly be denied that the laws against cruelty to animals are intended to foster the humane sentiments of the people, and thereby promote the public welfare. A true system of ethics will concede, to the animal, rights which man is bound to respect, but the animal, in relation with man, does not possess the equal rights which man possesses in relation with his fellowman. Cruelty to the animal is not a crime of the same order as injury to the person of one man by another.

It may be therefore that, like blasphemy and Sunday desecration, cruelty to animals is prohibited only to protect the citizens against nuisance, and the good order of society from disturbance. But scarcely anyone denies, and almost everyone takes satisfaction in believing, that the laws in question, whatever other purpose they may have been intended to serve, were intended mainly to foster humane sentiments in the breast of the citizen.

It would seem inconsistent therefore, to concede to the government the right to foster humanity, and deny its right to foster Christianity, especially since Christianity includes humanity, as the whole includes the part, or the genus the species. If the right in the latter case be granted, it is to be remarked that the fostering in both cases is confined to the prohibition of acts which are of the character of nuisance and tend to disturb the good order of society. It may be doubted, however, whether an act of outrageous cruelty to an animal perpetrated in seclusion whereof sufficient proof could be found, would escape the penalty on the plea of seclusion. But aside from this, the cases are not altogether alike. Difficulties would attend the exercise of the fostering function in the one case that do not attend it in the other. Strong religious feeling is not so prevalent among the people as the humane feeling. No one denies that it is a duty to be humane ; while many deny that it is a duty to be Christian. Besides, the advocates of the humane treatment of animals are not divided into sects, all differing in opinion as to what particular form of humanity ought to be fostered ; while another sect, of considerable strength, stands in opposition to them all, affirming that humanity is a factitious sentiment which interferes with the law of natural selection and tends to prevent the survival of the fittest. It seems, therefore, that as a matter of practical necessity, if not of principle, the exercise of the religious function of the government should be reduced to the last degree consistent with a proper regard for the feelings, convictions, and rights of Christian people.

Furthermore, when there is within the State a large and well-organized body, which has for its special object the propagation and fostering of Christianity, the natural law of efficiency in all organic bodies—specialization in the form and function of organs—would justify the government in leaving the whole work of fostering Christianity to the Church,—at least the use of all positive measures to that end. The government takes knowledge of Christianity as an organized system, not as an abstraction, an *imperium in imperio.* Were there no organized Christian church, and were the people Christian, it might be the duty of the government, not only to foster, but to inculcate Christianity, just as it is the duty of the lowest animal organism to use any and every part of its body, as mouth, legs, and arms.

It may be remarked that if the government abstain from fostering Christianity while it does foster humanity, there is all the more ground for maintaining that it should abstain with the most scrupulous care from doing anything adverse to Christianity. If the case were such that it could leave the fostering of humanity to an organization better fitted than itself for the purpose, it would be passing strange if it should make occasion of that fact to profess itself to be inhuman, or even neutral ; and stranger still if it should be found actually fostering inhumanity.

In accordance with the principles just set forth, the State ought to abolish all distinctions between ministers of the gospel and other citizens in the disqualifications for office. Up to 1846 the Constitution of New York contained the following prohibition, viz.:

"Art. VII. Sec. 4. And, whereas, the ministers of the gospel are by their profession dedicated to the service of God and the care of souls, and ought not to be diverted from the great duties of their function ; therefore, no minister of the gospel or priest of any denomination whatsoever shall at any time hereafter, under any pretence or description whatever, be eligible to or capable of holding any civil or military office or place within this State."

The Constitutions of eleven other States have contained similar prohibitions. These disqualifications were not intended to operate towards a divorce of Christianity from the State, but, as is expressly stated, to more fully secure its influence for the benefit of the State. They were no more intended to be derogatory to Christianity than the provision found in all the State constitutions which prohibits any member of Congress or other person holding office under the United States being a member of the State legislature or holding any other office under the State, was intended to be derogatory to the general government. In both cases the intention was to promote efficiency and purity in office by requiring exclusive devotion to its duties. The disqualifications imposed on ministers of the gospel were intended to foster Christianity as a means of promoting the welfare of the State. The fact has become manifest that Christianity does not need the fostering of the State, and there has been a tendency of late years towards the withdrawal of these disqualifications, so that now they remain in the Constitutions of only three States, Delaware, Kentucky, and Tennessee, the first giving no reason for the disqualification, and confining it to the time that the minister "continues in the exercise of the pastoral or clerical functions."

The fostering of any particular Christian sect, by making appropriations to it from the public treasury, is a wrong so obvious as to need no special consideration. Were it the duty of the government, however, to foster Christianity in general, a sect seeking an appropriation might plead that it was simply doing its own share in bringing the government to a performance of its duty, and that the other sects, instead of condemning it, ought to follow its example. It might refer in support of its plea to the appropriations lately made by the federal government to different Christian denominations for the carrying on of schools among the Indians; but the fact referred to would give no support to the plea. It was not the intention of the government in making those appropriations to foster Christianity in general, by fostering all the sects, in particular; for it did not propose to give appropriations to more than a few of the leading denominations. The intention of the government was to foster Christianity among the Indians, a work which as we have already seen, it was under obligation to do, and which it might better have done directly than indirectly by selecting certain denominations for the purpose, assigning territory to them severally, and making appropriations to them, which with so much color of reason could be called sectarian. The public sentiment against making appropriations from the public treasury to any Christian sect upon any pretence whatsoever, whether of promoting education or charity, is so widespread and firmly established and the conditions in which such appropriations can be obtained are so unlikely to occur and so repugnant to the feelings of personal independence that no other safeguard is thought to be necessary to prevent the wrong.

On the 14th of December, 1875, Mr. James G. Blaine, in accordance with a recommendation of President Grant, proposed in the House of Representatives the following amendment to the Constitution of the United States, viz.:

"No State shall make any law respecting an establishment of religion, or prohibiting the free exercise thereof; and no money raised by school taxation in any State for the support of public schools, or derived from any public fund therefor, nor any public lands devoted thereto, shall ever be under the control of any religious sect; nor shall any money so raised, or land so devoted, be divided between religious sects or denominations."

While the matter was pending in the House, both the great political parties happened to hold their quadrennial conventions, and both included in their platforms an approval of the measure, either in form or in principle. In the platform of the Republican party is the following declaration, viz. :

" The public school system of the several States is the bulwark of the American Republic, and with a view to its security and permanence, we recommend an amendment to the Constitution of the United States, forbidding the application of any public funds or property for the benefit of any schools or institutions under sectarian control."

In the platform of the Democratic party was the following declaration, viz.:

" The public schools, of which the establishment and support belong exclusively to the several States, and which the Democratic party has cherished from their foundation, and is resolved to maintain without prejudice or preference for any class, sect, or creed, and without largesses from the treasury for any. . . ."

The amendment, with an added clause, was approved by the House of Representatives August 4, 1876, by a vote of one hundred and eighty for and seven against. In the Senate it was further amended and as the vote stood twenty-eight for and sixteen against it was defeated, Art. V. of the Constitution requiring a vote of two thirds in both houses for the proposing to the people or the legislatures of the States of amendments to the Constitution. The matter has since that time not been deemed of sufficient urgency to be revived and pressed to a conclusion.

Only one Christian sect (the Roman Catholic) now seeks or shows any willingness to accept any such appropriations, and the amendment in question has therefore seemed to contain a direct condemnation of that particular division of the Church, a thing which a generous people would forbear inflicting until there should be a practical necessity. In the present state of public sentiment it is possible to obtain such an appropriation only in particular localities, and only when the sect seeking it includes in its membership votes enough to make a balance of power between the contending political parties, is able to control the votes of its members, and is willing to make corrupt bargains with the political parties for the disposal of those votes.[1]

[1] From 1886 to 1893 the Roman Catholic church received, from the United States government, for contract schools among the Indians, $2,366,416 and all the Protestant denominations received, during the same period, for the same purpose, $937,977. This vast disproportion may be attributed to greater vigilance, persistence, and better organized efforts, in solicitation. But that is only the proximate cause. No Protestant denomination could hope to have obtained a like amount by a like effort. The ultimate cause, the cause without which the result could not have been accomplished, was nothing else than the control of Catholic votes by the Catholic clergy. The methods of the Jesuits, and the control exercised by the clergy over the people in secular affairs, are two surviving follies of the Roman Catholic Church, surprising anachronisms in this country and in this age. That church has the advantage of a venerable antiquity, of an imposing ecclesiastical organization, and of a system of theology built up by ages of earnest thought, and it might be expected to hold its own more securely and extend itself more rapidly did it, like Protestant denominations, rely upon the power of intellectual conviction, and the vigor of spiritual life, rather than upon the force to be exerted through an ecclesiastical machine. Its methods cause it to be regarded

Furthermore, experience has shown that while a minority wielding such a power may enjoy its unrighteous gains for a time ; yet, with a powerful public moral sentiment against it, the success it achieves is likely to be in the end more disastrous than defeat.   The great public which suffers from the wrong may be slow to move, but there is a point beyond which its forbearance will not go, and the temerity the offender gains from his successes will tend to hasten the retribution.   A far-sighted prudence therefore would restrain any sect from seeking to obtain the fostering of the government by appropriations from the public treasury.   This, together with the rare occurrence of the conditions in which such fostering is possible, and the odiousness of those conditions when they occur, render any legal prohibition practically unnecessary.   Yet such a prohibition would prevent the rising of a desire for such fostering, and the vexation which would be produced on the one side by its occasional success and on the other side by its defeat.

2d. To give preference and favor to Christianity.—While the State ought not to adopt any positive measures for the fostering of Christianity ; yet when Christianity is brought to its notice in such a way as to require positive action, it ought to give preference and favor to Christianity.   It ought to do so, not on the ground that being a person it must have a belief on the subject of religion, and being a person in authority,

with contempt by all self-respecting people, and to be suspected, as a dangerous political factor, by all patriotic citizens, outside of its own communion.   It may be, however, that a comprehensive paternalism belongs essentially to that form of church government which recognises, as its supreme and infallible head, one whose official title, in the official language, is *Papa*.

it is under obligation to pronounce one religion true and another false, but on the ground that Christianity is the religion of the people. Other religions are entitled to toleration and protection, but not to favor. A foreign language is entitled to toleration, and persons who prefer it are entitled to protection in the use of it, but the English language alone is entitled to favor. The favor is not given to Christianity and the English language because they are so essential to the government, or so identified with it, that it could not exist if either were to be changed. The one being the religion of the people, and the other the language of the people, public policy requires that both should receive preference and favor from the State.

The Constitution of Illinois requires that, " All laws of the State of Illinois and all official writings and the executive, legislative, and judicial proceedings, shall be conducted, preserved, and published in no other than the English language." [1]

Upon the appeal of William McCoy from a decision of the Circuit Court of Cook County, the Appellate Court of Illinois decided as follows, March, 1889, Gary, P. J.

" Upon a bill filed by a tax-payer of the City of Chicago to enjoin it from entering into any contract for, or the paying out of any money for publishing in the German language, matters and things required by law or ordinance to be published in a newspaper, this court holds that under the State Constitution such publication must be in the English language alone. . . . If the city may publish at public expense in German, why may it not pass ordinances and conduct its business in Greek? . . . The decree of the Circuit

[1] Schedule, §18.

Court dismissing the bill is reversed, and the cause remanded with directions to perpetually enjoin the city as prayed in the bill. . . ." [1]

We might ask in passing upon what ground the English language can be legally recognized as the language of the people which would not entitle Christianity to be legally recognized as the religion of the people. The urgency of the public policy, it must be admitted, is greater in the one case than in the other, but if the English language can be made the established language of the State so far as to prohibit the use of any other language in the conducting, preserving, or publishing of official business, Christianity upon the same principle may be made the established religion of the State so far as to prohibit any other than Christian religious services to be conducted by appointment of the State and to be paid for out of the treasury of the State.

3d. To give equal protection to Christians, Non-Christians, and Anti-Christians.—The State ought to protect Jews, Mohammedans, and pagans dwelling among us in their worship when that worship is orderly and not connected with immoral practices, punishing all unnecessary and malicious disturbance thereof.

It ought also to protect all orderly meetings of unbelievers, even when assembled on the Lord's Day, for the purpose of controverting the doctrines and disproving the evidences of the Christian religion. Such protection would no more imply indifference to Christianity, than the protection of the subjects of a king from mob violence when met within our borders in an orderly manner, to advocate the principles of monarchy, would imply indifference to republican institutions.

[1] McCoy *v.* City of Chicago *et al.*, 33. *Appellate Court Reports*, 576.

The protection ought to be impartially given as between the believer and the unbeliever. Care ought to
be taken, lest an ill-defined and untenable theory as to
the character of the government should produce a bias
and lead to a discrimination against Christian people.
If with Mr. Anderson (see p. 295) we are to regard the
common law, which makes blasphemy, Sunday desecration, and the disturbance of religious assemblies,
indictable offences, as simply providing protection
against nuisances, we have a right to insist that as
much consideration be given to the religious feelings
of Christian people as to the mere bodily senses of the
public in general.

It may be said that the law requiring that a rendering establishment, or a slaughter-house, be removed
outside of city limits, had regard only to the effect of
the odors upon the health of the people, and no regard
whatever to their comfort as affected by the stench.
But while there is ground for the presumption that
some unpleasant odors are detrimental to health, it is
not certain that all are.   It has not been positively as-
certained that the workmen in the establishments just
mentioned are especially subject to disease.   The motive force that produces legislation in such cases comes
from the people, and the most energetic motive is the
one which is most likely to be foremost in action, and
that is, in this case, the feeling of discomfort.   The
probability, therefore, is that legislation as to nuisances
is based in a large measure upon the feelings of the
people.   Were an action to be brought to secure the
removal of an establishment that filled the air with
offensive odors, it is not at all likely that the complainant would be required to prove that the odors
were noxious as well as offensive.   The religious feel-

ings of the Christian are certainly as worthy of protection from offence, as the feelings excited by the sense
of smell. The State ought, therefore, to prohibit such
acts, displays, and demonstrations on the Lord's day
as offend those feelings. The Christian ought not to
be required either to have no religious feelings, or to
suffer the pain of the offence as a penalty for having
them.

Christian people, also, have a right to protection in
the training of their children in what they regard as a
matter of very great importance. People who desire
to secure for their children the benefits of education,
have a right to demand that bear dances, brass bands,
and military parades shall not be obtruded upon the
attention of their children in such a way as to interfere
with the attainment of the desired end. Should those
who were engaged in these exercises sincerely believe
that education made people worse instead of better,
yet, as every one will readily see, they have no right
thus to defeat the efforts of those who think best to
educate their children.

The Supreme Court of Pennsylvania, in the case of
Johnston *v.* Com., 10 Harris, 102, Woodward, J., said :
" The right to rear a family with a becoming regard to
the institutions of Christianity, and without compelling them to witness the hourly infractions of one of
its fundamental laws ; the right to enjoy the peace and
good order of society, and the increased security of
life and property, which result from a decent observance of the Sabbath, are real, substantial rights, which
the legislature sought to secure by this enactment (and
when has legislation aimed at higher objects ?) and as
much the subjects of governmental protection as any
other right of person or property." This decision was

23

quoted by the Supreme Court of New York with approbation in the case of Lindenmuller *v.* The People, 33 Barbour, 560.

For these very plain reasons business houses ought not to be allowed to be open on Sunday, nor should military companies, or brass bands, be allowed to parade on the streets on Sunday, nor should base-ball games or other shows be allowed even outside of city limits, when they obtrude themselves on the public, by the throngs on the streets going to or coming from the place of exhibition. The law of nuisance should be impartially enforced. Even if the government is to be regarded as destitute of positive Christian character ; if the statutes which make blasphemy and Sunday desecration offences, are to be regarded as simply providing protection against nuisances, it is a wrong to discriminate against Christian citizens in the enforcement of the laws. If, however, it is true that our government is necessarily, rightfully, and legally Christian, such discrimination would become a still greater wrong. That there is a tendency towards such discrimination is indicated by the fact that some of the States have no law against blasphemy, and one (California) has repealed its Sunday laws, and has made Sunday merely a holiday, with no distinction between it and any other holiday.

It may be that Christian people have become so imbued with their Master's spirit of meekness that blasphemy and desecration of the Sabbath do not now provoke to a disturbance of the peace of society ; but they still have feelings, and it is to be presumed that increased meekness has been attended with increase in the strength and tenderness of feeling. Therefore, the nuisance in question is to them more aggravated now than ever before ; and there is more reason now than ever before for making and enforcing laws for their protection.

4th. **Not to adopt any sectarian Christian doctrines, nor protect bequests for pious uses.**—The State ought not to take any action which involves the adoption or establishment of any sectarian Christian doctrine. The courts may interpret the doctrinal standards of all the Christian denominations ; not, however, to declare which are true or false, but just as they would interpret a contract, a deed, a will, or any other document, to compel the fulfilment of any obligation that may be dependent thereon. The State may protect bequests for charitable purposes, and may decide what purposes are charitable. It may grant incorporation to churches, theological schools, and missionary societies, which being corporate persons have the right that belongs to all other persons to receive gifts and bequests for the promotion of their proper work. Notwithstanding that the bequests made to these institutions are intended to aid in the teaching and promulgation of certain Christian doctrines, yet the State in granting them protection does not make any decision upon the character of those doctrines ; not any more than it approves of the theology of any other person whom it protects in the enjoyment of property received by bequest. It has been held, however, that the State cannot protect bequests that have been made for what are technically called *pious uses.* Boards of trustees may become incorporated, but a trustee in the technical sense of the term is not a corporate person. A corporate body is created by the State. The trust, however, is created by an individual, and the trustee is appointed by him, and it falls therefore to the courts to pass judgment upon the object of the trust when it is brought before them for action. The appointing power of the creator of the trust is absolute ; he may appoint an alien enemy or a minor, and the trustee may have become a felon or a lunatic. Equally absolute is the power of choosing the object of his benevolence. The trust may be in contra-vention of the policy of the law, as for the creation of a perpetuity, "a thing, odious in law and destructive to the commonwealth ; stopping commerce and preventing the circulation of riches in the kingdom ; and therefore not to be countenanced in equity." Or it may be for purposes connected with immoral practices, as for the support of illegitimate children that may happen in the future to be born. The State, in granting protection to a trust, acting through its courts, must give judgment approving of both the trustee and the object of the trust. It is only upon the ground of such approval that the protection asked can be given. If the State grant protection to a bequest, placed in the hands of a trustee for *pious uses*, it must be regarded as approving of the special doctrine upon which the use is based. If the doctrine be, as it may often happen to be, a mere superstition, the State in protecting the bequest would be giving its approbation to the superstition, and also acting in contra-vention of public policy,—diverting funds from productive business, fruitful of benefits to mankind, to a use which can be fruitful only of evil. Whatever it may do in the case it must decide whether the doctrine upon which the *pious use* is founded be a superstition or not. In England a devise for a fund to circulate a book teaching the supremacy of the Pope in matters of faith ; to provide prayers and masses for the good of the soul of the testator ; to maintain a taper forever before our Lady, has been held to be void, as being for a superstitious use. The State ought not to decide upon the truth or falseness of any sectarian Christian doctrine ; and if the protection of a bequest for *pious uses* necessarily involves such a decision the protection ought not to be given.

In the case of Andrew *v.* The N. Y. Bible and Prayer Book Society, 4 Sandford's Superior Court Reports. 180-184, the question at issue was whether a legacy given for the purpose of promoting the circulation of the Book of Common Prayer in New York could be sustained upon the ground of its being a *pious use*. The court said : ". . . The use attached to this legacy is not a charitable use, in the usual and legal sense of the term. It is strictly a *pious use :* not otherwise charitable than as the noblest office of charity is the dissemination of religious truth ; but it is impossible for a court of justice to sustain a use upon this ground, unless in a country where the truths of religion have been settled and defined by law, or judges have discretionary power to determine and declare them. . . . Under a Constitution which extends the same protection to every religion, and to every form and sect of religion, which establishes none and gives no preference to any, there is no possible standard by which the validity of a use as pious can be determined ; there are no possible means by which judges can be enabled to discriminate between such uses as tend to promote the best interests of society by spreading the knowledge and inculcating the practice of true religion, and those which have no other effect than to foster the growth of pernicious errors, to give a dangerous permanence to the reveries of a wild fanaticism, or encourage and perpetuate the observances of a corrupt and degrading superstition. Hence, unless all uses that may be denominated pious shall be subjected to the same rule as other trusts, we shall find no escape from this alternative ; either all uses for a religious purpose, whether the religion they are intended to aid be true or false, rational or absurd, must be upheld and enforced, or the uses connected with a particular form of religion must be selected as the special and exclusive objects of favor and encouragement. If we adopt the first course, we renounce the principle upon which pious uses were first introduced, and upon which alone their defence can be rested, namely, their tendency to benefit society by diffusing the knowledge and practice of true religion. We disregard and deny the eternal distinctions between truth and falsehood, and give the sanction of law to the pernicious absurdity that all religions, however contradictory in their tenets and in their precepts, have a just and equal claim, not merely to the protection, but to the favor of the government, and are not simply to be tolerated but encouraged. If we adopt the second alternative, we violate that equality between different religions and different forms and sects of religion which the principles of our government and the provisions of our constitution are designed to secure ; we create an odious distinction between different classes of our citizens ; and by declaring that the religion which we favor is alone true we establish it, in a restricted sense it is true, but in a definite sense, as the religion of the State.

" We are quite aware of the answer that has been given to this objection. Christianity, it has been asserted, is now in a modified sense the religion of the State. It is so as a part of the common law which our ancestors introduced and we have retained. Christianity, therefore, furnishes the test that is desired, so that in judging of the validity of a use as pious we have only to inquire whether it is in harmony with the doctrines that Christianity teaches. The maxim that Christianity is part and parcel of the common law has been frequently repeated by judges and text writers, but few have chosen to examine its truth or attempt to explain its meaning. We have however the high authority of Lord Mansfield and of his successor, the present Chief Justice of the Queen's Bench, Lord Campbell (Campbell's *Lives of Chief Justices*, vol. ii., p. 513) for stating, as its true and only sense, that the law will not permit the essential truths of revealed religion to be ridiculed and reviled. In other words, that blasphemy is an indictable offence at common law. The truth of the maxim in this very partial and limited sense may be admitted. But if we attempt to extend its application we shall find ourselves obliged to confess that it is unmeaning or untrue. If Christianity is a municipal law, in the proper sense of the term, as it must be if a part of the common law, every person is liable to be punished by the civil law who refuses to embrace its doctrines and follow its precepts ; and if it must be conceded that in this sense the maxim is untrue, it ceases to be intelligible, since a law without a sanction is an absurdity in logic and a nullity in fact.

"Let it be admitted, however, that Christianity is a part of the common law in any sense of the maxim, which those who assert its truth may choose to attribute to it. The only effect of the admission is to create new difficulties quite as impossible to overcome as those that have already been stated. How, we would then ask, in judging of the validity of a use as pious, are we to apply the test which Christianity is said to furnish ?

It will not be pretended that the common law has supplied us with any definition of Christianity. Yet without a judicial knowledge of what Christianity is, how is it possible to determine whether a particular use, alleged to be pious, is or is not consistent with the truths which Christianity reveals? No religious use has been or can be created that does not imply the existence and truth of some particular religious doctrine, and hence when we affirm the validity of a use as pious, we necessarily affirm the truth of the doctrine upon which it is founded. In a country where a definite form of Christianity is the religion established by law, the difficulty to which we refer is not felt, since the doctrines of the established church then supply the criterion which is sought ; but with us, it can readily be shown that the difficulty is not merely real and serious but insurmountable.

" Let us suppose that a Roman Catholic had devised his whole estate, real and personal, to trustees, to apply the income forever, one half to the purchase of indulgences for the benefit of such as might seek them, and the other moiety to the payment of daily masses for the safety of his soul, and that the validity of this devise were the question to be determined. In England such uses are held to be void, as superstitious ; but the statute by which they are declared so we have repealed, and some other rule or principle must be found to govern our decision. The uses, it is manifest, imply the existence and truth of certain important doctrines. They imply that the Saviour has delegated to the Pope, as His vicar on earth, the absolute and unconditional power of pardoning sin. They imply the existence of purgatory, and the duty and efficacy of prayers for the dead. Such is the necessary import of the uses upon the validity of which, guided by the light of Christianity, we are required to pronounce. Shall we, by sustaining them as pious, declare that the doctrines which they imply belong to the class of truths which the New Testament reveals ; or shall we, by rejecting them as superstitions, condemn as false and corrupt the ancient faith which so large a class of our citizens avow and follow ? Are these questions, over which we, as judges, whatever we may privately think, have any jurisdiction ? Are they questions which any court of justice in this State, at any time since the formation of our present government, could rightfully entertain and decide ? Such are the questions that must be considered and decided, if uses inconsistent with the general rule of law are to be sustained as pious, and the proper test of their legality as such is their correspondence with the true doctrines of Christianity.

" For ourselves, if the case we have supposed were now before us, we should not hesitate in pronouncing our judgment, abstaining from any remarks upon the nature and tendency of the uses, neither admitting them to be pious, nor condemning them as superstitious. We should hold the devise to be entirely void, as repugnant to those wise and salutary rules of law which forbid the citizen to withdraw his property, beyond a limited period, from that free circulation which the interests of commerce and the healthful action and permanence of our Republican institutions alike demand ; and if this would be a proper decision in the case supposed, it is manifest that the same judgment ought to be pronounced in every case where a trust which involves a perpetuity is sought to be maintained upon the sole ground of its piety. We may be disposed to regret that a perpetual trust for the distribution of that sublime manual of true devotion, perhaps the noblest of human compositions, the Book of Common Prayer, cannot be sustained ; but the regret must cease when we reflect that it can only be sustained upon a principle that would render just as valid a similar trust for the circulation of the monstrous fables of the Talmud, or the gross impostures of the Koran.''

5th. Not to give favor and protection to a trust created with purpose hostile to Christianity.— The State ought not to give favor and protection to a trust created with hostile purpose towards Christianity. (See Webster's argument before the Supreme Court of the United States, in the case of Vidal and others *v.* the Executors of Stephen Girard, *Works*, vol. vi., pp. 133–177 ; also the decision of the court in that case, Reports, vol. xv., 2, 3 Howard, pp. 83–87, both referred to and quoted in part, p. 139. All persons, whether real or corporate, Christian or anti-Christian, are entitled to freedom of opinion and of speech, and are to be protected in the decent and orderly promulgation of their doctrines ; but a trust is not a person in any sense of the term. Christianity, in a proper sense, is the established religion of this nation ; established, not by statute law, it is true, but by a law equally valid, the law in the nature of things, the law of necessity, which law will remain in force so long as the great mass of the people are Christian. And notwithstanding some implications in the decision just cited, our courts are just as competent to decide between Christians and non-Christians, what the general principles of Christianity are, as they are to decide between Christians on the one part, and Mormons or pagans on the other part, what the principles of morality are.

When it grants incorporation to societies of Jews, Mohammedans, pagans, and atheists, in order that they may be enabled to hold property, sue and be sued, it creates a corporate person, which may be anti-Christian in its purpose, but the act no more implies the adoption or the exercise of a positive agency in the promulgation of the doctrines of those societies than granting incorporation to the congregations, theological schools, and missionary organizations of the various Christian sects implies the adoption or the promulgation of the sectarian doctrines those bodies were organized to teach. It may grant incorporation to societies of disbelievers and unbelievers, just as it may grant license for marriage to individual disbelievers and unbelievers, notwithstanding that its act results in the one case in the creating, and in the other (as is to be presumed) in the begetting of an anti-Christian person. It may refuse to create a corporate person intended to promote immorality, just as it may refuse license for the marriage of idiots and lepers ; but, excepting in such cases, the person, whether created or begotten, is entitled to protection in the freedom of opinion, of speech, and publication, when that freedom is not used in an indecent and disorderly manner. A trust, however, is not a person, and the denial of favor and protection to a trust created for a purpose hostile to Christianity is not inconsistent with the granting of incorporation to bodies which may be presumed to be hostile to that religion.

6th. **Not to discontinue any Christian practice for any reason derogatory to Christianity.**—The government ought not to discontinue any Christian practice or exercise which has become established by custom ; such as the opening of the daily sessions of the Congress of the United States and of the legislatures of the States, with prayer; the employment of Christian ministers as chaplains in the army and navy, in the prisons, hospitals, and homes under its charge; and the opening of the daily sessions of the public schools with religious exercises. If such exercises should be discontinued in any case, it ought not to be for any reason that is derogatory to Christianity.

The objection that the sessions of the courts, supreme and subordinate, the meetings of the President's Cabinet, of the Governor's council, of City Councils, and Boards of Education, though all needing divine guidance as much as the Congress, the legislature, and the public school, are not opened with prayer, and that the principle, if it be a right one, ought to be made general; we are fully warranted in pronouncing a mere cavil, for there are obvious reasons for an opening with prayer in the one class of cases which do not exist in the other.

A strong impression of greatness or importance produces an exalted state of feeling, which is kindred to and naturally awakens the religious feeling. Great perils, great calamities, great deliverances, cause the most of men to think of the Almighty. Mountain pinnacles fill the soul with awe and point to God. The meeting of large numbers of men for a common object, especially if the meeting be a formal one, is impressive, and excites an emotion which naturally tends upward. It is perfectly natural that the great National and State political conventions should be opened with prayer; not so natural that the meetings of the National executive committees should be opened with prayer; perfectly natural that the National and State Teachers' Associations should be opened with prayer; not so natural that the meetings of sections and committees should be so opened ; perfectly natural that the daily sessions of Congress and the legislature should be opened with prayer ; not so natural that the meetings of their committees should be so opened ; perfectly natural that the daily sessions of the public school should be opened with prayer ; not so natural that the meetings of the Board of Directors should be opened with prayer. It would be hardly just for the unbeliever to say that in these cases of omission the public authorities have come over to his ground, and that to be consistent they ought to make the omission general. They have not come over to his ground. They have not made the omissions for his reasons at all.

7th. Either to exempt church property from taxation or change principle of exemption.—The customary exemption of property used for Christian worship from taxation may very well be continued ; indeed, in the present state of the case, ought not to be discontinued, for the discontinuance would involve a discrimination against Christianity. There can hardly be a doubt that it was the Christian sentiment of the people prompted the exemption at the beginning, but it is doubtful whether the continuance can be properly based on any obligation which the government, as Christian, owes to Christianity. If the exemption is based upon the supposed duty of the government to foster Christianity, then it must follow that the places of worship used by all non-Christians,—Confucians, Buddhists, Mohammedans, and even the synagogues of the Jews, are to be denied the like exemption ; for it would be a self-stultification to foster contradictory systems of religion. A Christian people animated by the true spirit of Christianity will not desire that the government shall foster their religion by laying upon the followers of other religions burdens from which they are exempt. Such fostering would possess the essential character of persecution.

The exemption may very properly be made on the general principle that all property which is used for a public purpose, and not for pecuniary profit, is to be exempt from taxation; the principle upon which the property of educational and charitable institutions, of public libraries, agricultural, horticultural, mechanical, and philosophical societies, is exempt. To make exemptions upon such a principle, and not to exempt the property used for Christian worship, would be to discriminate against Christianity; and not to exempt at the same time the property used for other forms of religious worship would be to discriminate against all religion. It cannot be denied that the exemption in the case of the institutions and societies just mentioned has a fostering purpose; a purpose which as we have seen cannot be applied to Christianity without involving the persecution of other religions; and cannot be applied to all religions without involving the absurdity of fostering contradictory systems. To give them all perfect freedom is one thing; to foster them all is another thing.

It would be better, perhaps, to abandon altogether this principle of exemption, and exempt only Federal, State, County, and Municipal property, on the ground that it is the product of taxation. Two good reasons may be given for the abandonment of this principle: 1st. It would inflict no hardship or injustice on anybody. 2d. The principle is one which cannot be consistently carried out. If the principle was made really general and was consistently carried out, it would require that all the private pleasure-grounds and art galleries of the wealthy which are open to the public at stated times, the club-houses of the city, the houses and other property of boating and yachting clubs, should be exempt, for this property is all employed for a public use, and not for pecuniary gain, if not exactly, yet very nearly in the same sense in which the houses of religious worship are so employed. In accordance with this principle the streets and pleasure-grounds of Pullman, a suburb of Chicago, containing 11,000 inhabitants, but owned entirely by the Pullman company, ought not to be taxed ; while the church which is owned by the company and rented to the congregation worshipping in it, just as all the other houses in the place are rented, ought to be taxed.

8th. Conform its actions on moral questions to the precepts of Christianity.—The State, when it acts upon a moral question, ought to conform its action to the precepts of Christianity. The courts, however, are not to be deemed competent to enforce by penal inflictions any of the precepts of Christianity which have not been incorporated with the statutes. But the legislature ought to be regarded as under obligation to frame the statutes on moral questions in accordance with the precepts of Christianity. It should not profess to have discovered by speculation, or to have deduced from the writings of sages, or from the experience of mankind, the moral code upon which it bases its requirements ; nor should it pretend that its moral requirements are based upon such a code, to the entire exclusion of all considerations that may be drawn from the precepts of Christianity. Ethics may have been advanced in these latter days to the position of a science, but it is not an exact science, its promoters not

being agreed, as yet, even upon its fundamental principles. For this reason, if there were no other, it is ex-
ceedingly doubtful whether the State can rightly launch
out upon the sea of speculative ethics, and require a
Christian people to accept its discoveries, as the rule
of their action or the basis of their laws. An abstract
code of morals for the State, independent of the moral
convictions of the people, is a fiction. The code by
which legislation is to be governed is the code of the
people ; and in this country, it is the code of Christianity. To impose any other code than that, or even
that as modified by unbelief, or by a debased moral
sentiment, would be a wrong ; an evil root which can
be expected to produce none but evil fruit.

Upon the subject of marriage and divorce, the State
ought to conform its regulations to the precepts of
Christianity, and not to any social code supposed to
have been derived from an extra Christian source. All
Christian people, Roman Catholics and Protestants
alike, believe that on this subject the Bible is a divinely given rule of practice, and that there can be
therefore no departure from that rule but to the injury
of the public welfare.

No more serious mistake could be made than to reduce marriage to the condition of a mere civil contract,
as those are disposed to do who contend that the government ought to be destitute of all religious character.
Marriage is a relationship, having its basis in nature
and in the ordinance instituted by nature's God. The
contract is an incident, necessary to the beginning of
the relationship, but of small importance compared with
the relationship itself. The atoms of Oxygen and Hy-
drogen in water were brought into contact and held
together by the force of gravitation, inherent in each,

but that contact was only a necessary incident to the
union which afterwards took place, and which constituted a permanent relationship, making of twain one
new thing. To dissolve the relationship and force back
the connection into one of mere contact would be destructive to the constitution of the world. Scarcely
less destructive to the constitution of society would it
be to reduce marriage to the condition of a mere civil
contract. The consequences of such a step would
speedily demonstrate that the law of Christ, in this
matter, is a law of nature. Much nearer to the true
law of social life is the doctrine of the Roman Catholic
Church which makes marriage a holy sacrament.

There is one instance in nature in which we have contact without relationship. The Oxygen and Nitrogen
of the atmosphere are in contact but not in union, and
beneficently so. The Oxygen, however, is no free-
lover ; and it is ever ready to enter into permanent relationship with some one of its affinities ; and when
the union is once consummated it would be perpetual,
did no extraneous force produce a dissolution. The
Oxygen in the atmosphere is like one of the sexes in
the period of minority, ever ready to convert the accidental condition of contact into one of permanent relationship, from which, obedient to the laws of nature, it
never seeks release. Marriage is more than contract,
as chemical union is more than contact.

9th. **To observe the Lord's day as a day of rest
and conform its regulations to the view held by
the majority of the people.**—The government should
observe the Lord's day as a day of rest, and should
conform the regulations it prescribes for the observance
of that day to the view which is held by the majority of
Christian citizens. It has no right to inquire into or

24

decide upon the merits of the different sectarian views that may be held upon that subject. It has passed far beyond that stage of development in which it would possess any such right.

It should observe and appoint the first day of the week as the day of rest ; not however upon the ground that it has rejected the views of the Sabbatarians and adopted the views of those who hold to the divine obligation of what is called the Christian Sabbath, but upon the ground that the good order of society and the attainment of the object of the institution require that a particular day should be appointed by law, and that as the vast majority of Christian citizens observe the first day of the week the appointment of that day will be attended with the least hardship.

It ought to observe the day and order all its regulations for the observance, in accordance with the prevailing view as to the proper mode of the observance. To observe the day, and order all its regulations for the observance thereof in accordance with the view which prevails on the continent of Europe, while the prevailing view in this country is the one which is known as the Puritanical view, would be as unjust as to adopt and enforce the Puritanical view while the people were holding the continental European view. In either case the government would be a self-constituted propagator of a particular religious doctrine ; and more than that, it would be putting its power in the hands of a minority to offend and wrong the majority. It is no part of the proper function of government to propagate any particular form of Christian doctrine, whether liberal or rigid, so called. To say that in adopting any Sunday legislation at all it must of necessity adopt and propagate the one view or the other ; that it must be

regarded therefore as perfectly free to make its choice
between the two, and that the principles of liberty require it to choose the so-called liberal view, is to mistake
the facts in the case and the proper relation of the government to the whole question.[1] The fact that the
Puritanical view has been the prevailing one in this
country from the time of the first landing on the banks
of James River and Plymouth Rock cannot be questioned.   It is found in the legislation of all the Colonies, of all the original States, and of nearly all the
other States.   It has been established in the sentiments,
traditions, and customs of the people from the beginning.   That this view has been the prevailing one in
this country is shown by the fact that on the continent
of Europe, it is known and designated, not as the Puritanical, but as the English and American view.   The
government has not been free, and is not now free to
make any choice in the matter.   For the government
to adopt and enforce any other view of the Sabbath

[1] The use of the word *liberal*, in connection with a question
of truth or right, is mere cant ; for there can be no place for
liberality in the determination of such a question.   Think of
a surveyor set to ascertain the exact dimensions of a piece of
ground ; or of an engineer sent out to ascertain the exact level
at which a section of railroad should be laid ; or of a chemist
employed to find the exact constituents of a compound body ;
appending to his report the statement that he had taken in
a large amount of *liberality* as a factor in the investigation !
That very admission would be ground enough for the rejection
of his whole work as worthless.   To confess liability to error is
not liberality ; it is honesty.   Liberalism claims to have gone
beyond the limits of what is required ; Honesty professes that
it has endeavored to come up to those limits.   Liberalism is
proud ; honesty is humble ; liberalism is boastful, honesty is
modest ; liberalism is censorious, honesty is charitable ; liberalism is the pharisee of the parable, honesty is the publican.

than the one which prevails among its Christian citizens would be to exercise the power of a spiritua' despot.

It is undoubtedly true that a part of the population of this country, not by any means inconsiderable in point of numbers, would prefer the continental European mode of observing the Sabbath. And it might be pleaded that in strict justice the government ought, in its own conduct and in the regulations it prescribes, to follow a middle course between the two views. The justice of this plea would have to be conceded, perhaps, were the people of this country who hold the view in question equal in numbers to those who hold the Puritanical view, and were they of like character with those who hold the other view in Europe. But the equality in numbers and the likeness in character are both wanting. In Europe the doctrine of the Sabbath there prevailing is held considerately by the most sincere and earnest Christians. They regard their doctrine as founded on important Christian principles. They hold that the observance of the Lord's day as a day of rest and public worship is necessary to the highest Christian life, and therefore obligatory; the duty arising entirely from the value of the spiritual end to which it is a means, and not in any degree from a sanctity belonging to the hours of the day in themselves. To hold that the day now possesses a holiness which can be profaned by acts, otherwise allowable, even if done through inadvertence or an error in reckoning,—to assume, for instance, that by the divine ordinance the day was made to begin with the evening, and then hold, that to engage in such worldly occupations and recreations as are lawful in themselves, from sunset till midnight on Saturday, would be a profana-

tion, the sinfulness of which could not be blotted out
by the most devout and scrupulous observance of an
equal number of hours after sunset on Sunday would
be, in their view, to go back into the bondage of the
Old Testament ceremonial law, from which Christ
made his people free. They believe that in this doctrine of the Christian Sabbath they are following the
most eminent reformers.[1] The people in this country,
however, who desire the establishment of the European
Sunday are not of such a character ; nor is their conduct
in the matter governed by any such principles. It can
hardly be regarded as a breach of charity to say that
they are, with slight exceptions, irreligious, including
in their number all that are positively anti-Christian,
and a large proportion of the vicious and criminal
classes.

The government possesses a positively religious character ; it is Christian, and to modify its regulation of

[1] A note made by the late Rev. William B. Sprague, D. D.,
of Albany, N. Y., of a visit to the late Dr. Aug. Neander will
serve to show the view of the Sabbath which is held by some of
the most eminent Christians in Germany. He says :

" Neander was the first person upon whom I called at Berlin.
. . . He spoke in a manner that indicated the highest reverence and respect for the King, and when I asked him concerning the King's religious character he remarked that he had
no doubt he was a truly pious man. I expressed some astonishment at that, from having seen it stated in a French newspaper
that I had taken up that he attended the theatre on the Sabbath. ' But,' says Neander, ' I suppose you know that the same
views of the Sabbath are not entertained in Germany as in England and America. I do not entertain them myself. . . . I
would not go to the theatre any day of the week, but there is
nothing that I would do at any time that I would not do on
Sunday, if convenience required it.' . . .

" Immediately on my introduction to Neander he asked me

a Christian observance in accommodation to the views
of the irreligious or the anti-Christian would be the
same as to modify the syntax and orthography of its
statute books, its records, and public documents in accommodation to the usages of the illiterate ; or to
modify its laws relating to property in accommodation
to the doctrines of anarchists; or to modify its laws
against brutality in accommodation to the views of
those who frequent the prize-ring and the dog-pit.
The government being Christian, and so long as it is
Christian, may very properly make accommodation
between the different views on the positive side of the
question ; but not between the views of the positive
and those of the negative. A general may have regard
to the views of the different arms of the service, in
disposing his forces for battle, but not to the views
of the enemy. If the government is Christian, the anti-
Christian must be regarded as in that respect an enemy.

if I would dine with him the next Sunday ; and as it presented
to me the alternative of dining in a Christian family or in a
hotel, I had no scruples in accepting the invitation. . . . In
due time the servant announced that dinner was ready, and
what was my astonishment as I entered the dining-room to
find as many guests there as the room could possibly accommo-
date. . . . The manner in which the afternoon was spent
was quite in accordance with the German doctrine in respect to
the Sabbath ; and as the good-humored, not to say boisterous,
demonstrations were all in German, I must confess that I was
for once more than reconciled to my ignorance of the language.
What aggravated the case to me was that I had no reason to
doubt that the dinner party had been made on my account.
. . . I am sure he did not intend to do violence to my feelings, and I am equally sure that if he had had any adequate
appreciation of the manner in which we regard the Sabbath, I
should not have been placed in a situation so painful to me."
—*Visits to European Celebrities*, pp. 131-135.

Any officer in the civil or military service of the government who assumes that the government is destitute of all religious character, or that the continental European doctrine of the Sabbath is the established doctrine of this government, and, upon that assumption, requires his subordinates to do unnecessary work on Sunday, commits an offence against the people and inflicts a wrong upon his subordinates. An officer, so offending, ought to be rebuked and restrained by his superiors.

10. **To require that all teaching in high schools, State universities, military and naval academies be in accordance with the fundamental truths of Christianity.**—The government ought to provide Christian teaching and nurture for all those citizens to whom it stands *in loco parentis.* This duty we have already considered to some extent (see p. 243), but we proceed, now, further to say that the State is under obligation to require that all the teaching in the high schools, universities, military and naval academies, be in accordance with the fundamental truths of Christianity. Here is ground upon which there can be no neutrality. A large range of subjects is taught in these institutions, in which the teaching must be either for or against Christianity. Theism ; a divine production of all finite things (in one way or another) ; the dependence of nature's laws upon the divine will for their existence and their constancy ; the distinction between matter and spirit, body and mind ; are fundamental postulates of Christianity. If these be denied Christianity cannot be believed ; and it is impossible to teach Physics, Metaphysics, Philosophy, History, Geography, Chemistry, Astronomy, or Biology, as they ought to be taught, without making af-

firmations that involve the acceptance or rejection of one or another of the postulates mentioned. To teach any of these subjects and make no affirmations on these postulates, were the same as to teach optics or acoustics and make no affirmation upon the doctrine of vibrations ; or to teach Chemistry and make no affirmation on the doctrine of atoms ; or to teach Biology and make no affirmation on the origin of life. A State university that should so teach on these subjects would speedily fall into the lowest rank, and would soon become extinct. Since, therefore, there must be teaching in these institutions which is either for or against Christianity, the State, in a Christian land, is bound to require that the teaching be not in contradiction to, but in conformity with the fundamental truths of Christianity. The matter should not be left to accident, with the secret hope that it will turn out favorably to the Christian public. The State university, however endowed, has no more independence of the people than the public school, for there is no mystic source of revenue, in the heights of heaven or in the depths of ocean, whence the State may obtain money, and leave untouched the amount the people have saved from the earnings of their toil. Every cent of the funds of the State university, whatever may be the immediate source, has come out of the pockets of the people, just as really as though it had been raised by direct taxation ; and to spend the money of a Christian people for the support of a state university and not give positive legislative guaranty that the teaching therein shall not contradict the truths of the Christian religion, merely hoping that it will turn out favorably to them, were as great a wrong as it would be to take the people's money out of the treasury of the State and lend it without taking note or security, hoping that the borrower when the time of re-payment comes will be found in such a financial condition, and in such a moral mood, that the transaction will inflict no wrong upon the people.

Furthermore, when Christian people pay their taxes for the support of State schools, and a number of them, in addition to that, expend large sums of money for the founding of institutions of learning in which they shall have the guaranty in question, it cannot be just for the State to use the proceeds of taxation to institute a competition which will tend to cripple or ruin those institutions. Still greater will be the injustice if advantage should be taken of the special interest of a Christian people in institutions of their own founding, to convert the State university into the preserve of a class, composed of atheists, agnostics, and the irreligious, to be managed in accordance with their peculiar views on the subject of religion.

If persons, belonging to this class, desire an institution of learning in which all the teaching shall be in accordance with their views, no one will deny their right to found such an institution. Let the State grant them a charter; let them endow the institution with their own money, and let them proclaim openly its object; but let them not attempt to accomplish their purpose, covertly and cheaply, by the use of funds which have been derived, almost wholly, from a Christian public. Even if the State were not Christian, if it were neutral on the subject of religion, the effort to make the principles of atheism rule the teaching in a State university would be a violation of right. In that case, the teaching ought to be perfectly neutral, which, as we have shown, would be an impossibility. But a State, composed of Christian people, as we have also shown, is not, and cannot be, neutral; it is, and of necessity must be Christian.

If it be said that Christian people are in the majority and have only themselves to blame for the wrongs they suffer, it is to be replied that when they express their will by the ballot the issue is always complicated with other political questions; that they share in the general confusion of ideas on the relation of religion to civil government; and that a zealous minority may very easily avail itself of these circumstances to exercise over them the power of a despot. Despots have always been a minority, and they have always established their power by taking advantage of favoring circumstances. Mere opportunity does not make despotism right.

Large accumulations of wealth cannot be expected to endure in this country beyond two or three generations, neither can they be used to found a hereditary aristocracy; the Constitution of the United States having prohibited both the United States and the States granting any title of nobility. There will always, therefore, be a strong tendency to employ superabundant wealth in the founding and endowment of institutions of charity and learning; and the history of the higher education in this country amply sustains the opinion, that private munificence will be a sufficient reliance for the purposes of such education. The State university is in fact of sentimental origin. It was provided to meet no real want, or at best, only a prospective want, which was already being provided for by private enterprise. The older States, with their provisions, privately made, Massachusetts, with her Harvard, Amherst, and Williams; Connecticut, with her Yale; Rhode Island, with her Brown; New York, with her Columbia, Union, Hamilton, and

Cornell ; New Jersey, with her Princeton and Rutgers ; and Maryland, with her Johns Hopkins need, no State university. If it be admitted that, where there is a State university of high rank, no other similar institution is needed ; it must be admitted also, that the existence of such an institution will tend to prevent the flow of private wealth into educational channels. It may be doubted whether Michigan, with her Ann Arbor, will ever have an institution of learning, privately founded, equal in endowment and equipment to Chicago University in Illinois ; which, considering the exposure of a State institution to political and anti-Christian influences ; and weighing justly all the other considerations that enter into the question, can hardly be regarded as the best provision for the higher education of a Christian people.

If, however, a State could organize its university so as to be entirely free from the influence of State politics, and should give guaranty that the teaching therein should not be subversive of Christianity, the abundant funds available to put it, at once, in the condition of the highest efficiency, would be an advantage.

A further advantage might then be easily obtained by the adoption of a system which would bring all the private institutions into some sort of relation to the State institution, such as that of colleges to a university, thus specializing the work, getting the utmost benefit from the expenditure, and making, of the whole, one true university. Or, that failing, then, if the State institution, and one or more of the private institutions, should be made universities in reality as well as in name, their competition would act as a perpetual stimulus, inciting all to the attainment of the highest excellence.

The contingencies, in which the State university may be so managed as to inflict injustice upon Christian people, are so likely to occur, that the State ought, either not to establish such an institution, or ought, in establishing it, to adopt legislative safeguards sufficient to prevent any such infliction.

But, the question of justice aside, when education ascends above the requirements of merely mundane utility, and aims at culture, not in the vulgar, but in the full and proper sense of the word—the development of a perfect man,—it enters the domain of religion ; just as the blade, springing up from the buried seed, enters the domain of light. To exclude religion from such education would be to exclude the possibility of the education itself. As well attempt to produce a perfect development of plant or animal without sunlight, as to produce a perfect development of man without the religion of Him who is " the light of the world."

CHAPTER XX.

CONCLUSION.

THE survey we have taken of the relation of religion to civil government will justify us, we think, in saying that in the United States of America religious liberty has made its farthest advancement ; and that, a few of the older States being excepted, has reached the ultimate stage of its progress. The State is without a Church, but not without a religion. The government is Christian, but is not sectarian ; nor is it an oppressor of its non-Christian citizens. It exercises a just regard for the feelings and convictions of the unbeliever, as well as for those of the believer; indeed, it has come to be the case in some of the younger States, by reason of the confused ideas and inchoate theories of some Christian people, that if there is any difference in its treatment of the two parties it is in favor of the former rather than the latter.

Having dislodged injustice from its stronghold in that borderland where the domain of religion overlaps that of civil government, we may cherish the hope that our government will maintain the purest justice in all else, and thus become strong and enduring. As the atoms of the opaque and amorphous rock, coming out of solution or fusion, form the crystal, so the principles of liberty, coming down to us out of the past ages, have given us a political structure, beautiful in its form, strong in its constitution, and open to the light. Like the stone which Nebuchadnezzar saw in his dream, "cut out without hands," it has grown and become a great mountain. We may not expect, or even desire, that like that mountain, it shall fill the whole earth, but we may expect that it will grow wider-based and higher as the years go on. It may well excite our patriotic admiration as we behold it crowned, not with the frowning battlements and black enginery of war, but with the white-walled temple of peace, sparkling with the light that beams down from the heavenly habitations of righteousness, and sending that light abroad over the earth as a hope-inspiring illumination.

So long as it shall continue to be truly Christian and scrupulously just, deriving its character from a people who love the Lord their God, and delight in obedience to his righteous law, it may be looked upon as at least one of the anti-types of that holy mountain which the inspired singer of Israel praised as " the joy of the whole earth."

INDEX.

AMERICAN HISTORY

American Orations. From the Colonial Period to the present time, selected as specimens of eloquence, and with special reference to their value in throwing light upon the more important epochs and issues of American history. Edited, with introductions and notes, by Alexander Johnston, Professor of Jurisprudence and Political Economy, College of New Jersey. Three volumes, 16mo, uniform with "Prose Masterpieces" and "British Orations," pp. 282, 314, 405 . . . . . . $3 75
The same, half calf 7 50

Constitutional History of the United States as Seen in the Development of American Law. Comprising a Course of Lectures Delivered before the Political Science Association of the University of Michigan, with an Introduction by Prof. Henry Wade Rogers, Dean of the Law School of the University of Michigan. 8vo, pp. 296 . . . . . . $2 00

Documents Illustrative of American History, 1606–1863. By Howard W. Preston. With introduction and references. Second and cheaper edition. 8vo, pp. 320 . . . $1 50

The Federalist. By Alex. Hamilton, John Jay, and James Madison. A Commentary on the Constitution of the United States. Being a Collection of Essays Written in Support of the Constitution Agreed upon September 17, 1787, by the Federal Convention. Edited, with Introduction and Notes, by Henry Cabot Lodge. 8vo, pp. xlv. + 586 . . . . . $2 00

GOODNOW. Comparative Administrative Law. An Analysis of the Administrative Systems, National and Local, of the United States, England, France, and Germany. By F. J. Goodnow, Professor of Administrative Law in Columbia College. Part I. Organization. Part II. Legal Relations. 2 vols., 8vo, cloth, each $3 75

Great Words from Great Americans. Comprising the Declaration of Independence; the Constitution of the United States, with notes; Washington's Circular-Letter of Congratulation and Advice to the Governors of the Thirteen States; Washington's First and Second Inaugural Addresses and his Farewell Address; and Lincoln's First and Second Inaugural Addresses and his Gettysburg Address. With an Index to the Constitution, and an Appendix. With portraits of Washington and Lincoln. 18mo, pp. 207 75

G. P. PUTNAM'S SONS
NEW YORK AND LONDON

HOFFMAN. The Sphere of the State; or, The People as a Body Politic. With Special Consideration of Certain Present Problems. By Frank Sargent Hoffman, A.M., Professor of Philosophy, Union College. 12mo $1 50

PAINE. The Life of Thomas Paine. By Moncure Daniel Conway, author of "Omitted Chapters of History, Disclosed in the Life and Papers of Edmund Randolph." 2 volumes, 8vo. Illustrated. Pp. xviii. + 380 + 489 . . . . $5 00

RANDOLPH. Omitted Chapters of History, Disclosed in the Life and Papers of Edmund Randolph. By Moncure D. Conway. With portrait, 8vo, pp. vi. + 401 . . $3 00

ROOSEVELT. The Winning of the West. By Theodore Roosevelt. Author of "The Naval War of 1812," "Hunting Trips of a Ranchman," "The Wilderness Hunter," etc. 3 vols., octavo, gilt top, with maps, each $2 50
Vol. I. From the Alleghanies to the Mississippi, 1769–1776.
Vol. II. From the Alleghanies to the Mississippi, 1777–1783.
Vol. III. The Foundling of the Trans-Alleghany Commonwealths, 1784–1790.

ROPES. The Story of the Civil War. A Concise Account of the War in the United States of America between 1861 and 1865. By John Codman Ropes, Member of the Massachusetts Historical Society, The Military Historical Society of Massachusetts, Fellow of the Royal Historical Society. Author of "The Army Under Pope," "The First Napoleon," "The Campaign of Waterloo," etc., etc. To be complete in three parts, printed in three octavo volumes, with comprehensive maps and battle plans. Each part will be complete in itself and will be sold separately. Part I. Narrative of Events to the opening of the Campaign of 1862, with 5 maps, 8vo $1 50

STERNE. The Constitutional History and Political Development of the United States. An Analytical Study. By Simon Sterne (of the New York Bar). Fourth edition, revised with additions. 12mo, pp. xx. + 361 . . . . $1 25

STRAUS. The Origin of Republican Form of Government in the United States of America. By Oscar S. Straus. 12mo, pp. ix. + 140 . . . . $1 00

TAUSSIG. The Tariff History of the United States, 1789–1888. By Prof. F. W. Taussig. Comprising the material contained in "Protection to Young Industries" and "History of the Present Tariff," together with the revisions and additions needed to complete the narrative down to 1892. 12mo, pp. vii. + 269.
$1 25

G. P. PUTNAM'S SONS
NEW YORK   AND   LONDON

AMERICAN HISTORY

American Orations. From the Colonial Period to the present time, selected as specimens of eloquence, and with special reference to their value in throwing light upon the more important epochs and issues of American history. Edited, with introductions and notes, by Alexander Johnston, Professor of Jurisprudence and Political Economy, College of New Jersey. Three volumes, 16mo, uniform with "Prose Masterpieces" and "British Orations," pp. 282, 314, 405 . . . . . . $3 75
The same, half calf 7 50

Constitutional History of the United States as Seen in the Development of American Law. Comprising a Course of Lectures Delivered before the Political Science Association of the University of Michigan, with an Introduction by Prof. Henry Wade Rogers, Dean of the Law School of the University of Michigan. 8vo, pp. 296 . . . . . . $2 00

Documents Illustrative of American History, 1606–1863. By Howard W. Preston. With introduction and references. Second and cheaper edition. 8vo, pp. 320 . . . $1 50

The Federalist. By Alex. Hamilton, John Jay, and James Madison. A Commentary on the Constitution of the United States. Being a Collection of Essays Written in Support of the Constitution Agreed upon September 17, 1787, by the Federal Convention. Edited, with Introduction and Notes, by Henry Cabot Lodge. 8vo, pp. xlv. + 586 . . . . . $2 00

GOODNOW. Comparative Administrative Law. An Analysis of the Administrative Systems, National and Local, of the United States, England, France, and Germany. By F. J. Goodnow, Professor of Administrative Law in Columbia College. Part I. Organization. Part II. Legal Relations. 2 vols., 8vo, cloth, each $3 75

Great Words from Great Americans. Comprising the Declaration of Independence ; the Constitution of the United States, with notes ; Washington's Circular-Letter of Congratulation and Advice to the Governors of the Thirteen States ; Washington's First and Second Inaugural Addresses and his Farewell Address ; and Lincoln's First and Second Inaugural Addresses and his Gettysburg Address. With an Index to the Constitution, and an Appendix. With portraits of Washington and Lincoln. 18mo, pp. 207 75

G. P. PUTNAM'S SONS
NEW YORK   AND   LONDON

HOFFMAN. **The Sphere of the State; or, The People as a Body Politic.** With Special Consideration of Certain Present Problems. By Frank Sargent Hoffman, A.M., Professor of Philosophy, Union College. 12mo $1 50

PAINE. **The Life of Thomas Paine.** By Moncure Daniel Conway, author of "Omitted Chapters of History, Disclosed in the Life and Papers of Edmund Randolph." 2 volumes, 8vo. Illustrated. Pp. xviii. + 380 + 489 . . . . $5 00

RANDOLPH. **Omitted Chapters of History, Disclosed in the Life and Papers of Edmund Randolph.** By Moncure D. Conway. With portrait, 8vo, pp. vi. + 401 . . $3 00

ROOSEVELT. **The Winning of the West.** By Theodore Roosevelt. Author of "The Naval War of 1812," "Hunting Trips of a Ranchman," "The Wilderness Hunter," etc. 3 vols., octavo, gilt top, with maps, each $2 50
Vol. 1. From the Alleghanies to the Mississippi, 1769-1776.
Vol. II. From the Alleghanies to the Mississippi, 1777-1783.
Vol. III. The Foundling of the Trans-Alleghany Commonwealths, 1784-1790.

ROPES. **The Story of the Civil War.** A Concise Account of the War in the United States of America between 1861 and 1865. By John Codman Ropes, Member of the Massachusetts Historical Society, The Military Historical Society of Massachusetts, Fellow of the Royal Historical Society. Author of "The Army Under Pope," "The First Napoleon," "The Campaign of Waterloo," etc., etc. To be complete in three parts, printed in three octavo volumes, with comprehensive maps and battle plans. Each part will be complete in itself and will be sold separately. Part I. Narrative of Events to the opening of the Campaign of 1862, with 5 maps, 8vo $1 50

STERNE. **The Constitutional History and Political Development of the United States.** An Analytical Study. By Simon Sterne (of the New York Bar). Fourth edition, revised with additions. 12mo, pp. xx. + 361 . . . . $1 25

STRAUS. **The Origin of Republican Form of Government in the United States of America.** By Oscar S. Straus. 12mo, pp. ix. + 140 . . . . $1 00

TAUSSIG. **The Tariff History of the United States, 1789-1888.** By Prof. F. W. Taussig. Comprising the material contained in "Protection to Young Industries" and "History of the Present Tariff," together with the revisions and additions needed to complete the narrative down to 1892. 12mo, pp. vii. + 269.
$1 25

G. P. PUTNAM'S SONS
NEW YORK   AND   LONDON